I0124293

Houman M. Sarshar is an independent scholar and director of publications at the Center for Iranian Jewish Oral History (CIJOH) in Los Angeles. He is consulting editor of Judeo-Persian Studies for the *Encyclopaedia Iranica*, and has edited and co-edited a number of books on Iranian Jews, including *Esther's Children: A Portrait of Iranian Jews* (CIJOH, 2002) and *Jewish Communities of Iran: Entries on Judeo-Persian Communities Published by the Encyclopædia Iranica* (New York, 2011). He holds a Ph.D. in comparative literature from Columbia University.

For Angel

THE JEWS OF IRAN

The History, Religion, and Culture of a
Community in the Islamic World

Edited by
HOUMAN M. SARSHAR

I.B.TAURIS
LONDON • NEW YORK • OXFORD • NEW DELHI • SYDNEY

I.B. TAURIS
Bloomsbury Publishing Plc
50 Bedford Square, London, WC1B 3DP, UK
1385 Broadway, New York, NY 10018, USA

BLOOMSBURY, I.B. TAURIS and the I.B. Tauris logo are
trademarks of Bloomsbury Publishing Plc

First published in Great Britain 2014
Paperback edition printed 2019

Copyright Editorial Selection and Introduction q 2014 Houman M. Sarshar

Copyright Individual Chapters q 2014 Mojgan Behmand, Orit Carmeli, Judith
L. Goldstein, Vera B. Moreen, Jaleh Pirnazar, Parvaneh Pourshariati, Nasrin Rahimieh,
Shalom Sabar, Haideh Sahim, Martin Schwartz, David Yeroushalmi.

Houman M. Sarshar has asserted his right under the Copyright,
Designs and Patents Act, 1988, to be identified as Author of this work.

All rights reserved. No part of this publication may be reproduced or
transmitted in any form or by any means, electronic or mechanical,
including photocopying, recording, or any information storage or retrieval
system, without prior permission in writing from the publishers.

Bloomsbury Publishing Plc does not have any control over, or responsibility for,
any third-party websites referred to or in this book. All internet addresses
given in this book were correct at the time of going to press. The author and
publisher regret any inconvenience caused if addresses have changed or sites
have ceased to exist, but can accept no responsibility for any such changes.

A catalogue record for this book is available from the British Library.

ISBN: HB: 978 1 78076 888 5
PB: 978 1 78831 926 3
eISBN: 978 0 85773 710 6
ePDF: 978 0 85772 765 7

A catalog record for this book is available from the Library of Congress.

Typeset by Jones Ltd, London

To find out more about our authors and books visit
www.bloomsbury.com and sign up for our newsletters

CONTENTS

LIST OF ILLUSTRATIONS

LIST OF CONTRIBUTORS

Parvaneh Pourshariati is Associate Professor of Islamic and Iranian Studies at The Ohio State University. A specialist in Late Antique and early medieval history of Iran and the Middle East, her recent publications include *Decline and Fall of the Sasanian Empire* and as Guest Editor, a double issue of the *Journal of Persianate Studies*.

Martin Schwartz is Professor Emeritus at the University of California, Berkeley, where he taught Iranian Studies from 1970 until his retirement in 2011. Before Berkeley, he taught Iranian Studies and Sanskrit at Columbia University. His publications include studies on a variety of Old and Middle Iranian languages and texts, historical linguistics, Zoroastrianism, Manicheism, and ethnobotany and art history in Iranian contexts. In recent years, his work has focused on the compositional structure, style, and meaning of the Gathas of Zoroaster. He has also published on interactions between the Iranian and Jewish worlds, particularly in the history of magic. His most recent publication, "On Some Iranian Secret Vocabularies, As Evidenced by a Fourteenth-Century Persian Manuscript" in *Trends in Iranian and Persian Linguistics* (2018), builds on and expands the scope of some of the material set forth in detail in the article in the present volume.

ADDENDUM (November 2018): My thesis (above, pp. 51–53) that the spread of Iranian Jewish exclusionary jargon into Muslim argot began in early Buyid Gorgan (in the city of Astarabad) is supported by the evidence of a for Jews of that period constituting a speech community in Gorgan in the relevant period, as per the close linguistic analysis of a 10th–12th century C.E. magical fragment from the Cairo Geniza (Shaul Shaked, "An Early Geniza Fragment in an Unknown Iranian Language," in *A Green Leaf: Papers in Honour of Jes P. Asmussen*, ed. W. Sundermann, J. Duchesne-Guillemin, and F. Vahman [Leiden, 1988, pp. 219–235], which, after further examination, led Habib Borjian ("Judeo-Iranian Languages," in *Handbook of Jewish Languages, Revised and Updated Edition*, ed. Lily Kahn and Aaron D. Rubin [Leiden, 2015]. pp. 235–279, here p. 238) tentatively to label the language as "Judeo-Gurgani;" for Jews earlier in Gorgan, see Pourshariati in the present volume, pp. 14–15. My exposition of Iranian Jewish and Muslim exclusionary vocabularies is now revised an much expanded in Martin Schwartz, "On Some Iranian Secret Vocabularies, As Evidenced by a Fourteenth Century Persian Manuscript," in *Trends in Persian and Iranian Linguistics*, eds. A. Korangy and C. Miller (Berlin and Boston, 2018), pp. 69–79.

Vera B. Moreen is a visiting associate professor at several colleges and universities and has written and co-edited several books, with *Miniature Paintings in Judaeo-Persian Manuscripts* nominated for the National Jewish Book Award. She was recently named co-editor of the *Encyclopaedia of Jews in the Islamic World*.

David Yeroushalmi teaches Persian language and Iranian cultural history at Tel Aviv University's Department of Middle Eastern and African History. His main area of research and publication deals with the history and cultural heritage of Iranian Jewry, with his latest book entitled *The Jews of Iran in the Nineteenth Century: Aspects of History, Community, and Culture*.

Haideh Sahim has taught Persian language and literature and the history of Iran and Islam at New York University, Hofstra University and Queens College, CUNY. She has lectured on various subjects related to Iran, most recently in 2012 at the Middle East Studies Association Conference, and has published widely on the subjects of Iranian dialects and the Jews of Iran.

Shalom Sabar is Professor of Jewish Art and Folklore at the Hebrew University of Jerusalem. His research concentrates on the history of Jewish art from Biblical times to the present, and the rituals and material culture of Jewish communities in Europe and the lands of Islam. He has published dozens of essays and reviews related to these topics. Among his books are *Mazal Tov: Illuminated Jewish Marriage Contracts, Jerusalem – Stone and Spirit: 3000 Years of History and Art, The Life Cycle of the Jews in Islamic Lands*, and *The Sarajevo Haggadah: History & Art*.

Orit Carmeli is an Independent Researcher / Art Historian. Her field of study is Jewish art from Islamic lands and she specializes in the material culture and ritual objects of the Jews of Iran. Her main area of research and publication deals with the illuminated Judeo Persian manuscripts.

Judith L. Goldstein is a cultural anthropologist who has done ethnographic and archival research in Iran (Yazd), Israel, Paris, and Rome. Her publications on Iranian Jews in Iran and in the diaspora include: "The Jewish Miracle Worker in a Muslim Context" (1980), "The Paradigm of Protection" (1981), "Iranian Ethnicity in Israel: the Performance of Identity" (1984, 1998), "Iranian Jewish Women's Magical Narratives" (1986), "How Mulla Daoud was Lost and Found in Lebanon or the Politics of Ethnic Theater in a Nation at War" (1990), " The Tear Jar" (2009) and several encyclopedia articles on Jews in the Islamic world.

Jaleh Pirnazar teaches Persian language and literature and Iranian cinema at the University of California, Berkeley, where she has taught in the Department of Near Eastern Studies for over thirty years. Her research interests, various publications in Persian and English, and encyclopaedic entries include topics in literary criticism, film reviews, and the history of Iranian Jews.

Nasrin Rahimieh is Howard Baskerville Professor of Humanities and Professor and Chair of the Department of Comparative Literature at the University of California, Irvine. Her teaching and research are focused on modern Persian literature, the literature of Iranian exile and diaspora, contemporary Iranian women's writing. Among her publications are *Missing Persians: Discovering Voices in Iranian Cultural History*, Forugh *Farrokhzad, Poet Of Modern Iran: Iconic Woman And Feminine Pioneer Of New Persian Poetry* co-edited with Dominic Parviz Brookshaw and *Iranian Culture: Representation and Identity*.

Mojgan Behmand is Associate Vice President for Academic Affairs and Professor of English at Dominican University of California. Her scholarship includes writings on the intertwining of contemporary Iranian novels such as Daneshvar's *Savushun* with the medieval Persian epic *Shahnameh* and the dramatic tradition of *ta'ziyeh* and history, in addition to publishing and presenting widely on curricular revision, faculty development, and Big History pedagogy. She is co-editor of *Teaching Big History* published by UC Press.

INTRODUCTION

Houman M. Sarshar

Jewish Iranian studies is at last entering the next and indeed exciting stage of scholarship where, relying in part on the foundational work of preceding scholars, researchers are now examining the social, historical, and cultural life of Jews in Iran with the objective of arriving at hypotheses that reach beyond a mere systematic archival documentation of facts. What is consequently coming to light with this new generation of works is an increasingly nuanced understanding of one of Iran's oldest sub-cultures as a community in a mutually influential dynamic with its environment. No longer burdened with the laborious yet hitherto indispensable challenge of piecemealing data about the life of Jews on the Iranian plateau over the past 2,700 years, the contemporary generation of researchers is now focusing on a more analytical examination of this history in contexts that reach beyond the more immediate perimeters of Judaism, Jewish history, or minority studies. As a direct consequence of this refreshing shift in perspective, the Jews of Iran are no longer being seen exclusively as a passive minority group victimized by the Zoroastrian or, later, Shi'ite hegemony, but also as an active factor in the development of Iranian history, society, and culture. Contemporary scholars are thus taking greater steps in raising our awareness about the fact that—whether as catalysts, harbingers, or markers of change—this ancient community of Iranians has consistently remained an inextricable thread in the complex fabric of greater Iran.

The present volume offers a collection of novel contributions to this new period of scholarship in Jewish Iranian studies. The majority of these articles were originally presented at the conference "Iranian Jewry: From Past to Present", which I convened at the University of Maryland in November 2008. Co-sponsored by The Joseph and Rebecca Meyerhoff Center for Jewish Studies and The Roshan Cultural Heritage Institute Center for Persian Studies, and co-hosted by The Hebraic Section and Near East Section, African and Middle Eastern Division of the Library of Congress, the three-day conference gathered scholars of Jewish Iranian studies from around the world to present new research in a broad range of categories. With the exception of Martin Schwartz and Orit Carmeli, who were not presenters at the conference, all the other contributors to the volume elected to develop their original presentation into the article-length version for this publication.

These contributions are loosely organized here in thematic or historical order, starting with Parvaneh Pourshariati's "systematic investigation into the pattern of the settlement of Iranian Jewry in Iran and the implications of this in the context of the history of Iran in Late Antiquity and early medieval periods." Pourshariati here outlines the concentration of Jewish Iranian settlements along the northern trade route that crossed the Iranian plateau during the Parthian and Sasanian periods. In her detailed analysis of various sources, Pourshariati provides many convincing hypotheses in relation to the long-standing enigma of why Jews gravitated mostly towards certain specific areas in Iran after their initial appearance on that land *c.*722 BCE and then again after the conquest of Babylon by Cyrus II the Great (b. *c.*600 BCE, d. 530 BCE) on October 29, 539 BCE. As is generally the case with groundbreaking scholarship, however, Pourshariati's findings raise as many questions for the reader as they answer. What, for instance, were the long-term consequences of these early choices both for the settling Jewish community itself and for the specific area as a whole? How, if at all, do these patterns play into the development of Judeo-Persian languages, the relationship of Jews with land ownership, or the cultivation of local art and artisanry? Might there be a coincidence between these settlements and the later establishment of centers of medical practice and teaching throughout Iran? Whether these or other questions might be addressed in the second part of Pourshariati's article (forthcoming) remains to be seen. What is certain, however, is that in tackling this long-standing lacuna in our knowledge of Jewish Iranian history, Pourshariati has demonstrated that in many ways the work of exploring the multifarious influences of Jewish presence in antiquities and pre-modern Iran has entered a new and exciting chapter with the promise of many lively debates to follow.

In the volume's second article, Martin Schwartz's analysis of Loterā'i (a Persian Jewish exclusionary argot essentially different from Judeo-Persian dialogues) traces the history of this sociolect from its earliest known samples to the present day to demonstrate its adoption by non-Jewish Iranian beggars and rascals and members of the early medieval Shi'ite underclass. And not unlike Pourshariati's article before, Schwartz's intriguing findings on many of the hitherto overlooked nuances of Loterā'i invite many questions from disciplines beyond the field of linguistics. For instance, how does this adoption shed light on the social status of Jews in medieval Iran? Does the fact that the Shi'ite underclass adopted their argot necessarily suggest a regular interaction between this Shi'ite subsegment and the entirety of the Jewish community? Or is it more indicative of a lateral exchange between the Shi'ite and Jewish communities' respective subclasses? Furthermore, how might this adoption reflect on questions of identity in the context of a self/other dynamic? While Schwartz himself sheds much valuable light on "the history of interethnic relationships and class in the Middle East and Asia" as demonstrated by the gradual gentilization of Loterā'i, his work also lays invaluable ground for complementary explorations of such questions.

In the volume's third article Vera Moreen and David Yeroushalmi offer a close examination of the intellectual parameters of Molla El'azar Hayim's *Hovot Rafa'el* (The Duties of Raphael) treatise. The article is an important addition to the field not only for its focus on a hitherto overlooked text, but further for its exploration of the nuanced "religious and polemical concerns of a learned and religious individual confronted by both internal [...] and external pressures." Moreen and Yeroushalmi's work thus helps provide an increasingly intimate understanding of Jewish intellectual life in Iran during the second half of the nineteenth century to provide us with a richer, more palpable experience of the time.

Haideh Sahim's article "Two Wars, Two Cities, Two Religions: The Jews of Mashhad and the Herat Wars" offers a new perspective on one of the more studied chapters of Jewish Iranian history. In her detailed examination of previously neglected documents, Sahim revisits the forced conversion of Mashhad's entire Jewish community on March 27, 1839 in the context of larger political dynamics of the time, ultimately to reveal formerly overlooked forces that might have sparked the flames of the Allāhdād and further determined the community's fate in the years following the event. Moreover, in investigating issues of nationality, religious identity, and the treatment of this community of forced converts by various influential members of Iran's ruling elite in the face of foreign affairs dynamics, Sahim also highlights important factors in Qajar history that had thus far remained obscure to researchers of modern Iranian history.

Following Sahim's article, Shalom Sabar's detailed study of the origins of the decorated ketubbah in Iran and Afghanistan complements Moreen and Yeroushalmi's addition to the study of Judeo-Persian manuscripts by exploring the artistic features of a specific subsection of this category. Starting with some of the earliest known samples of ketubbahs in Iran, Sabar traces the origin and development of some of the characteristic features of these documents, ultimately to present the convincing hypothesis that the decorated ketubbah from Iran serves "to bridge the great gap between the Genizah period and modern times" when compared to its counterparts from the medieval tradition. With this conclusion, Sabar adds a key piece to the puzzle of Jewish material culture, effectively demonstrating how a systematic examination of Judeo-Persian objects can expose otherwise imperceptible factors in the regional development of other Jewish communities' respective material culture.

Complementing Sabar's essay, Orit Carmeli's overview of the material culture and ritual objects of the Jews of Iran represents another important contribution to the filed of Judeo-Persian studies. Though inevitably general due to the piece's comprehensive scope in the comparably brief span of an article, Carmeli's essay is one of very few publications to date to examine Jewish Iranian material culture. Here, Carmeli discusses objects ranging from works on paper to metalwork to ceremonial art and textiles, with each category divided into respective subcategories such as miniature paintings, amulets, Torah ornaments, needlecraft, and carpets. It is arguably a testimony to the significance of her essay that Carmeli's work sheds as much light on her treated subject as it does on the lacuna of published scholarship on the material culture and artistic production of the Jews of Iran; a lacuna that speaks as much to the relative scarcity of produced objects by this 2,700-year-old community—this in and of itself being grounds for speculation about the general condition of life for Jews within Iran's predominantly Shi'ite society—as it does to the unfortunate lack of interest in the subject by historians of Jewish art in general. It has long been my personal view that the study of Judeo-Persian material culture merits a book-length study. Together, Sabar and Carmeli's respective essays have only strengthened my conviction, as they have each effectively demonstrated the new range of nuances that can come to light with respect to Iranian material culture in general, and of Jewish material culture in particular, when each is examined alongside the work of Jewish Iranian artisans.

The next and final four essays of this volume collectively represent the launch of a novel field in Judeo-Persian studies, while individually they each make valuable headway in the study of Jewish Iranian women's literary production. In "The Things They Left Behind", Judith Goldstein offers a keen reading of Dalia Sofer's *Septembers of Shiraz*, with a particular eye on the significance of the narrative's preoccupation with the characters' revealing connection to emotionally charged elements of their material world, astutely to show how ordinary objects of our daily life, such as a teacup, become containers for a web of emotions that take on a whole new set of values in the Iranian diasporatic life. Ultimately, through her analysis of the narrative's treatment of these objects, Goldstein succeeds in bringing to light delicate nuances in the characteristic emotional life of a community in exile.

Jaleh Pirnazar then examines the works of Farideh Goldin and Roya Hakakian to focus on both the common threads and diversity in the experience of Jewish Iranian women before and during the Islamic Revolution. Through Pirnazar's work, we come to realize how two symmetrically opposed experiences ultimately lead to identical resolutions. On the one hand we have Goldin, who chose to leave Iran in the mid-1970s to free herself from the constraints of her traditional patriarchal world, while on the other we find Hakakian forced to leave the initially emancipated atmosphere of post-revolutionary Iran. Thus the former willingly removes herself from an oppressive familial and community-wide patriarchy in an otherwise liberal country, while the latter is forced to leave the increasingly oppressive confines of a theocracy despite life in an otherwise liberal family environment. Yet both women meet at the crossroad of memoir writing in their respective attempts to heal from the trauma of obligatory emigration from a world of oppression.

Pirnazar's essay finds a complement in Nasrin Rahimieh's comparative analysis of the workings of memory in the quasi-autobiographical historical novels of Gina Nahai and Dalia Sofer who both, Rahimieh argues, "draw on fictional representation to develop an oblique relationship to the history of Jewish Iranian experience, to mine and interrogate communal memory and tradition, and to lay bare the mechanisms of subjection and how they produce themselves within the Jewish community." Rahimieh then convincingly hypothesizes that, free from the constraints of historicity, both Nahai and Sofer use fiction to "carv[e] out an imaginative site of potential for change and self-transformation." In the light of Rahimieh's hypothesis, one may expand upon Pirnazar's earlier view to suggest that self-imposed exile serves the same function in the life of the Jewish Iranian women memoirists as imagination does in the life of their novelist counterparts. Bound by the realities of life as a Jewish woman in Iran, the author of memoirs has no choice but to physically remove herself from these confines to actualize her respective potential for change and self-transformation within the sanctuary of an "other" time and space. The memoire writer's flight from geography is the fiction writer's flight from history.

In the volume's last article, Mojgan Behmand looks at Nahai's four novels as "narratives of transgression—transgression against established authority, traditional gender roles, received history and everyday laws of nature." One of the guiding lines in Behmand's analysis of these transgressions is the gradual shift in Nahai's primary concern from the interaction of her Jewish characters with the Shi'ite majority in Iran toward the increasingly prominent focus of "the female experience of life in the Iranian and Middle Eastern Jewish community." With particular attention to Nahai's use of magical realism as a narrative technique, Behmand demonstrates the potential of exile as one of the key engines of transgression.

All in all, the ten essays in this volume help advance the field of Judeo-Persian studies by raising our awareness about previously unknown factors in the life of Iranian Jews. I'm deeply grateful to all the contributors for their trust in me as editor and for granting me the opportunity to compile their work in this book. I am further grateful to Ahmad Karimi-Hakkak (Department of Middle Eastern Studies, University of Maryland), and Hayim Lapin and Marsha Rozenblit (Joseph and Rebecca Meyerhoff Center for Jewish Studies, University of Maryland) for their tireless work in organizing the "Iranian Jewry: From Past to Present" conference in November 2008. My last words of gratitude are for Meir Litvak and The Dr. Habib Levy Program in Iranian Jewish History of the Alliance Center for Iranian Studies at Tel Aviv University for their generous grant, without which this publication would not have been possible.

On a final note, I should simply like to point out that I have not employed a systematic transliteration system throughout the book, as I have omitted the great majority of diacritics from all but two articles. Given that Martin Schwartz's essay is a work of linguistics, the use of diacritics was inevitable. With respect to Haideh Sahim's article, while I felt that the text did not require transliteration per se, I nevertheless honored her wish to publish her copy exactly as she had it set.

CHAPTER 1

NEW VISTAS ON THE HISTORY OF IRANIAN JEWRY IN LATE ANTIQUITY, PART I: PATTERNS OF JEWISH SETTLEMENT IN IRAN[1]

Parvaneh Pourshariati

The study of the history of Iranian Jewry in Late Antiquity remains an important desideratum for future scholarship. The picture painted thus far of this history remains at best fragmentary and episodic and, individual and important studies notwithstanding, seriously devoid of any systematic analysis.[2] Scholars have sifted through the evidence provided by the Bible itself on the antiquity of the settlement of Iranian Jewry in various provinces of Iran, noting that these hark back to at least the eighth century BCE.[3] Through individual and important studies, piecemeal information on the settlement of Jewry in ancient Media,[4] Khuzestan, Azarbayjan,[5] Armenia,[6] Kurdestan,[7] Gilan, Tabaristan, and Khorasan[8] (though these last primarily deal with the later, post-Sasanian periods of Iranian history) have likewise been garnered. Thus, a very general maxim has been formed: when, sometime in mid-third century BCE, the Parthians (247 BCE – 224 CE) set out from the eastern regions of the Caspian Sea and began their westward journey through Parthava[9] and Media, they encountered an ancient community in Iran—that of the Iranian Jewry. What is known besides this, however?

Besides this very elementary understanding,[10] we still remain in the dark about many crucial aspects of this history. Thus, to date, the state-of-the-field remains predominantly the same as that which the late Walter Fischel had painted in the 1950s: the "spread and diffusion of the Jewish Diaspora beyond the Euphrates and Tigris into [. . .] Persia [. . .][11] still [remains] an obscure chapter of Jewish historical research."[12] Meager as our sources have been, however, and dim as the picture they present, there are yet vistas through which we can gain a better sense of this history. The present article is a preliminary attempt in explicating this perspective.

Though much has been said of the ostensible settlement of Iranian Jewry "on the trade routes" of the Near and Middle East in general—with comments that sporadically touch upon Iran[13]—to date no systematic effort has been made to isolate (i) the precise routes and (ii) the spatial arrangement of the settlement of Iranian Jewry *on the routes that traversed the Iranian plateau*, or (iii) the chronological time span of these settlement patterns. In other words, while we have long been preoccupied with garnering scattered information about the history of Jews in Iran, there has been no systematic investigation into the pattern of the settlement of Iranian Jewry in Iran and the implications of this in the context of the history of Iran in Late Antiquity and early medieval periods. At least two main routes crossed the Iranian plateau, with many roads bifurcating from these. On which of these routes do we find the most ancient settlements of Iranian Jewry? Once we have delimited these, the next important query presents itself, viz., what could possibly be the implications of our new understanding for the history of Iranian Jewry in Iran?

The present article, part one of a two-part study on the topic, has therefore, initially, a modest, albeit important aim: it is a preliminary work that seeks to trace the pattern of settlement of Iranian Jewry on the Iranian plateau and, specifically, the concentration of these settlements during the Parthian and Sasanian (224 BCE – 651 CE) periods. Briefly, in this first part, I will propose that the *concentration* of the settlement of Iranian Jewry on the Iranian plateau seems to have been predominantly along the *northern* overland trade route—namely, the road that crossed Iran at the foothills of the Alborz mountain range—and, significantly, *not* on the southerly route that crossed the country from Khuzistan to Fars and branched off in this last region. Once I have established this, in the forthcoming part two of this study, I will investigate the relationship of this pattern of settlement to crucial junctures of the history of Iranian Jewry in a period that spans roughly from the early fifth century CE to the Arab conquest of Iran in the early decades of the seventh century.[14]

Main Arteries of Trade through Iran:
The Northern and the Southern Routes

Before we proceed, and in order to give the reader a sense of the itineraries of the main overland northern and southern routes—and some of their important bifurcations—a brief examination of these routes is in order. The reader must bear with me while I briefly identify these, as acquiring a picture of the location of various cities on these routes is crucial to the thesis that I will be proposing.

As is well known, only a few roads cut through the imposing Zagros mountain ranges connecting the Iranian plateau to Mesopotamia and the west.[15] The most significant and celebrated of these roads was, of course, the northern route; what in the early medieval period was clearly identified as the Khorasan "highway,"[16] or, at times, the "Qumis road."[17] With minor variations dictated by the social and political requisites of various junctures of Iranian history, key urban centers astride this main northern highway had themselves an ancient history.[18] Due east, this highway began at one of the ancient trade entrepôts of Mesopotamia, Babylon/Seleucia/Ctesiphon (in Aramaic, Mahoza)/Baghdad and, following the course of the Arvand Rud (or Diyala river) northeast, ascended the mountains in order to enter the plateau.[19] The first major city reached on this itinerary was the ancient city of Hulwan.[20] Entering the Jibal at Hulwan through a "steep ascent," the main road reached Dinavar[21] and continued east to Hamadan before it arrived at the ancient city of Rayy in Tabatistan. From Rayy, due east, it proceeded through Qumis until it reached Nishspur and Tus in Khorasan. A northern road branched off from Rayy, and cutting across the Alborz range went through Amol before it reached the ancient city of Gorgan on the southeastern corner of the Caspian Sea.[22] From Rayy westwards, the road proceeded to Zanjan, at which point it bifurcated, one branch of it leading to the city of Ardabil in Azarbayjan, before continuing to Armenia.[23] The other branch from Zanjan continued westward to Miyanej (or Miyana)[24]—itself a very important trade entrêpot in later times—and thence to the region where Tabriz was later constructed.[25] The road that bifurcated from the Khorasan highway to Sinn Sumayrah or "Sumayrah's Tooth" in the Jibal, through Dinavar and Sisar, also led to Azarbayjan. This then was the main northern route and some of its main branches.

There was then the southern route. As Le Strange describes it, the southern road began in ancient Ubulla[26] (later Basra) and proceeded to Ahvaz[27] in Khuzestan, whence it continued eastward to the city of Shiraz in the Fars province. From Shiraz the road branched off. A northern route connected it to Isfahan and thence to the great Khorasan highway. After Shiraz, in Fars four roads took one in northeasterly, easterly, southerly, and southeasterly directions respectively. The important cities on the northeastern road were Yazd and Tabas, before the road connected to the Khorasan highway in Nishapur. On the road due east, one led to Kerman and Zaranj (in Sistan). The other two roads led to the Persian Gulf: (i) a southeastern road passed through Darabjerd, before going to Suru near the Persian Gulf; (ii) a southern route led to Siraf, the "chief harbor" of Fars.[28] These, then, were the main itineraries and bifurcations of the main northern and southern roads crossing Iran and the important urban centers located on these. Hulwan, Hamadan, Rayy, Qumis, Tus, and Nishapur—the last constructed only during the Sasanian period—and finally Gorgan were thus the most important ancient urban centers of the northern route before one reached Marv on the main road and proceeded further east. Ahvaz, Shiraz,[29] Kerman,[30] Yazd, and finally Zarang[31] in Sistan were some of the major towns on the southern route. Isfahan, being ideally situated as a north south urban connection, had a unique history, to which I will get in due course.

Now even a superficial investigation of the pattern of settlement of Iranian Jewry, of ascertaining where we find the *concentration* of their settlements, will lead to a significant observation: namely, that up until the restoration of the city of Shiraz in 693 CE,[32] the preponderance of the major Jewish settlements on the Iranian plateau during the Parthian and Sasanian periods was on the northern overland trade route.[33] While in this pattern of settlement the Jews of Iran were simply following the millennia-old human geography of the plateau,[34] and while much has been made of the settlement of Jews on trade routes, what is especially significant for the purposes of this study is that it was on this route, *and not the more southerly route*, that one finds the most populated and ancient centers of Jewry in Iran. This very important issue needs to be kept in mind in what follows, for as far as I have been able to ascertain, in none of the ancient and important cities that were located on the three main branches of the southern route (i.e., Kerman, Yazd, Tabas, and Zaranj in Sistan) have scholars established the existence of any substantial Jewish communities through the Parthian and Sasanian periods.

For the purposes of the present and future studies, another significant issue must be kept in mind, namely the intimate and amicable relationship that Iranian Jewry ultimately came to establish with the Parthians,[35] under whose rule they came to live for more than four centuries of their history in Iran. Naturally, this is a vast topic, a treatment of which is well beyond the confines of the present study.[36] It is hoped, however, that the conclusions of this and the sequel to this study will further substantiate this well-established scholarly consensus.

As we will see, when the Parthians began their journey through the plateau to Mesopotamia and the west, in almost every region that they set foot on the northern route and wherein they even constructed a capital, be it Hyrcania (Gorgan or "land of the wolves"),[37] Parthava, ancient Rhages (Rayy),[38] Ecbatana[39] (Hamadan), and whether in Armenia, where they established the Armenian Arsacid[40] or Arshakuni dynasty, and on their way to Mesopotamia through the important crossing of the Middle Zagros, Ḥulwān, they came across an ancient Jewish Iranian community.[41] It is on this itinerary, following in the footsteps of a traveler coming from the west, that we will begin our journey in search of ancient settlements of Jews in Iran. I will confine my treatment to major cities on this road in which Jewish settlements can firmly be established during the Parthian and Sasanian periods, namely Hulwan, Hamadan, Isfahan, Rayy, Gorgan, Marv, and finally Juzjanan.

Hulwan

The city of Hulwan was one of the main urban centers near the very entrance of the Zagros pass of the Paytak. Forming a "natural frontier between Babylonia and Media" during the later Sasanian period,[42] Hulwan or Shadh Piruz (or Khusrow Shadh Piruz) was one of the summer residences of Sasanian kings. All evidence underlines the fact that this strategic and important first relay of the Khorasan highway had an ancient and, to all appearances, very significant and substantial Jewish community. The earliest indicator of this fact dates back to the Parthian period, and underlines the jurisdiction of the Exilarchate[43] over the Jewish community in Hulwan.[44] Thus Rabbi Nathan, the Babylonian[45] who lived in the second century CE—and as the son of the Babylonian Exilarch was in a perfect position to be informed of such matters—already mentions Hulwan as being under the jurisdiction and leadership, or *rāshūt*,[46] of the Exilarch, observing that the latter received "150 golden coins (dinars)" yearly from Hulwan.[47] It should be observed at the outset that, besides its other sources of income, the Exilarch received one-fifth of the income from the population under its jurisdiction into its coffers. Whatever the worth of 150 gold *dinars*—which were probably Roman gold solidi[48]—it is safe to conclude that in the second-century Jewish community of Hulwan, we are probably not dealing with a low-income community.[49] How wealthy the Jewish community of Hulwan could have been at the time is not our present concern. The point, rather, is that in the second century CE, the Jewish community of Hulwan must have been extensive and productive enough to have afforded to pay such taxation to the office of the Exilarch. By the time the Bavli or Babylonian Talmud—composed through the third to the early sixth centuries—comes to comment on 2 Kings (18:11) about the Assyrian deportation of Jews to "Halah, along the Habor [and] the River Gozan, and in the towns of Media"[50] in *b. Kid 71b–72a*, the city of Halah is explicitly identified with Hulwan.[51] The point of course is not whether this identification was justified,[52] but rather that it was made at all. Thus, already in the *Kiddushin*—the chapter dealing with laws of betrothal in the Babylonian Talmud—we get further substantive and direct references to the city of Hulwan. In fact the Jewish community of Hulwan seems to have been so ancient and prominent by this time that in the genealogical warfare that was prevalent among a section of the Jewish population of Babylonia, one of the few communities to have been accepted as having "pure" and "good" genealogical pedigree was none other than the Jewish community of Hulwan.[53] Thus, once again, Hulwan is specifically singled out in the *Kiddushin:* In *b. Kid 71b–72a*, therefore, while "Bei Huzae (Khuzistan), Mesene, Elam,[54] [and] Media, [are] regarded as 'dead,' 'dying' or 'sick' as far as Jewish lineage was concerned,"[55] Hulwan, Nahrawan,[56] and communities in Upper Mesopotamia are deemed to have the "healthy lineage" of Babylonian Jewry.[57] At the very important and strategic entrance to the northern route at Hulwan, therefore, there certainly existed a substantive enough Jewish community during the Parthian and Sasanian periods. It was doubtless partly from this constituency that the active Christian population of the city had been later formed,[58] so that we have Nestorian bishoprics attested in the region in 554, 585, and 605 CE.[59] It is the history of this ancient Jewish community in Hulwan that, likewise, comes to form the legacy of the city in the tenth century, where a *darb al-yahud*, Gate of the Jews, led to the Yahudiya, or Jewish quarter, of the city. By this time Hulwan's synagogue was so noteworthy, and the Jewish settlement therein so substantial, that it solicited Shams al-Din al-Maqdisi's comparison with Jerusalem.[60] Whether or not the Jewish population of the city had increased by this time, we cannot ascertain in the current stage of our research. What is clear, however, is that by the time Maqdisi was writing from the "eight gates" of the town, besides the Khorasan gate, one was called the "gate of the Jewess," and another the "gate of the Jews."[61]

From Hulwan, and after crossing the mountains "diagonally" to the northeast and reaching the environs of Dinavar—wherein the existence of a substantial Jewish population during the medieval period[62] cannot be doubted—the traveler was presented with a choice. A northerly road took one through the valleys of the imposing Zagros mountains to the north to Azarbayjan, Armenia,[63] and the Caucasus. If one's destination was eastwards, however, the route of choice was the Great Khorasan highway. On this latter road, the next major city was the ancient capital of the Medes and the Achaemenids, the city of Ecbatana or Hamadan,[64] the Achmeta of Ezra (6:2) and of the apocryphal traditions (2 Macc. 9.3; Judith 1:1, 2, 14 and Tobit 3:7; 6:5; 7:1; 14:12, 14).

Hamadan

As we have long been aware, there is substantial evidence, primarily Biblical, that establishes Hamadan as one of the earliest settlement locations of Iranian Jewry in the post-exilic period. The earliest reference to Hamadan and Jewish settlement in this important capital of Media seems to be contained in the Pentateuch, where we are told that in 722 BCE a group of Israelites were brought by King Shamanaser of Assyria and "settled [...] in the cities of the Medes" (2 Kings 18.11). It is agreed that one of these major "cities of the Medes" was Hamadan.[65] In the Book of Ezra (6:2), attributed to a priestly scribe of the governor of Judah who functioned probably during the rule of Artaxerxes I (r. 465–425 BCE),[66] and in the apocryphal traditions (2 Macc. 9:3; Judith 1:1, 2, 14 and Tobit 3:7, 6:5, 7:1, 14:12, 14)—the latter two of which, as we shall see, were composed during the Parthian period—the continued centrality of Hamadan in Media to the post-exilic life of Iranian Jewry is amply underlined. Hamadan becomes so important in the historical memory of Iranian Jewry that the tombs of Queen Esther and Mordechai[67] later come to be located in the city, giving rise to a tradition that is attested neither in the Babylonian nor in the Jerusalemite Talmud, and significantly not recognized among non-Iranian Jewry.[68]

As far as Media and its ancient capital Hamadan are concerned, one other significant fact should be kept in mind, namely that the majority of the Judeo-Persian[69] dialects spoken in Iran to this day belong to the "Central or Median dialects, which occur in the central parts of Iranian plateau in a geographical area approximately between Isfahan, Hamadan, and Kashan."[70] Included in these, and naturally besides Hamadan, are the dialects of Jews living in Rayy, Kashan Isfahan, Natanz, Borujerd, Khomein, Arak, Nahavand, Malayer, and "many other cities" of Iran.[71] A glance at any map of Iran with the aim of locating these cities will make it clear that, significantly, these regions were in fact not only in the ancient territory of Media, but also along the trade routes connecting Isfahan to the north (Natanz, Kashan) and Rayy and/or Dinavar/Kermanshah to Isfahan (Nehavand, Borujerd, Malayer); in short, on roads that criss-crossed Media or western Parthava.

While the precise characteristic and historical evolution of various regional Judeo-Persian dialects themselves must remain the domain of the linguists, the predominance of the Central or Median dialect also gives evidence of two remarkable facts: first, it provides evidence of the interconnections of various Iranian Jewish communities through the ages;[72] second, and even more importantly, it underlines the regional focus and spread of this linguistic domain in Iran. We can thus comfortably assume that greater Media was *the* original homeland of Iranian Jewry, wherefrom they spread, predominantly to the northeast and the northwest. Before proceeding with our examination of Jewish settlement in the rest of the major cities on the northern route, a word needs to be said about Jewish settlement in Isfahan for, as mentioned above, the settlement of Iranian Jewry in Isfahan is in fact of particular interest for the purposes of our study.

Isfahan

In classical Arabic sources, the antiquity of the Jewish community of Isfahan[73] is traced to the post-exilic and Achaemenid periods of its history.[74] For example, Ibn Faqih Hamadani records a tradition according to which the first exiles, carrying a sample of the water and soil of Jerusalem, travelled from city to city until they found the water and soil of Isfahan resembling that of their holy city, and thus settled there.[75] Besides this lore, the historical context of which can naturally not be ascertained, our first documented evidence for this settlement pertains to the Sasanian period. It is contained in the account of the Armenian historian Moses Khorenats'i, where Moses traces the establishment of a Jewish settlement in Isfahan to the reign of Shapur II (r. 309–379). While describing Shapur II's campaigns in Armenia, Khorenats'i here claims that, in the course of these campaigns, the Sasanian king deported a multitude of Jews, as well as Armenians, from various cities in Armenia, and settled the Jews in Isfahan. It should be noted, however, that Khorenats'i's account of Shapur II's deportation of the Jews is itself based on the account of the anonymous *History of the Armenians* (*P'awstos Buzand*).[76] Whereas in the *P'awstos Buzand* Shapur II is said to have settled these captives "some in Asorestan, some in the country of Xuzhastan,"[77] Moses claims that they were settled in Isfahan. This last bit of information, we now know, was added by Khorenats'i himself.[78] Now, considering the caution with which we have been advised to view Khorenats'i's account of Jewish settlements and resettlements in Armenia,[79] and further considering the fact that Khorenats'i was most probably writing in the first two decades after the Abbasid revolution, it is quite likely that the author had the very recent and "formal founding" of the Jewish town of Yahudiya[80] in mind when making the connection between the resettlement of Armenian Jews and their final settlement in Isfahan.[81]

As far as we can ascertain, and as we will be arguing in more detail in the sequel to this study, the growth of the Jewish population of Isfahan seems to belong to the middle Sasanian period; specifically to the reign of Yazdgird I "The Accursed" (r. 399–420) when, rather unsuccessfully it seems and as a result of political exigencies,[82] Yazdgird attempted to reinvigorate the north–south highway crossing Iran by settling a trading community in Isfahan, the city that would eventually grow on this highway. Unlike Hulwan, Hamadan, Rayy, and Gurgan (see below), in which regions there is very little doubt about the existence of Jewish communities during the Parthian period, the earliest concrete and perhaps most reliable evidence that we currently possess of the settlement of Jews in Isfahan is contained in the Middle Persian source, *Shahrestaniha i Eranshahr*.[83] Here we are significantly informed that it was at the prompting of his Jewish wife, Shushandokht, that the Sasanian king, Yazdgird I, settled Jews in Isfahan.[84] While there is a possibility that Jews might have been settled in Isfahan prior to this, as even the *Shahrestaniha* seems to insinuate,[85] it is the association of the settlement of Jews in Isfahan with Yazdgird I, known in the *Xwaday Namag* tradition as "*bezeh-kār*" (The Accursed)[86] that is significant here.[87] As we shall see in the sequel to this study, it is in this context that we must consider the ostensible persecution of the Iranian Jewry by Piruz (459–484), specifically as it relates to the Jewish population of Isfahan.[88] While there is little doubt that, from at least the reign of Yazdgird I onward, there was in fact a Jewish settlement in the Yahudiya of Isfahan—as the very reaction of Iranian Jewry of the region to the Arab conquest, among many other indications, bears witness—it is also the case that it was only in the first two decades *after* the Abbasid revolution and the creation of Baghdad that we witness the formal founding and unprecedented growth in the prosperity of the Yahudiya of Isfahan.[89] The very growth of the city of Isfahan in fact dates back to this period, and as I will try to elaborate in subsequent works, this growth was directly related to the final and rather successful opening of the north–south road from the province of Fars, through Isfahan, to Rayy in this period.

Rayy

After Hulwan, Dinawar, and Hamadan, the next ancient and important city going northeast on the Qumis or Khorasan road was the city of Avestan and Biblical fame: Raga or Rayy.[90] As with Hamadan, Rayy became central to the ancient history of Iranian Jewry, so much so that a number of Biblical apocrypha are directly and intimately concerned with this important city on the northern overland route. Thus, Rayy appears as 'Ragau' in Judith (Judith 1:5, 15) and 'Rages' in Tobit[91] (Tobit 1:14; 4:1, 20; 5:5; 6:12; 9:2). While the historicity of many facts in the apocryphal story of Tobit[92] (dated to sometime between mid-first century BCE to mid-first century CE)[93] have been questioned by scholarship, and while the story of Tobit is more akin to a popular narrative, or novelette, there is no denying the fact that the cultural context of the Book of Tobit is heavily Iranian.[94] A substantial part of the fascinating story of Tobit, in fact, unfolds in Media, with Rages providing a crucial context for the story.

Briefly, according to the story the righteous Tobit, from the tribe of Nephtali, marries Anna, one of his own kindred, with whom he begets Tobias. Along with his family and brethren, Tobit is eventually led to captivity from the northern kingdom of Israel to Ninevah. In Ninevah, Tobit relates, by the grace of god he became the "purveyor" of Enemessar (i.e., the Assyrian king Shamanaser V (r. 727–722 BCE)). Early on in the story, we learn that Tobit goes to the city of "Rages" in "Media" where he leaves ten talents of silver in trust "with Gabael, the brother of Gabrias." It must be pointed out that if a talent of silver was equivalent to approximately £100, Tobit had ostensibly entrusted to Gabael the quite substantial amount of around £1,000 of silver! What is even more interesting is that this "sum of money becomes an important motif of the [whole] story."[95] And thus, even if in folkloric garb, we get a sense of the incredible wealth of Tobit and the fact that he had bequeathed this wealth to a close associate in, what is in the context of the story, the Parthian city of Rayy. As the story proceeds, Tobias sends Azarias, who is in fact none other than the angel Raphael, along with two camels and a servant, to Rages in order to fetch the wealth that his father had entrusted to Gabael. Presenting what is depicted as a "handwritten," presumably contract, of the loan to Gabael, Azarias then procures the bags that contained the talents of silver, and returns to Ecbatana along with Tobias and Gabael. In the finale of the narrative, after Tobias's parents are dead, he returns with his wife to Ecbatana, where they finally settle. The centrality of Rages, along with Ecbatana, in the story of Tobit, reflects not only the importance of these ancient cities on the northern route to the historical memory of the Iranian Jewry during the Parthian period, but also the interconnections of the Jewish communities of Rages and Ecbatana to each other, and the regions west, in this case Ninevah/Mawsul. As we know, in another apocrypha composed during the Parthian period, namely the story of Judith,[96] this memory of Rages/Ragau/Rayy is further maintained when the Median king, called Arphaxad in Judith (Judith 1:1, 5, 13, 15, etc.), the historical Cyaxares[97] who ruled in the sixth century BCE,[98] is said to have been defeated by Nebuchadnezzar II (r. 605–562 BCE) in the great plains on the borders of Ragau (Judith 1:5).

The close connection of Iranian Jewry to the ancient city of Rayy was maintained during the Sasanian period. For instance, Theophylact Simocatta underlines the financial support that the community gave to the great Parthian dynast of the house of Mehran, Bahram Chubin (r. 590–1) of Rayy, during the important rebellion of the latter against the Sasanians.[99] As others have noted—and I will discuss in the sequel to the study—the direct involvement of Iranian Jewry in this revolt had important and damaging consequences for the community once Bahram's rebellion was put down by Khusrow II Parviz (r. 591–628). This intimate connection of Iranian Jewry to Rayy was so forceful that its memory was even maintained in the works of later classical authors writing in Arabic. Thus, we find in al-Sahmi's biography of Abd al-Wasi in the *Tarikh Jurjan* that, according to Abd al-Wasi b. Taiba al-Jurjani, "it is *written in the Torah* that [. . .] al-Rayy [. . .] is one of the gateways of the lands [. . .], and {leading} to it are *the routes mankind follows for trade.*"[100] Of course, no such information can be found in the Torah as we have it. Whether or not the version of the Torah circulating in Abd al-Wasi's milieu in fact contained such a piece of information—as far as the author is concerned not an improbability—is a moot point. For what is fascinating about this account in the *Tarikh Jurjan* is the fact that

Abd al-Wasi was in fact underlining, and sanctifying no less, the importance of Rayy for what was most certainly a Jewish or Judeo-Islamic audience, by reference to the Jewish Holy scripture. It was from time immemorial, as witnessed in the Torah itself, he is reminding his audience, that Rayy had been the gateway of mankind and the route that it had followed for trade. Significantly, this lore seems to have been a highly popular one, for it is repeated in other classical accounts.[101] In the sequel to this study I will underline the network of cities—including Rayy, Gorgan, Marv, and Juzjanan—that connected the Iranian Jewry of Khorasan and Tabarestan on the eve of the conquest of Iran and thereafter. For now, it is important to continue to trace the footprints of Iranian Jewry on the Qumis road, to the east.[102]

Gorgan

An important and strategic center on one of the northeastern branches of the Khorasan highway was the ancient city of Gorgan or Hyrcania. Significantly, Hyrcania itself seems to have been closely connected to the Eastern Mediterranean since the Achaemenid period. The earliest evidence to this effect is contained in *Geography*, the important work of the Greek geographer and traveler Strabo (64/63 BCE–24 CE), which seems to have been written sometime in the first decades of the first century.[103] Here Strabo informs us that the Hyrcanian plain (Hiera Kome) of Lydia was "a name given [to the region] by the Persians, who brought colonists [there] from Hyrcania."[104] These settlements pertain to the Achaemenid (550–330 BCE) period, and are only part of the picture of the Achaemenid colonization in Asia Minor.[105] On the other hand, and even more important for the purposes of this study, is the evidence that we have of the settlement of Jews in Hyrcania at the end of this period. In his *Seven Books of History against the Pagans*, Paulus Orosius (375–418 CE) (the Christian Archbishop and student of St. Augustine who, after travelling and living in North Africa, moved to Jerusalem) tells us that the Achaemenid king Artaxerxes Ochus (r. 358–338 BCE),[106] "after having carried on a very extensive and long-lasting war in Egypt, forced a great many Jews to migrate and ordered them to live in Hyrcania near the Caspian Sea."[107] Hyrcania seems to have maintained its rather intimate connection with the Eastern Mediterranean and Palestine. A fortress, for example, was called Hyrcania in Palestine, on the wake of this same relationship; and Hyrcanian Jews seem to have immigrated back to Palestine. While some controversy surrounds the origins of the *nisba* "Hyracanus" adopted by important figures in Palestine, Neusner argues that "a Jew belonging to a family settled in Hyrcania, returning to Palestine, would at first be distinguished by the designation 'Hyracanian'." He therefore concludes that the rather well-attested *nisba*s of "Hyracanian" and "Hyrcanus" in Palestine (e.g., John Hyrcanus (d. 104 BCE) the Hasmonean High Priest, and the sage Eliezer b. Hyrcanus (*c*.90 CE)) are "best interpreted [. . .] to indicate familial origin, however remote, in Hyrcania."[108] There is, therefore, very little doubt about the antiquity of the settlement of Iranian Jewry in Gorgan. Orosius underlines the continued numerical strength of Iranian Jewry in Hyrcania during his own lifetime, in the fourth century CE, in the Sasanian period. It is "common belief," he maintains, that the Hyracanian Jews had remained in their new home "up to the present day, with ample increases in their race."[109]

Now Hyrcania was a region that was ideally positioned as a trade entrepôt and commercial hub. It was the terminus of seafaring trade across the Caspian sea,[110] and overland trade either through the Caspian coastlines or through the Khorasan highway. In this context, therefore, (i) the settlement of Iranian Jewry in this ancient land and (ii) the connection of the region to the Eastern Mediterranean through the Parthian period and thereafter become particularly telling. As I will argue in the sequel to the present work, Gorgan continued to be home to Iranian Jewry after the Arab conquest of the region; a conquest that, significantly, was finally effected only in 711 and the first half of the eighth century. The *Bab al-Yahud* (Gate of the Jews) of Gorgan and the Jewish quarter within the city therefore had an ancient history,[111] only the bare outlines of which we can reconstruct with the information currently at our disposal.

Marv and Guzgan

A brief discussion of two more ancient urban centers of the settlement of Jewry on the Khorasan highway will conclude our investigation of the easternmost itinerary pertaining to this study, namely the cities of Marv and, closely connected to it for the purposes of this article, Guzgan (or Juzjanan),[112] located half way between Marv and Balkh.[113] There is very little doubt of the settlement of Iranian Jewry in Marv during the Parthian and Sasanian periods: (i) excavations carried out at the "Erk-qala," the citadel of "Old Marv,"[114] have revealed Hebrew names inscribed on Parthian inscriptions dating to the first to the third centuries CE;[115] (ii) the Avodah Zarah tractate of the Babylonian Talmud provides information pertaining to the travel of one of the Babylonian Amora,[116] Shmuel bar Bisena, a member of the Jewish academy of Pumbedita (Peruz-Shapur, later Anbar, in Mesopotamia), to MRGW'N (Marv);[117] and finally (iii) sixth-century ossuaries with Hebrew inscriptions have been unearthed in a necropolis west of Marv;[118] all of which confirm the existence of a Jewish community in Marv during the Parthian and Sasanian periods.[119] As in all the other cities under review here, it was this older Jewish settlement in Marv that, most probably, formed the Jewish heritage of the city in the Later Antiquity.[120] Finally, located half way between Marv and Balkh, on the main caravan road, was the chief city of Juzjanan, namely its Yahudiya. As I will argue in the sequel to this study, and as was the case with Hamadan and Rayy, from the eve of Arab conquest of Transoxiana in the middle of the seventh century well into early Abbasid period, there was a very direct and intimate connection between the Jewish communities of Marv, Juzjanan, Gorgan, and finally Rayy. This connection, I suspect, was formed in earlier centuries.

This, then, was a bird's eye view of the settlement pattern of Iranian Jewry on the northern route during the Parthian and Sasanian periods. Leaving aside Azarbayjan and Armenia, the roads towards which branched off from the Khorasan highway west of Rayy and north of Dinawar in the Zagros mountains, the paramount issue is that by the time the Sasanians entered the scene—and leaving aside their settlement in southwestern Iran—the concentration of the settlement of Iranian Jewry in Iran in fact closely followed the itinerary of the northern *overland* trade route. From Marv to Gorgan, to Rayy, to Hamadan, and finally to Isfahan, and on the egress of the Khorasan highway to Mesopotamia in Hulwan where the northern trade route traversed or bent, there too communities of Iranian Jews had been establishing themselves since at least the Parthian period. Of this settlement pattern, in other words, we ought to have little doubt for the period under consideration here. This leaves out of the picture the regions in the north, for which our evidence of settlement pertains *only* to Later Antiquity and early medieval periods.

As opposed to this pattern of settlement, however, and again leaving aside Khuzestan, we have, comparatively speaking, an astounding dearth of evidence for Jewish settlement in any of the major urban centers that lay astride the southern route and roads that bifurcated from these during the Parthian and Sasanian periods. This was the case with the major centers of Kerman,[121] Yazd,[122] Sistan and Zarang.[123] The Kerman Jewish community, as far as we can ascertain, for example, was established in the modern period.[124] There seems to be next to no evidence, at least none that we could locate, about ancient Jewish settlement in Sistan. This leaves the city of Yazd. Here, significantly, the earliest evidence that has been thus far garnered pertains to the ninth century, and interestingly enough is reflected in the "ninth century Hebrew manuscript of the Old Testament (section of the Latter Prophets), produced by Jewish scholars in Yazd."[125] As I pursue the present study in the sequel to this paper, what is of interest here is that both the Jewish communities of Isfahan and Yazd seem to have experienced rather simultaneous growth subsequent to the Abbasid revolution and, more specifically, following the foundation of Baghdad in the middle of the eighth century. We seem to have very little information on the history of the city of Yazd itself, even for the Sasanian period.[126] At any rate, in all likelihood there were no substantial Jewish communities to speak of in the region during the period under study. After the conquest, however, and by the ninth century, the community seems to have grown to such extent that it was producing its own manuscripts of the Old Testament.

This then was a synopsis of our givens for the pattern of Jewish settlement in Iran during the Parthian and Sasanian periods. Khuzestan set aside, Jews did *not* settle in "all provinces of Iran," as the Book of Esther repeatedly claims (3:6, 8; 8:5, 12; 9:20). In fact, the significant fact that must be underlined here is that the very composition of the Book of Esther itself has been (only) dated to the Parthian period, in the third or second century BCE.[127] Likewise, Iranian Jewry did *not* settle on all trade routes that crossed the Iranian territory during the period under consideration, but settled primarily only on the northern route. As I will propose in the sequel to this study, if we accept this new theorem, we will be able to go a long way in explicating the history of Iranian Jewry from the early fifth century through the Arab conquest, and thence through the post-Sasanian centuries. In my forthcoming work, I aim to explicate how the deterioration of the Jewish relationship with the Sasanians during the reign of Yazdgird II (r. 438–57) and Piruz (r. 457–84), and intermittently thenceforth, was precisely related to the ancient and amicable ties that Iranian Jewry had come to establish with the Parthian dynastic families; a relationship that was itself occasioned by their long-time settlements and direct involvement in the overland trade route that passed through Parthian lands during Late Antiquity.[128] These same set of conditions, I will argue, accounted for the support that Iranian Jewry appear to have given to the rebellion of the Parthian Bahram Chubin (r. 590–1), and to the Mehranid general of Khosrow Parviz, and the conqueror of Jerusalem, Shahrbaraz, in 614; not to mention the reception that Iranian Jewry gave to the Arab conquerors in the middle of the seventh century. All of this, and hopefully more, I relegate to the sequel to this study.

Acknowledgements

I would like to thank my colleague Haideh Sahim for reading the present article and for giving me valuable suggestions, saving me from a number of infelicities. For those that remain, I take full responsibility.

Notes

All online resources last accessed June 2012.

1   This is the first part of a two-part study, the second segment of which the author hopes to publish shortly.

2   See Houman Sarshar, "Judeo-Persian Communities i. Introduction," *Encyclopaedia Iranica* [online journal] <http://www.iranicaonline.org/articles/ judeo-persian-communities-of-iran-i-introduction>, where a synopsis of the state of field is given along with references to works thus far published.

3   See, for example, the works cited in Sarshar, "Judeo-Persian Communities;" Mayer I. Gruber, "Judeo-Persian Communities ii. Achaemenid Period;" *Encyclopaedia Iranica* [online] <http://www.iranicaonline.org/articles/judeo-persian-communities-ii-achaemenid-period> and Jacob Neusner, "Judeo-Persian Communities: iii. Parthian and Sasanian Periods," *Encyclopaedia Iranica* [online] <http://www.iranicaonline.org/articles/judeo-persian-communities-iii-parthian-and-sasanian-periods>.

4   Walter J. Fischel, "Isfahan: The Story of a Jewish Community in Persia," in *The Joshua Starr Memorial Volume* (New York, 1953), pp. 111–28.

5   Walter Fischel, "Azarbaijan in Jewish History," *Proceedings of the American Academy for Jewish Research*, 22 (1953), pp. 1–21, here p. 4.

6   Jacob Neusner, "The Jews in Pagan Armenia," *Journal of the American Oriental Society*, 84:3 (Jul.–Sep., 1964), pp. 230–40.

7   Abraham Ben-Yaacob, Amnon Netzer, and Edith Gerson-Kiwi, "Kurdistan," in *Encyclopaedia Judaica* [online facsimile], ed. Michael Berenbaum and Fred Skolnik (2nd edn, Detroit, 2007), Gale Virtual Reference Library <http://go. galegroup.com/ps/>, vol. 12, pp. 389–93.

8   For a brief assessment of these, see below. Also see Edwin Yamauchi, "The Reconstruction of Jewish Communities During the Persian Empire," *Journal of The Historical Society*, 4:1 (Winter, 2004), pp. 1–27.

9   Roughly corresponding to the present boundaries of the province of Khorasan originally, the later boundaries of Parthava comprised an extensive territory that "was bounded in the east by Gurgan, in the north by the Caspian Sea, and in the southwest by the region between Khuzistan and Media" (Parvaneh Pourshariati, *Decline and Fall of the Sasanian Empire: The Sasanian–Parthian Confederacy and the Arab Conquest of Iran* (London, 2008), p. 36).

10 Neusner's in-depth studies of the history of Jewry in Babylonia remain an exception.

11 Fischel had naturally also included the Caucasus, India, and China in his list. An assessment of these last, however, is beyond the confines of the present study. W. Fischel, "Azarbaijan in Jewish History," p. 1.

12 Ibid.

13 Much has been said about the settlement of Jewry on the "East–West" trade routes. The settlement of the community in isolated cities on these "routes" has

likewise been underlined. See, for example, Richard Foltz, "Judaism and the Silk Route," *The History Teacher*, 32:1 (1988), pp. 9–16. As far as we know, no study has proposed the thesis offered presently.

14 For now, I offer a synopsis of this in the conclusion to this study, below.

15 The classic work on trade and communication routes remains Guy Le Strange, *The Lands of the Eastern Caliphate: Mesopotamia, Persia, and Central Asia from the Moslem Conquest to the Time of Timur* (Cambridge, 2011).

16 Naturally, there were many roads that connected to and bifurcated from the Khurasan highway. It is the stages of the most direct route that are usually depicted in medieval geographical treatise. It is thus that we get, for example, Estakhri's assessment that the distance from "the valley (*wādī*) of Balkh to Iraq, is around sixty stages (*marḥala*)" (Abu Eshaq Ebrahim b. Mohammad al-Faresi, Estakhri, *Masālek va'l-Mamālek*, ed. M. J. de Goeje (Leiden, 1870), p. 12). Also see 'Izz al-Din Ibn al-Athir, *al-Kāmil fi'l Tarikh* (Beirut, 1965), vol. 3, p. 111.

17 Abu 'l-Hasan Ali b. Zayd al-Bayhaqi, Ibn Funduq, *Tārikh-e Bayhaqi*, ed. Ahmad Bahmanyar, with an introduction by Muhammad Qazvini (Tehran, n.d.), p. 46.

18 For detailed itineraries of this route, see, among others, Le Strange, *The Lands of the Eastern Caliphate*, pp. 9–10; Christopher Brunner, "Geographical and Administrative Divisions: Settlement and Economy," in E. Yarshater (ed.), *The Cambridge History of Iran*, vol. 3(2): *The Seleucid, Parthian and Sasanian Periods* (Cambridge, 1983), pp. 747–78.

19 M. Kasheff, "Arvand-Rūd," *Encyclopaedia Iranica* [online] < http://www.iranicaonline.org/articles/arvand-rud>.

20 "[I]dentified with [...] present-day village of Sar-i Pul-i Dhhāb, which is 33 km east by south of Ḳaṣr-i Shīrīn, Ḥulwān was called Khalmanu in Assyrian times." The district of Hulwan, possibly attached fiscally to the "Quarter of the West," was often the summer residence of the Sasanian kings. L. Lockhart, "Ḥulwān," in *Encyclopaedia of Islam* [online], ed. P. Bearman, Th. Bianquis, C. E. Bosworth, E. van Donzel, W. P. Heinrichs (2nd edn), Brill Online, 2014. < http://referenceworks.brillonline.com.proxy.lib.ohio-state.edu/entries/encyclopaedia-of-islam-2/hulwan-SIM_2945>, vol. 3, 571:2.

21 Built probably during the Seleucid period, Dinavar was situated to the northeast of Kermanshah, and became an important fortified center in the Jibal during the Sasanian period. Kermanshah was, most probably, a Sasanian construction. See L. Lockhart, "Dīnawar," in *Encyclopaedia of Islam* [online] < http://referenceworks.brillonline.com.proxy.lib.ohio-state.edu/entries/encyclopaedia-of-islam-2/dinawar-SIM_1867>, II:299:1; C. E. Bosworth, "Dinavar," *Encyclopaedia Iranica* [online] < http://www.iranicaonline.org/articles/dinavar>.

22 Le Strange, *The Lands of the Eastern Caliphate*, pp. 364–81, especially p. 381.

23 Le Strange, *The Lands of the Eastern Caliphate*, pp. 220–30.

24 See C. E. Bosworth, "Miyāna," in *Encyclopaedia of Islam* [online] < http://referenceworks.brillonline.com.proxy.lib.ohio-state.edu/entries/encyclopaedia-of-islam-2/miyana-SIM_5243>, VII:189:2.

25 Le Strange, *The Lands of the Eastern Caliphate*, p. 230. The regions surrounding Tabriz are initially said to have been purchased on behalf of Zubayda, the wife of the Abbasid caliph, Harun al-Rashid (r. 786–809). At the time, it developed into a small village. It was only after the rebellion of Bābak was put down, under the caliph Mutawakkil (r. 847–61), that the village was turned into a fortified town. W. Barthold, *An Historical Geography of Iran* (Princeton, 1984), p. 217. For trade routes through Azarbayjan, see below.

26 J. H. Kramers, "al-Ubulla," in *Encyclopaedia of Islam* [online] <http://referenceworks.brillonline.com.proxy.lib.ohio-state.edu/entries/encyclopaedia-of-islam-2/al-ubulla-SIM_7673>, X:765:2.

27 L. Lockhart, "al-Ahwāz," in *Encyclopaedia of Islam* [online] <http://referenceworks.brillonline.com.proxy.lib.ohio-state.edu/entries/encyclopaedia-of-islam-2/al-ahwaz-SIM_0437>, I:305:2, and C. E. Bosworth, "Ahvāz," *Encyclopaedia Iranica* [online] <http://www.iranicaonline.org/articles/ahvaz-a-town-of-southwestern-iran#pt3>.

28 Le Strange, *The Lands of the Eastern Caliphate*, pp. 10–11.

29 Shiraz seems to have grown substantially only after the Arab conquest of Fars, when, significantly again for our future purposes, it became the center of the province. See Shapur Shahbazi, "Shiraz i. History to 1940," *Encyclopaedia Iranica* [online] <http://www.iranicaonline.org/articles/shiraz-i-history-to-1940>.

30 A. K. S. Lambton, "Kirmān," in *Encyclopaedia of Islam* [online] <http://referenceworks.brillonline.com.proxy.lib.ohio-state.edu/entries/encyclopaedia-of-islam-2/kirman-COM_0521>, V:147:1.

31 C. E. Bosworth, "Zarang," in *Encyclopaedia of Islam* [online] <http://referenceworks.brillonline.com.proxy.lib.ohio-state.edu/entries/encyclopaedia-of-islam-2/zarang-SIM_8123>, XI:458:1.

32 Shiraz was probably restored by Mohammad, the brother of Hajjaj b. Yusof. See Ann K. S. Lambton, "Shīrāz," in *Encyclopaedia of Islam* [online] <http://referenceworks.brillonline.com.proxy.lib.ohio-state.edu/entries/encyclopaedia-of-islam-2/shiraz-SIM_6958>, IX:472:2.

33 This excludes the ancient settlements of Jews in Khuzestan (namely in the ancient centers of Susa, or Shushan, and Shushtar), itself an extension of the Mesopotamian plane, and therefore a region that partook in the southern overland trade route. On Susa/Shushan, see Adele Berlin, Marc Zvi Brettler and Michael Fishbane, *The Jewish Study Bible* (New York, 2014), Nehemiah 1:1; Esther 1:2, 5; 2:3, 3:15, 9:11; Daniel 8:2. On Shushtar, see J. H. Kramers and C.E. Bosworth, "Shūshtar," in *Encyclopaedia of Islam* [online] <http://referenceworks.brillonline.com.proxy.lib.ohio-state.edu/entries/encyclopaedia-of-islam-2/shushtar-SIM_6995>, IX:512:1.

34 Heinz Gaube, "Iranian Cities," in Salma K. Jayyusi, Renata Holod, Attilio Petruccioli and André Raymond (eds), *The City in the Islamic World*, vol. 2 (Leiden, 2008), pp. 2 and 159–81. Also see W. B. Fisher, "Physical Geography," in *The Cambridge History of Iran*, vol. 1 (Cambridge, 1968),

pp. 3–111; and X. de Planhol and Judith A. Brown, "Geography of Settlement," ibid., pp. 409–68.

35 Though, as Neusner observes, we have "no information on Parthian and Babylonian and Mesopotamian Jewish relations before the first century AD" (J. Neusner, "Jews in Iran," in *The Cambridge History of Iran*, vol. 3(2): *The Seleucid, Parthian and Sasanian Periods* (Cambridge, 1983), pp. 909–24).

36 For the history of Babylonian Jewry during the Parthian period, see J. Neusner, *A History of the Jews in Babylonia*, vol. 1: *The Parthian Period* (Leiden, 1969). Also see Neusner, "Jews in Iran," ibid; and G. Widengren, "Iran and Israel in Parthian Times," in *Temenos: Nordic Journal of Comparative Religion*, vol. 2 (1966), pp. 139–77. As is well known, the intimate association of Jews with the Parthians is highlighted in the community's messianic expectations, reflected in the often repeated quote of the first century Palestinian Rabbi, R. Simeon b. Yohai, who is said to have declared: "If you see a Persian horse tethered (to a grave) in the land of Israel, look for the footsteps of Messiah" (see Neusner, *A History of the Jews in Babylonia*, vol. 1, here p. 85). It is probably this same history also that provides the context for the claim contained in the Acts of Apostles (2:9–11), composed sometime *c*.85 CE, where, in the list of pilgrims who gathered in Jerusalem on the day of Pentecost, we find not only the Medians, but "Elymaeans," and the Parthians (Joseph A. Fitzmyer, *The Acts of the Apostles: A New Translation with Introduction and Commentary* (New York, 1997), p. 4, 2:9–11). It should be noted that the reference to the Elymaeans in the list pertains, in all likelihood, to the Elymais, the "descendants of the traditional Elamite[s]" who lived as a "semi-independent state frequently subject to Parthian domination [. . .] in the territories of Ḵūzestān (Susiana), in southwestern Persia" (see John F. Hansman, "Elymais," *Encyclopaedia Iranica* [online] < http://www.iranicaonline.org/articles/elymais> and Michael Zand, "Bukhara vii. Bukharan Jews," *Encyclopaedia Iranica* [online] < http://www. iranicaonline.org/articles/bukhara-vii>. Medes, of course, refers to the inha bitants of Media.

37 A. D. H. Bivar, "Gorgān v. Pre-Islamic History," *Encyclopaedia Iranica* [online] < http://www.iranicaonline.org/articles/gorgan-v>; R. Hartmann and J. A. Boyle, "Gurgān," in *Encyclopaedia of Islam* [online] < http://referenceworks. brillonline.com.proxy.lib.ohio-state.edu/entries/encyclopaedia-of-islam-2/ gurgan-SIM_2565>.

38 V. Minorsky, "al-Rayy," in *Encyclopaedia of Islam* [online] < http://referenceworks. brillonline.com/entries/encyclopaedia-of-islam-2/al-rayy-COM_0916>, VIII:471:1.

39 Stuart C. Brown, "Ecbatana," *Encyclopaedia Iranica* [online] < http://www. iranicaonline.org/articles/ecbatana> and Xavier de Planhol, "Hamadān iii. Historical Geography," *Encyclopaedia Iranica* [online] < http://www.iranicaon line.org/articles/hamadan-iii>.

40 For Jewish presence in Armenia, see below. For a short account on the Arsacids in Armenia and bibliographical information, see, among others, C. Toumanoff,

"Arsacids vii. The Arsacid Dynasty of Armenia," *Encyclopaedia Iranica* [online] <http://www.iranicaonline.org/articles/arsacids-index#pt7>.

41 As we will see below, Azarbayjan proves to be an enigmatic case in this research.

42 Michael Morony, "Continuity and Change in the Administrative Geography of Late Sasanian and Early Islamic al-'Irāq," *Iran*, 20 (1982), pp. 1–49, here pp. 21 and 41.

43 The Exilarchate was the lay authority over the Jewish communities of the Diaspora, and the "oldest institutions of the central institutions to merge in Diaspora." Its leaders claimed Davidic descent and had complete authority over the affairs of the Jewish community. "In keeping with Persian custom, they maintained courts of their own, possessed considerable property and income, indulged in pomp and ceremony, and surrounded themselves with courtiers, servants and slaves." For the Exilarchate see Moshe Gil, "The Exilarchate," in Daniel Frank (ed.), *The Jews of Medieval Islam: Community, Society, and Identity* (Leiden, 1995), pp. 33–67, here pp. 33–4. Also see Jacob Neusner and Eliezer Bashan, "Exilarch," in *Encyclopaedia Judaica* [online], vol. 6, pp. 600–7.

44 J. Neusner, *A History of the Jews in Babylonia*, vol. 3: *The Early Sasanian Period*, 1966, pp. 241–3.

45 See J. Neusner, *A History of the Jews in Babylonia*, vol. 1: *The Parthian Period*, pp. 79–86, where he puts forth the interesting conjecture that the father of Rabbi Nathan was in fact a Parthian official and that the controversy in which the Rabbi himself was engaged upon his return to Palestine was motivated by his desire to carry forward Parthian foreign policy in the region.

46 For *rāshūt*, meaning "leadership," as in "the area or sphere in which the authority, leadership, appointments, finances and judgments, are controlled by one of the heads of the four authoritative centers of the diaspora: the Exilarch, the Sura Yeshiva, the Pumbita Yehshiva, and the Palestinian Yeshiva," see Moshe Gil, *Jews in Islamic Countries in the Middle Ages* (Brill, 2004), pp. 92–5, here p. 92. For the place of Hulwan under the Exilarch's *rāshūt*, see ibid., p. 520.

47 Moshe Gil, *Jews in Islamic Countries*, p. 520.

48 Solidi (sing. solidus) were Roman gold coins first introduced under Diocletian (r. 284–305) and reintroduced by Constantine I (r. 306–37), weighing about 4.5 g. Alan Bowman, Averil Cameron and Peter Garnsey (eds), *The Cambridge Ancient History*, vol. 12: *The Crisis of the Empire, AD 193–337* (Cambridge, 2005), p. 103.

49 As my good colleague and mentor, Michael Bates, observes, it "would not be surprising if moneychangers, merchants and other wealthy people, as well as some state officials, had *solidi* in their treasure chests in Hulwan" (personal communication, August 3, 2011).

50 Berline and Brettler, *The Jewish Study Bible*, 2 Kings, 18:11. It must be reiterated that we are not concerned here with whether or not the Halah of 2 Kings, 18:11 in fact referred to Hulwan, but with its later identification.

51 Thus, "R. Ika b. Abin said in the name of R. Hananel in Rab's name: Halwan
    and Nahawand are as the Exile in respect to genealogy [... And] Halah is
    Hulwan; Habor is Adiabene; the river of Gozan is Ginzak [...] And three ribs
    were in his mouth between his teeth. Said R. Johanan: This refers to Hulwan,
    Adiabene and Nesibin, which it [Persia] sometimes swallowed and sometimes
    spat out." I am grateful to my colleague, Daniel Frank, for providing me with
    the completed translation and reference to this passage of the *Kiddushin* tractate
    (*Babylonian Talmud*, tractate *Kiddushin* 71b–72a, in *The Babylonian Talmud*, tr.
    and ed. I. Epstein (London, 1935–52)). Also cited in Jacob Neusner, *A History
    of the Jews in Babylonia*, vol. 3, p. 243.
52 In fact the precise identity of the cities mentioned in 2 Kings (18:11) still
    remains unsettled.
53 Jacob Neusner, *A History of the Jews in Babylonia: The Early Sasanian Period*,
    Studia Post Biblica, Supplements to the *Journal for the Study of Judaism*, 11:2
    (1997), pp. 241–3.
54 Probably Elymaeans. See note 36.
55 Hayim Ben-Sasson (ed.), *A History of the Jewish People* (Cambridge, 1985), p. 374.
56 For Nahrawan, "a town and canal system in the lower Diyala (Tamarra) region
    east of the Tigris River," see Michael Morony, "Nahrawān," in *Encyclopaedia of
    Islam* [online] <http://referenceworks.brillonline.com.proxy.lib.ohio-state.
    edu/entries/encyclopaedia-of-islam-2/al-nahrawan-SIM_5760>.
57 *Babylonian Talmud*, tractate *Kiddushin* 71b–72a; Haim Hillel Ben-Sasson (ed.),
    A History of the Jewish People (Cambridge, 1985), pp. 373–4. I am once again
    indebted to my colleague Daniel Frank for kindly providing me with the full
    reference for this citation.
58 For this and numerous other significant observations about Hulwan, see
    Michael Morony, *Iraq After the Muslim Conquest* (New Jersey, 2006), *passim.*
59 Morony, "Continuity and Change", p. 21.
60 Shams al-Din Maqdisi, *Ahsan al-Taqāsīm fī Maʿrifat al-Aqālīm*, ed. de Goeje
    (Leiden, 1906), p. 123. Moshe Gil, *Jews in Islamic Countries*, p. 520.
61 Maqdisi, *Ahsan al-Taqāsīm fī Maʿrifat al-Aqālīm*, p. 123.
62 Ahmad b. Abu Yaʿqub (al-Yaʿqubi), *Al-Buldān*, ed. G. Juynboll (Leiden,
    1861), pp. 46–7. While the contours of the history of Dinavari Jews in the
    Parthian and Sasanian periods need to be reconstructed, there is no doubt that
    the Jewish community of the region was an ancient community. In so far as it
    has been argued that "Jewish communities in Adiabene and elsewhere seem to
    have formed the nucleus of the new Christian communities in the Parthian
    empire," furthermore, the existence of a substantial Christian population in
    Dinavar as early as the sixth century might also give one a sense of the potential
    cultural and numeric strength of the Dinavar's Jewish population prior to this. See
    Amnon Netzer, "Conversion iv. Of Persian Jews to other religions," *Encyclopaedia
    Iranica* [online] <http://www.iranicaonline.org/articles/conversion-iv>; J. P.
    Asmussen, "Christians in Iran," in *Cambridge History of Iran*, vol. 3(2), pp. 924–
    6; G. Widengren, "The Status of the Jews in the Sassanian Empire," *Iranica*

Antiqua, 1 (1961), pp. 117–62, here p. 125, n. 1. As we know, an East-Syrian school existed at Tel Dinavar in Bet Nuhadra, where there was found a "damaged colophon from a copy of Gospels dated to 599/600." See Samuel Rolles Driver, *Studia Biblica: Essays in Biblical Archaeology and Criticism and Kindred Subjects* (Clarendon Press, 1891), p. 52; Adam H. Becker, *Fear of God and the Beginning of Wisdom* (Pennsylvania, 2006), p. 155. Also see P. Pourshariati, "The *Akhbār al-Ṭiwāl* of Abū Ḥanīfa Dīnawarī: A *Shuʿūbī* Treatise on Late Antique Iran," in R. Gyselen (ed.), *Sources for the History of Sasanian and post-Sasanian Iran*, collection *Res Orientales* XIX (Bures-sur-Yvette, 2010), pp. 201–89; Abū Ḥanīfa Aḥmad Dīnawarī, *Akhbār al-Ṭiwāl*, ed. Abd al-Munʿim ʿĀmir (Beirut, 1990), pp. 253–61. At any rate, the city that was most probably constructed as early as the Seleucid period had by the tenth century a village in its proximity, namely the village of Kurkan, the Jewish community of which used to hold large fairs. Moshe Gil, *Jews in Islamic Countries*, p. 521. Also see Le Strange, *The Lands of the Eastern Caliphate*, pp. 188–90.

63 For a brief examination of these regions, see below.

64 Yaʿqubi, *al-Buldān*, p. 48. In the later medieval period, from Hamadan, one road took one to Nehavand and Karaj. For our future purposes, it is important to keep in mind that Karaj was only constructed by ʿIsa b. Idris and his descendants, the Dolafids, in the course of the early ninth century. The Shiʿite Dolafids and their troops had an active role in subduing the rebellion of Babak. It was from Hamadan, as well, that one set out for Qum. Yaʿqubi, *al-Buldān*, pp. 48–9 and 49–50. For the Dolafids, see Fred M. Donner, "Dolafids," *Encyclopaedia Iranica* [online] <http://www.iranicaonline.org/articles/dolafids>.

65 Houman M. Sarshar, "Hamadān viii. Jewish Community," in Houman M. Sarshar (ed.), *Jewish Communities of Iran: Entries on Judeo-Persian Communities Published by the Encyclopaedia Iranica* (New York, 2011), pp. 104–18. We know, of course, that Biblical Shamanaser was in fact the Assyrian king, Sargon II (r. 722–705 BCE).

66 M. A. Dandamayev, "Bible i. As a Source for Median and Achaemenid History," *Encyclopaedia Iranica* [online] <http://www.iranicaonline.org/articles/bible-i>.

67 For Esther and Mordechai, see Amnon Netzer, "Esther and Mordechai," *Encyclopaedia Iranica* [online] <http://www.iranicaonline.org/articles/esther-and-mordechai>. For the clearly Iranian background of the Scroll of Esther, or the Book of Esther, dubbed the "most characteristically Iranian book of the Bible in both its setting and its language," see, among others, Almut Hintz, "The Greek and Hebrew Versions of the Book of Esther and Its Iranian Background," in *Irano-Judaica III* (Jerusalem, 1994), pp. 34–9. Besides Esther and Mordechai, the Jews of Iran consider the tomb of the prophet Habakkuk to be in Hamadan as well, serving as a local shrine in Tuysarkan, to the south of Hamadan. How ancient this tradition might be remains an open question. See S. Sorudi, "Ḥabaquq, Tomb of" *Encyclopaedia Iranica* [online] <http://www.iranicaonline.org/articles/habaquq-tomb-of->.

68 Amnon Netzer, "Esther and Mordechai"; Moshe Gil, *Jews in Islamic Countries*, p. 522. To what period of their ancient history one can trace the belief of the

Hamadani Jews that they were the descendants of the tribe of Simeon, of the 12 Tribes of Israel, is not clear. See Habib Levy, *Comprehensive History of The Jews of Iran (The Outset of the Diaspora)*, tr. George W. Maschke (Los Angeles, 1999) (cited in Houman M. Sarshar, "Hamadān viii. Jewish Community").

69 For Judeo-Persian, "a term [...] referring to a group of very similar, usually mutually comprehensible, dialects of Persian, spoken or written by Jews in greater Iran over a period of more than a millennium," see Thamar E. Gindin, "Judeo-Persian Communities viii. Judeo-Persian language," *Encyclopaedia Iranica* [online] < http://www.iranicaonline.org/articles/judeo-persian-viii-judeo-persian-language>.

70 As Haideh Sahim observes, "Aramaic dialects were spoken mostly in the western parts of Iran, in Kurdistan area and western Azerbaijan [...] Jews of some parts of Kurdistan, such as Sanandaj and Saqqiz, also speak Aramaic dialects." Haideh Sahim, "Languages and Dialects of the Jews of Iran and Afghanistan" in Houman Sarshar (ed.), *Esther's Children: A Portrait of Iranian Jews* (Beverly Hills, 2002), pp. 283–94, here p. 287.

71 Even the Jewish dialects of Na'in, more centrally located, and that of part of the Jewish population of Yazd, who speak Judeo-Yazdi, belong to this Central Median Jewish dialect (see Haideh Sahim, "Languages and Literatures of Jews of Iran and Afghanistan," in Reeva Spector Simon, Michael Menachem Laskier and Sara Reuger (eds), *The Jews of the Middle East and North Africa in Modern Times* (New York, 2002), pp. 133–41, here p. 135).

72 The Jews of the northern sections of the Jewish quarter of Yazd speak Persian and have a Yazdi accent, for example, because they seem to have moved to Yazd from Hamadan. This development and the settlement of Jews in Yazd—which was located on one of the branches of the southern route—pertains to the modern period of the city. Thamar E. Gindin, "Yazd iv. The Jewish Dialect of Yazd," *Encyclopaedia Iranica* [online] < http://www.iranicaonline.org/articles/yazd-iv-the-jewish-dialect-of-yazd>. Moreover, it is significant to note the fact that, as Yarshater observes, whereas "the non-Jewish inhabitants of these regions, who spoke a Median dialect in the north and west of Iran down to Isfahan province, eventually gave up their language to Persian, which began to exert its influence from Sasanian times onward, the Jewish communities, being generally rather secluded from the Iranian populations, have kept their non-Persian Iranian dialects" (Ehsan Yarshater, "Judeo-Persian Communities x. Judeo-Persian Jargon (Loterāi)," *Encyclopaedia Iranica* [online] < http://www.iranicaonline.org/articles/judeo-persian-x-judeo-persian-jargon-loterai>.

73 Amnon Netzer, "Isfahan xviii. Jewish Community," *Encyclopaedia Iranica* [online] < http://www.iranicaonline.org/articles/isfahan-xviii-jewish-community>.

74 Abi Bakr Ahmad b. Muhammad b. al-Hamadani, Ibn Faqih, *Kitab al-Buldan*, ed. M.J de Goeje, *Bibliotheca Geographorum Arabicorum,* vol. 5 (Leiden, 1895), pp. 361–2. Besides Ibn Faqih, see for example, al-Maqdisi, *Aḥsan al-Taqasim*, vol. 3, p. 388.

75 Ibn Faqih, *Ketab al-Buldan*, pp. 361–2.

76 For Thomson's analysis of Moses's treatment of Jewish colonies in Armenia, see
   Thomson's introduction to Moses Khorenats'i, *History of the Armenians*,
   translation and commentary by Robert W. Thomson (Cambridge, 1980),
   pp. 28–9. P'awstos Buzand, *History of the Armenians*, translated from classical
   Armenian by Robert Bedrosian (1996), Robert Bedrosian's Homepage
   <http://rbedrosian.com/hsrces.html> accessed 2011, IV:55.

77 Khorenats'i, *History of the Armenians*, III:35, p. 293.

78 Thomson's introduction to Khorenats'i's *History of the Armenians*, pp. 28–9.

79 See Thomson's introduction to Khorenats'i's *History of the Armenians*, p. 28.

80 Yahudiya is said to have been founded by its Abbasid governor, Ayyub b. Zeyad
   al-Kendi; see J. Hansman and *EIr.*, "Isfahan iv. pre-Islamic Period," *Encyclopaedia
   Iranica* [online] <http://www.iranicaonline.org/articles/isfahan-iv-pre-islamic-
   period>.

81 As Gaube, citing Walker, observes, "the transfer of the center of activity from
   Jay/Khūshninān to Yahūdiyya is confirmed by numismatic evidence. There are
   coins struck between 695 and 746 with the mintmark of Jay, *whereas all later
   coins bear the mintmark of Isfahan* [emphasis mine]" (H. Gaube, "Iranian Cities,"
   p. 165). J. Walker, *A Catalogue of Arab-Byzantine and post-Reform Umaiyad Coins*
   (London, 1956), LXf.

82 Our detailed discussion of this will be forthcoming in the sequel to this study.

83 Josef Markwart, *Analecta Orientalia*, vol. 3: *A Catalogue of the Provincial Capitals
   of Ērānshahr (Pahlavi Text, Version and Commentary)*, ed. Giuseppe Messina
   (Rome, 1931), pp. 27–30.

84 Daryaee, *Šahrestānīhā ī Ērānšahr*, Bibliotheca Iranica: Intellectual Traditions
   Series 53 (Costa Mesa, 2002), p. 28.

85 Ibid.

86 Ferdowsi, *Shahnameh*, vol. 6, ed. Khalegi-Motlagh (New York, 2005), p. 361.

87 As I will be arguing in the second part of this study in detail, it underlines
   Yazdgird II's attempts at undermining the Pahlav (Parthian) dynasts' control of the
   northern route, a policy that was aggressively pursued by the important Sasanian
   king Piruz (r. 457–84) as well, and intermittently thenceforth by successive
   Sasanian kings. For the history of Parthian–Sasanian relationship, see
   P. Pourshariati, *Decline and Fall of the Sasanian Empire*, passim.

88 Ḥamza Iṣfahānī, *Ta'rīkh Sinī Mulūk al-'Arḍ w' al-'Anbīyā* (Beirut, 1969), p. 50.
   Parvaneh Pourshariati, "Ḥamza al-Iṣfahānī and Sasanid Historical Geography
   of Sinī Mulūk al-'Arḍ w' al-'Anbīyā," in Rika Gyselen (ed.), *Res Orientales* 17,
   Des Indo-Grecs aux Sassanides: données pour l'histoire et la géographie historique
   (Leuven, 2007), pp. 111–41.

89 The "formal founding of the town of Yahudiya is dated to the early Abbasid
   period and is attributed to Ayyub b. Ziyād al-Kendī [...]. *What may have been,
   in the Sasanid period, a relatively small Jewish settlement* [...] was later known to
   the Arab writers as the larger of the two towns [emphasis mine]" (J. Hansman
   and *EIr.*, "Isfahan iv. pre-Islamic Period," *Encyclopaedia Iranica* [online]
   <http://www.iranicaonline.org/articles/isfahan-iv-pre-islamic-period>). Even

so, as Xavier de Planhol observes, it was not until the emergence of the Seljuqs that conditions that led to the full exploitation of the strategic location of Isfahan were realized.

90 For Rayy also see Rocco Rante, "Ray i. Archealogy," *Encyclopaedia Iranica* [online] <http://www.iranicaonline.org/articles/ray-i-archeo>; and Pourshariati, *Decline and Fall, passim.*

91 See Amy-Jill Levine, "Tobit," in John Barton and John Muddiman (eds), *The Oxford Bible Commentary* (Oxford, 2001), pp. 626–32.

92 See, among others, Joseph A. Fitzmyer, *Tobit: Commentaries on Early Jewish Literature* (Berlin, 2003); and the review of the book by John J. Collins, *Journal of Near Eastern Studies*, 64:2 (April 2005), pp. 139–40. For a synoptic overview of the history of the manuscript recensions in Tobit, see Robert J. Littman, *Tobit: the Book of Tobit in Codex Sinaiticus* (Leiden, 2008), pp. xix–xxv.

93 Amy-Jill Levine, "Tobit," p. 626.

94 For the Iranian elements in the Book of Tobit, see James Russell, "God is Good: On Tobit and Iran," *Iran and the Caucasus*, 5 (2001), pp. 1–6. For the demon of lust, Asmodeus, in Tobit, the Aeshma (*aēšma*), the agent of wrath already attested in the Gathic Avesta, and in the Younger Avesta, see J. P. Asmussen, "Aēšma," *Encyclopaedia Iranica* [online] <http://www.iranicaonline.org/articles/aesma-wrath>. Also see M. Hutter, "Asmodeus," in Pieter van der Horst, Karel van der Toorn, and Bob Becking (eds), *Dictionary of Deities and Demons in the Bible* (2nd edn, Leiden, 1999), pp. 106–8.

95 Amy-Jill Levine, "Tobit."

96 Briefly, the story of Judith revolves around a beautiful and devout widow who, disillusioned by her countrymen's refusal to trust God in their delivery from the foreign enemy, takes matters into her own hands, and going to the camp of the Assyrian enemy general, Holofernes, dupes and decapitates him, thus dispersing the Assyrians and saving the Israelites. See Morton S. Enselin, *The Book of Judith: Greek Text with an English Translation, Commentary and Critical Notes* (Leiden, 1972), pp. 7–13.

97 I. M. Diakonoff, "Cyaxares," *Encyclopædia Iranica* [online] <http://www.iranicaonline.org/articles/cyaxares-gk>; and I. M. Diakonoff, "Media," in *The Cambridge History of Iran*, vol. 2: *The Median and Achaemenian Periods*, ed. I. Gershevitch (Cambridge, 1985), pp. 36–148, here pp. 112–13 and *passim*.

98 While deemed as a historical novel, the clear anachronistic nature of the Book of Judith seems to be well-established. While some have dated the composition to the early Persian period in the fifth or fourth century BCE, it seems to be now acknowledged that the book was composed in the late Hasmonean (*c*.140–63 BCE) period. See M. S. Enselin, *The Book of Judith*, pp. 26–31; also see "Judith, Book of," *Jewish Encyclopaedia* [website] <http://www.jewishencyclopedia.com/articles/9073-judith-book-of>, where it is maintained that the writer of the story "was a well-informed man, familiar with foreign geography." As far as I can ascertain, the Persian dimensions of the Book of Judith have yet to be properly examined, and should remain an interesting desiderata for future research.

99   This is how Theophylact Simocatta renders it: "For the support which Baram
     had received from the Jews for his usurpation had not been inconsiderable. For
     at that time there was living in Persia a large number of the said race, who had
     abundant wealth. For after the capture of Jerusalem by the emperor Vespasian
     [Titus Flavius Vespasianus (r. 69–79 AD)] and the burning of the temple,
     many of the Jews, shrinking from Roman might, migrated from Palestine to
     the Medes and returned to their primal nurse, whence their forefather Abraham
     had in fact come. Then these people, by trading in valuables and journeying
     across the Red Sea, had through financial transactions invested themselves with
     great wealth ..." (see Theophylact Simocatta, *The History of Theophylact
     Simocatta: An English Translation with Introduction and Notes*, ed. Michael and
     Mary Whitby (Oxford, 1986), p. 258).

100 Abul-Qasim Hamza b. Yusuf b. Ibrahim al-Sahmi, *Tarikh Jurjan* or *Kitab
     ma'rifa 'ulama' ahl-i Jurjan*, ed. Muhammad Abd al-'Amid Khan (Haydarabad,
     1387/1967), p. 200, as cited in Richard Bulliet, *Islam: the View from the Edge*
     (New York, 1995), p. 61.

101 So that Ibn Faqih narrates that "some say that it is written in the Towrat that
     Rayy is one of the gates of the world (*al-arḍ*) to which the people converge for
     trade (*wa ilayhā muttajar al-khalq*)" (Ibn Faqih, *Kitab al-Buldan*, p. 270).

102 Thus far, our information for Jewish settlement in other urban centers on the
     northern route, or other northern regions of Iran, seems to pertain to later
     periods. Such is the case, for example, with the settlement of Iranian Jewry in
     the southern Caspian provinces of Daylam and Gilan, as well as the Jewish
     settlements scattered in Gilliard of Damavand, and Rudbar, Qumis, and
     Nishapur. For Gilan see Amnon Netzer, "Gilān," in *Encyclopaedia Judaica*
     [online], vol. 7, p. 596. For a number of interesting pictures of the cemetery of
     Gil'ad or Gilliard, see http://www.7dorim.com/tasavir/Giliard.asp. Also see
     Davud Gohariyan, "Gurestan-e Giliyard: Pareh-i az Tarikh o Tamadon-e Iran,"
     Tehran Jewish Committee (Iran) [website] < http://www.iranjewish.com/Essay/
     Essay_36_giliyard.htm>. As many have remarked, Benjamin of Tudela (1130–
     73) also mentions the existence of 20,000 Jews in Rudbar, among whom were
     "many learned and rich men," but who nevertheless lived under "great
     oppression[!]" (see Benjamin of Tudela, *The Itinerary of Benjamin of Tudela:
     Critical Text*, translation and commentary by Marcus Nathan Adler (London,
     1907), p. 53). For Qumis, the evidence of Daniel ben Moses al-Qumisi (the
     important Karaite leader of the ninth–tenth century who finally immigrated
     to Jerusalem) indicates that there must have been a substantial Jewish
     community in Qumis in prior centuries, a community in which al-Qumisi
     found his intellectual training. For al-Qumisi, see "Daniel ben Moses Al-
     Qūmisī," in *Encyclopaedia Judaica* [online], vol. 5, p. 428. Nishapur was itself a
     city constructed during the Sasanian period. In so far as we know that Christian
     communities existed in the region during the rule of the Sasanian king Piruz
     (r. 457–84), however, and in so far as this implies the prior existence of a
     Jewish community in the region, we can safely conjecture that there were

indeed Jews living in Nishapur during the Sasanian period. For the Christians who are said to have martyred themselves in the region during the rule of Piruz, see, among others, Sebeos, *The Armenian History Attributed to Sebeos*, translated with notes by Robert Thomson, historical commentary by James Howard-Johnston with assistance from Tim Greenwood (Liverpool, 1999), vol. 2, p. 2 and notes 10 and 12. As we know, much later on, Benjamin of Tudela, "probably from hearsay," talks about the Jews living in the mountains of Nishapur, and reports that they claimed lineage from the ten lost tribes (see Moshe Gil, *Jews in Islamic Countries in the Middle Ages*, p. 529). For a synopsis of information on the Jews of Khorasan in general see Walter Fischel and Amnon Netzer, "Khurasan," in *Encyclopaedia Judaica* [online], vol. 12, pp. 118–19.

103   Strabo, *Geography*, ed. H. C. Hamilton, Esq., W. Falconer, M.A. (London, 1856), XIII:4:13.

104   And continues to add that "the plain of Cyrus, in like manner, had its name from the Persians" (Strabo, *Geography*, XIII:4:13).

105   Lydia, of course, was only one of the regions in Asia Minor in which the Iranian had settled (see Mary Boyce, "Diaspora Iranian i. In Pre-Islamic times," *Encyclopaedia Iranica* [online] < http://www.iranicaonline.org/articles/ diaspora#pt1>). For Achaemenid colonization, see, for example, Nicholas Victor Sekunda, "Achaemenid Colonization in Lydia," *Revue des Études Anciennes*, 87 (1985), pp. 7–29; ibid, "Achaemenid Colonization in Caria, Lycia, and Greater Phrygia," in A. Kuhrt and H. Sancisi-Weerdenburg (eds), *Achaemenid History*, vol. 6: *Asia Minor and Egypt: Old Cultures in a New Empire* (Leiden, 1991), pp. 83–143; and finally, ibid, "Persian Settlement in Hellespontine Phrygia," in A. Kuhrt and H. Sancisi-Weerdenburg (eds), *Achaemenid History*, vol. 3: *Method and Theory* (Leiden, 1988), pp. 175–96.

106   Some seem to have argued—quite improbably—that the king in question was the Sasanian, Ardashir I (r. 226–42 CE). For references to this, see Jacob Neusner, *A History of the Jews in Babylonia*, vol. 1 (Leiden, 1969), p. 11, n. 2.

107   Paulus Orosius, *The Seven Books of History against the Pagans*, translated with an introduction and notes by A. T. Fear (Liverpool 2010), p. 119, 7:6. Quoting from the Byzantine Chronicler, Georgius Syncellus (d. *c*.810 CE) who himself quotes from Julius Africanus (160–240 CE), the seventeenth-century Archbishop James Ussher also repeats this information: "Ochus, the son of Artaxerxes, made a journey into Egypt. He led away some Jews as captives. He settled some of them in Hyrcania, near the Caspian Sea, and the rest in Babylon. There they continue to this day as many Greek writers stated" (James Ussher, *The Annals of the World* (Green Forest, 2007), p. 209 and the references cited therein).

108   Jacob Neusner, *A History of the Jews in Babylonia*, vol. 1 (Leiden, 1969), p. 11, n. 2.

109   Paulus Orosius, *The Seven Books of History against the Pagans*, p. 120, 7:6.

110   According to Ibn Khurdadbih's *Kitab al-Masalik wa'l-Mamalik* (composed between 846 and 885 CE), one of the routes taken by the Jewish Radhanite merchants in later centuries took them from Khamlij (or Atil), the capital of

the Khazars, across the Caspian Sea, to Gorgan where they would disembark (see, among others, Ibn Khurdadbih, *Kitab al-Masalik wa'l-Mamalik*, ed. M. J. de Goeje (Leiden 1889), p. 154). I hope to deal with this extensively in my forthcoming work.

111 al-Sahmi, *Tarikh Jurjan* (Hyderabad, 1950), pp. 17, 34, 411.

112 Ibn Khurdadbih, *Kitab al-Masalik wa'l-Mamalik*, p. 32; R. Hartmann, "Djuzdjan," *Encyclopaedia of Islam* [online] < http://referenceworks.brillonline. com.proxy.lib.ohio-state.edu/entries/encyclopaedia-of-islam-2/djuzdjan-SIM_2134>.

113 Evidence of a substantial Jewish community in Balkh is also reflected in the fact that one of its gates was called the "Gate of the Jews" (*bab al-yahud*) (Moshe Gil, *Jews in Islamic Countries*, p. 530). The antiquity of this community is perhaps best reflected in the fact that the original Persian name of one of its Jewish quarters was *Jahudanak*, which was later changed to *Yahudiya* in Arabic texts.

114 V. A. Livshits, Z. I. Osmanova, "New Parthian Inscriptions from Old Merv," in Shaked and Netzer (eds), *Irano-Judaica*, vol. 3: *Studies Relating to Jewish Contacts with Persian Culture through the Ages* (Jerusalem, 1994), pp. 99–105.

115 Interestingly enough, the vessel has been identified to be a "cult vessel intended for some ritual use" (see Livshits and Osmanova, "New Parthian Inscriptions," p. 101).

116 Amora is "a term which designates the 'interpreter,' who communicated audibly to the assembled pupils the lessons of the rabbinic teacher. It is also used as a generic term for the rabbis of the post-mishnaic period, whose activities were centered on the interpretation of the Mishnah" (Shmuel Safrai, "Amora," in *Encyclopaedia Judaica* [online], vol. 2, pp. 88–9). "[W]hen used as a proper noun ('the Mishnah') it designates the collection of rabbinic traditions redacted by Rabbi *Judah ha-Nasi (usually called simply 'Rabbi') at the beginning of the third century" (see Stephen G. Wald, "Mishnah," in *Encyclopaedia Judaica*, vol. 14, pp. 319–31).

117 Babylonian Talmud, tractate 'Avodah Zarah, 31b, *Soncino Babylonian Talmud* [online], translated into English with notes, glossary and indices, under the editorship of Rabbi Dr. I. Epstein < http://www.halakhah.com/zarah/zarah_31. html>. It has been postulated that, as a "number of Babylonian Jewish religious authorities were engaged in the silk trade," and as "Marv stood on the Silk road," "bar Bīsěnā's journey may also have been undertaken in connection with the silk trade" (M. Zand, "Bukhara vii. Bukharan Jews").

118 Gabriele Puschnigg, *Ceramics of the Merv Oasis: Recycling the City* (London, 2006), p. 230.

119 This must have been the Jewish community that, centuries later, was headed by a figure called "Akiva the Jew." Akiva is said to have protected the community *c.*738–9 during the governorship of Nasr b. Sayyar in Khorasan (see Tabari, *The History of al-abari*, vol. 16: *The Waning of the Umayyad Caliphate*, tr. Carole Hillenbrand (New York, 1989), p. 24).

120 Walter Fischel, "The Jews of Central Asia (Khorasan) in Medieval Hebrew and Arabic Literature," in *Historia Judaica*, 7 (1945), pp. 29–50, here pp. 35–6.

121 Amnon Netzer, "Kerman," in *Encyclopaedia Judaica* [online], vol. 12, pp. 86–7.

122 It has been claimed that the Jewish community in Yazd "is one of the oldest in Persia." Side by side with the former claim, it has also been maintained that the community "had never been large" (see Thamar E. Gindin, "Yazd iv. The Jewish Dialect of Yazd").

123 I have not been able to gather any information on the potential existence of a Jewish community in Sistan, certainly none for the Parthian and the Sasanian periods.

124 See Amnon Netzner, "Kerman," in *Encyclopaedia Judaica*, where he argues that "as far as we know, the Jewish community there is relatively new. Oral tradition indicates that because of severe famine in Yazd/Yezd about 150 years ago, several Jews of that city immigrated southward and eventually settled in Kerman. Historically this may be true, because the Jews of Kerman are not mentioned in the two Jewish chronicles, that of Babai ben Lutf (17th century)—except for a mention of 'ignorant Yezdi-Kermani people' who extracted money from the Jews of Yezd—and that of Babai ben Farhad (about 1730), nor are they referred to in other Jewish and non-Jewish travelogues from the first half of the 19th century."

125 David Yeroushalmi, personal communication, August 5, 2011. I am grateful to Professor Yeroushalmi for providing me with this information, and for the following references. For the Jewish community in Yazd, see the short notice of Walter Fischel, "Yezd," in *Encyclopaedia Judaica* [online], vol. 21, pp. 327–8; and "for the exact bibliographical reference to the above mentioned biblical manuscript," see Alexander Marx, "Die Bucher und Manuskripte der Seminars-Bibliothek auf der Ausstelung der New Yorker Stadtbibilothek," *Soncino-Blatter*, 2 (1927), p. 114. For the city of Yazd in general, see Ann K. Lambton, "Yazd," in *Encyclopaedia of Islam* [online] < http://referenceworks.brillonline. com.proxy.lib.ohio-state.edu/entries/encyclopaedia-of-islam-2/yazd-COM_1363>, XI:302:1

126 Yazd is not mentioned, for example, in the *Shahrestaniha i Eranshahr*. The account given in the fifteenth-century *Tarikh-i Yazd*, that the city was constructed by Yazdgird II, is, in all likelihood, only an instance of popular etymology (see Ja'far b. Muhammad b. Hasan Ja'fari, *Tarikh-i Yazd*, ed. Iraj Afshar (Tehran, 1959), p. 13).

127 Shaul Shaked, "Esther, Book of," *Encyclopaedia Iranica* [online] < http://www. iranicaonline.org/articles/esther-book-of>.

128 For a detailed analysis of the role of the Parthian dynastic families during the Sasanian period, see P. Pourshariati, *Decline and Fall of the Sasanian Empire*, *passim*.

CHAPTER 2

LOTERĀI[1]: JEWISH JARGON, MUSLIM ARGOT

Martin Schwartz

The Scope of this Study

Loterā'i, Lutrā('i) and similar names, when used by Jews, refers to special substitutive vocabularies, now gradually disappearing, traditionally used by Iranian Jews as part of their local Iranian languages (different from ordinary vocabularies of these Judeo-Iranian languages, whose grammar is, however, the same) when they do not want non-Jews to understand. Much of this vocabulary, which differs somewhat from region to region, clearly has words of Hebrew, and less Aramaic, as well as words of less clear origin. The term Loterā'i etc. is most often explained by Jews as a Hebraic adjective meaning "not of the Torah;" however, the same term or similar terms (Luter, Luterā, etc.) also occur, in Persian sources from the tenth century onward—the earliest reference notes the speech for Astarābād in Gorgān, for a secret kind of speech, and these sources do not mention Jews, nor is a Jewish source evident for such words of this speech as are cited by the early sources.

This article will address these paradoxes and trace the history of this exclusionary vocabulary from the earliest period of Jews in Iran to the present day. It will show how the exclusionary speech of the Jews, beginning with the tenth century in the Caspian area in the

Buyid period, became part of an argot of non-Jewish Iranian beggars and rascals, best attested in the marginalia of a fourteenth-century Persian manuscript which richly attests this vocabulary as used by a Shi'ite underclass. This vocabulary, through its correspondences with twentieth-century Jewish Loterā'i, very much illustrates how Aramaic (as one can now understand the term Loterā'i = non-Toraic = the non-Hebrew Jewish spoken language) was originally the chief source of the Semitic component of the Jewish exclusionary language, as is confirmed by re-examining even earlier non-Jewish linguistic material.

Such Aramaisms also passed from the Shi'ite argot, along with other vocabulary, into the speech of Persian-speaking Gypsies and other itinerant groups, as is documentable from their argots in twentieth-century Iran and Central Asia. Of this material, the vocabulary of Gypsies of Astarābād, published in 1904, shows a significantly large Aramaic vocabulary of many words not found in the overall similar speech of related communities. This confirms the first entry of Jewish Loterā'i into gentile speech in Gorgan. The fact that a Jewish presence in the Middle Eastern underworld was a factor in the dissemination during this period is also shown by the argot vocabulary of material from terms (of Jewish Aramaic origin) referring to underworld scams, in tenth-century Arabic poetry composed under Iranian Buyid patronage and describing the world of beggars, charlatans, and thieves.

Yarshater's Study and the Issues it Raises

Yarshater's pioneering scientific study of Loterā'i,[2] based on fieldwork in various Jewish communities of Iran, in effect entails the following questions: (1) Is the term Loterā'i (etc.) indeed, as believed by Iranian Jews, etymologically from Hebrew "non-Toraic"? (2) What would be the precise feature to which the latter etymology, if correct, refers? (3) How can the Jewish etymology be reconciled with the fact that: (a) the earliest allusion to Loterā'i (lwtr'), in the tenth-century Ḥodud al-ʿĀlam, stating that lwtr' is one of the two languages of Astarābād, does not mention Jews; and (b) allusions to this speech in early

Persian lexica and poetry of the twelfth century cite words not
known from Jewish Loterā̃'i (henceforth JLtr) and, again, do not
mention Jews? Note also that the use of the term *lotar(ā)/lutar(ā)* for an
exclusionary language, found in the old dictionaries of Classical Persian
(as detailed by Yarshater), and the present-day use of the term outside
of Jewish communities, is used generically, without reference to Jews.
(4) What is the relative chronology of the heavily predominant
Hebrew component and the smaller Aramaic component of JLtr, and
(how) is this relevant to the foregoing questions? (5) What of the verbs
(etc.) of hitherto unidentified origin?

The Chief Non-Jewish Data

The medieval Muslim (Shi'i) Persian argot is attested by the
anonymous *Ketāb-e sāsiān ba-kamāl* (henceforth *KS*) "The Book of
Accomplished Grifters," extant *inter alia* (as a probably late copy)
in a fourteenth-century Persian manuscript in Tashkent, within the
marginalia of five pages, of which I have obtained photo scans.
A series of argot words, with Persian glosses, is given in the opening
section of *KS* in nine thematic chapters. Many of the words recur
at the end of *KS* in verses with some Persian annotations. Previously
a brief list of some of the words was given (with occasional
misreading) by Ivanow[3] and another brief list was given by
Troitskaya, this almost exclusively for comparison with words from
her Uzbek argot data. It should be noted that there are no Indic
words in the *KS*, although Indic matrial abounds in the Gypsy,
mendicant, and musician argots of Iran and Central Asia.

Linguistic Sources and Relevant Abbreviations

JLtr of regions in Iran: Bor(ujerd);[4] Isf(ahan), Gol(pāyagān),
Kāsh(ā)n, Kerm(ān), Khom(eyn), Mash(had), Shir(az), Teh(ran), and
Yazd.[5] Some JLtr words and phrases from Iran are given without
provenience in Hanina Mizrahi's study.[6] Her(at) Jewish argot (found
in Zarubin) is a form of JLtr.[7] In this article, all JLtr words from
Iranian are from Yarshater's two articles, unless otherwise indicated.

Twentieth-century non-Jewish argots:

PG = Gypsies of Eastern Iran.[8]

PD = mendicant dervishes of Eastern Iran.[9]

Djougi (i.e. Jugi), the term used by de Morgan for the speech of Gypsies of Astarābād.[10]

AG = Ḡorbati of Arāk, a Gypsy argot whose word-formation and lexicon shares features with PG, Djougi, and the Jugi of Tajikistan.[11]

Mus = Argot of traditional musicians of Iran, specified as to performance (Sāzanda, Mehtar), Gypsy provenience (Luti, Toshmāl), or locality (Chāli, Torbat-e Jām).[12]

LG = Argot of Gypsies of various localities of Iran (Fārs, Kermān, Osof).[13]

Abd(oltili) "language of itinerants" designates the argots of Uzbek-speaking artisans and musicians, preachers and qalandars.[14]

Argots of Tajik-speaking Gypsies of the Ḥeṣār Valley are: Ar(abcha) = Tashkent (Luli), Chist(oni), Ju(gi), Kāv(oli), S(am)arkand L(uli), and Sogut(arosh);[15] Mag(ati), an argot of Persian-speaking Gypsies.[16]

AD = argot in the tenth-century Qaṣida Sāsāniya of Abu Dolaf Yanbuʿi (Ḵazraji).[17]

SD = argot in the fourteenth-century Qaṣida Sāsāniya of Ṣafi-al-Din Ḥelli.[18]

LuJ = Luter-e (lwtr) Jāberi, argot (with some lexical affinities to Gypsy argots of Iran and Central Asia) of itinerant Kurdish-speaking traders of the Jāber community in the village of Badra, Ilām province, southwestern Iran.[19]

Other abbreviations: Aram = Babylonian Jewish Aramaic; Heb = Hebrew; OIr = Old Iranian; J = Jewish; Pers = Persian.

The Aramaic Component and Achaemenid Origins of the Jargon

I begin with question (4) above. JLtr nouns and adjectives of Aramaic origin in Yarshater's data are Bor *yumā* "day"; Gol *lihhā*

"heart"; Khom *rešā* "head"; Shir *rakka* "thin"; Gol *pasilā* "gentile"
< *pɔsīl* "unqualified" (i.e., "ritually unclean", cf. Judeo-Persian *pasul*
(< Heb) = "Mohammad (rasul)");[20] and, integrated with
conspicuous phonological change, Shir *yārtak* "boy" < *yaldā*, and a
few other words noted below. More significant are the JLtr verbs of
Aramaic origin. Clear examples are: Gol *nazq-un-*, Kash *nask-en-* "to
kill, hit" (Aram *nazq-* "to injure"); Shir *za(w)n-*, Teh *dev-*, Isf *dam-* "to
sell" < *zabben-*; Shir *deyl-* "to fear," denominative from *deḥel* "fear,
fright"; and Mash *meštā-*, Her *meštō-* "to say" < Aram *mešta ʿē*
"saying," whose agreement is chronologically noteworthy. Other
verbs of Aramaic origin will be noted below.

Particularly in view of "fear" and "sell," Yarshater wondered
whether at the time of the inception of Loterāʾi the Jews of Persia
were not Aramaic speaking and that only later in the course of time
were increasing Hebrew elements imported.[21] The latter situation
is confirmed by (1) evidence I shall present that JLtr began in the
Achaemenid period; (2) the Aramaic origin of words cited as *lwtrʾy* in
a twelfth-century poem by Suzani of Samarkand; and (3) data of the
KS and later argots of Iran and Central Asia.

We may start with the fact that Shir *bika* "egg" must go back to an
Old Aramaic form of the early Achaemenid period in which the
antecedent of later Aramaic and Syriac *bē(y)ʿā*, Heb *bēṣā*[b] and Arabic
bayḍa(t-) "egg" had for the second consonant a sound that is spelled as
qōf in other words which show the same correspondences—e.g., Old
Aram *ʾrqʾ* (cf. Pahl. Aramaeogram ALKA), later Aram and Syriac
ʾarʿā, Heb *ʾereṣ*, Arabic *ʾarḍ*, the change to the sound/letter *ʿayin*
taking place in the late sixth century BCE.

Another Mash-Her agreement, *nund-* "to give," is also found in *KS*
nwndydn "to give" (Pers gloss *dādan*), bnwnd "give!" (Pers *be-deh*), cf.
Her *be-nond* "id." (stem *nund-*), which I take as denominative from
Old Aram **nudn-* "(dowry-)gift" from Late Babylonian (ninth
century BCE) *nudnū, nudni* "dowry," cf. Neo-Assyrian (ninth to
seventh century) *nundunnû, nudannu*; Aram *nɔdunyā* "dowry," all
< Akkad *n-d-n* "to give." For semantics, cf. English *endow* < Old
French *endouer*, Lat *dotāre* "give dowry" < *dōs dōtis* "dowry" = **"gift
par excellence," Latin *dō* "give."

Matching *bika* and *nund-* as early Achaemenid residues in JLtr are what I explain as fossils from Old Iranian. Some examples:

(1) Shir *āj-* = Her *huj-* (**hoj-*) "to come" < OIr **hāčaya-* mid. *"to lead oneself," cf. Avestan *hācaiia-* (Y 5.18, etc.) "to lead, direct, persuade" (*contra* Lazard, p. 253, Her *huj-* is not related to Neh *hez-*, etc., for which see *s.v. KS* hzyδn below).

(2) Neh *viāj-* "sell, finish with" < OIr **abi-hāčaya-* or **api-hāčaya-*, cf. Avestan *upaŋhācaiia-* (< **upa-hāčaya-*) "to come to agreement with someone" (Mash *velāj-* = Neh *viāj-*, or < OIr. **upari-hāčaya-?*).

(3) Shir *čed-* "know, understand"; Kash *če(-V)-*, *čā(-C)-* "know, see"; Isf, Yazd, Kerm *čer-* "see, know, understand, recognize"; *KS* jhstn "to see" (Pers *didan*), bjh "see!" (Pers *be-bin*), < OIr *č(a)it/θ-* "recognize, perceive" (Old Avestan *cōiθaṯ*, *acistā*, *čikōitərəš*). The *KS* forms (with past stem like that of Pers *dānestan* "to know") represent **č(a)iθ-* > *čVH-* > Kash *čā-/če-*, whereas OIr **č(a)it-* > *čēd*, with West Iranian development, and Isf etc. *čer*, with "Tatic" development, cf. Judeo-Yazdi *šerin* "I went," with *šer-* < *šuta-*.

(4) Bor *čaːn* "good, pretty" *KS* jhn = *čahn "good, beautiful" (Pers *niku*) < OIr *čaxnuwāh perfect participle "delighting," cf. Old Avestan *cāxnārə* "they delight" (-*xn-* > -*hn-*, cf. OIr *tauxmā* > Middle Pers *tōhm* > -*tōm* "family" in Pahl mltwm = Man. Middle Pers mrdwhm "mankind").

(5) Mash *z(ə)vā-* "to say" < OIr *zvā-* (Old Avestan *zbā-* = */zuā-/) "to call, invoke." *KS* bwzfʔ (with f representing *β, a bilabial fricative fully written as the Arabic letter f with three dots instead of one superscript dot) "say!" (Pers *be-guy*), wzf[ʔʔ]ydn "to say" (Pers *goftan*) < OIr *(abi-)zvā-* "to call" (cf. Pahl *āzbāy-*); the JLtr may have labial dissimilation.

Other JLtr/argot words of Iranian origin cannot be certainly dated to Old Iranian: Mash and Her *ruj-*, Gol *rej-* etc. "see, know" < root *rauč-* "(be) illumine(d)"; Shir *kelows-* "to laugh" < root *xraus-* "to shout"; Shir and Teh *margun-* "to hit" < "make dead", cf. Shir. *kod* "hit, kill" < Aram *q-t-l* or *q-ṭ-l* "to kill". *KS* mlk "man, male" (Pers *mard*) (scribal error, probably based on *KS* mlkʔ "ruler" [Pers *amir*]

< Aram *malkā* "king") probably for correct **m ᵓk*, an early spelling for /*mak(k)*/, cf. Ju, Chist, AG *mak(k)*, Mus Čāli *makak*, LG Osof *makk* "man, male". JLtr has the comparable form *mak(k)eyhū* = Modern Heb *ha-iš* "the man"[22] (*-eyhū* < Aram demonstrative?). I take *mak(k)* from **martk* < **martaka-* "man".

Aramaic Material in the Non-Jewish Sources

Expectably, early JLtr had Aramaic forms that have disappeared from modern JLtr; thus may be explained the designation lwtrᵓy for < dx > and < zyf > in Suzani's poem. I take these from Aram *daxyā*, *dɔxē* "clear, pure, (ritually) correct" and *zayif* "false." KS collocates dx (Pers *nik* "good") and zyf (Pers *bad* "bad"). Not only is *dax* found for "good" in PG, PD, Djougi, and all the argots of Central Asia, but PD, Abd, Ju, Chist, and Ar also keep the original Aram meanings "clean, pure, right, correct." Remarkably, AG has *dax* "good, right" and *daxiyā* "pure."

As shall be seen, the *KS* and related sources show a clear predominance of Aramaic over Hebrew etyma, and many of these words have correlations in twentieth-century JLtr. Accordingly, for Loterāᵓi, indeed < **Loᵓ-Tōrāᵓī* "non-Toraic," the reference was "having a vocabulary not from Hebrew, but from Aramaic." Indeed, our materials cover the span of Aramaic spoken by Iranian Jews, from the early Achaemenid period (see *bika* and *nund-* above) to forms paralleling Jewish Neo-Aramaic of Iraq: KS nᵓšy "common people" (Pers ʿ*avām*), cf. Turkish Yürük nomads *naš* "people," Abd *noši* "a copper coin,"[23] all reflecting late Aram *nāšē* (as in JNeo-Aram) < ᵓ*ɔnāšē* "people" (the Abd form refers to the coin's bearing the image of a human face; thus too SD *mard* "dirham" < Pers *mard* "man").[24] Similarly, KS ᵓmᵓ "a hundred" (Pers ṣ*ad*) < late Aram ᵓ*ɔmmā* (as in Neo-Aram) < Aram *mɔᵓā* "a hundred."

Early Preponderance of Aramaic Over Hebrew in *KS*

The preponderance of Aramaic over Hebrew in the earlier phase of JLtr is evidenced by the fact that the verbs in *KS* that are

of Semitic origin are from Aramaic. The following correspond to
JLtr verbs:

(1) kʾlydn = *gʾlydn (Pers *raftan*) "to go." Shir *gāl-* "go," past
stem *gāled-* < Aram *g-l-y*, ptc. *galy-* "to go out."

(2) hzyδn "to go" (Pers *mesloho* "like that, {i.e., like the preceding
word, = Pers *raftan* "to go"}") bhz "go!" (Pers *borow*), kh
hznd "that they go." The synonymy of kʾlydn and hzyδn is
also indicated by Pers *va* "and" before hzyδn. Neh *hez-* "go,"
behez- "go!" cf. Gol. etc. *ez-* "id." < Aram. ʾ-z-l.

(3) tknydn "to make, to do" (Pers *kardan*), ntkn "don't make/do!"
(Pers *makon*), also aux. tkyn-, tykyn-. Mash *teken* (not *tek-en-*),
Her *tikin-* "to fix, make," Aram *taqqen*, "to establish, fix" (also
> Shir *taːn-* "id.").

(4) hʾlmdn "to sleep" (Pers *kospidan*), hʾlmwth "asleep" (Pers
kofta), Aram *h-l-m*, ptc. *halm-* "to dream." The same semantic
relationship in Ham etc. *dar halum-* "to go to sleep": Heb
halōm "a dream" points to a replacement (probably widespread)
within JLtr of Aramaic by the Hebrew cognate. Cf. e.g.
ʾʾxʾlydn below. The rendering of Aram and Heb *ḥ* by *h* is
consistent throughout JLtr, from whose medieval form *KS* and
thence the argots of Iran and Central Asia also have *h*; this
contrasts with *ḥ* > *x* in Neo-Aramaic.

(5) *KS* dhlydn "to fear" (Pers *tarsidan*), mydhlm "I fear" (Pers
mitarsam), *midahlad* "he fears," *ne bedahl* "don't be afraid."[25] Isf
dalan = *tarsan* "to fear" (both words are given together with
čandan and glossed by Pers *tarsidan* in a general {i.e., non-
Loterā'i} vocabulary of Judeo-Isfahani).[26] Ju *medahlum* "I fear,"
Chist *dal-* "to fear," PG *mīdella* "fears," and PG *dōl(iden)* "to
fear" < Aram *d-ḥ-l* "to fear," ptc. (participle) *daḥl-*. Cf. Shir
deyl- "to fear" < Aram noun *deḥel* "fear."

(6) *KS* ʾʾxʾlydn "to eat" (Pers *kᵛordan*), cf. Ju *oxolīdan* "id.," *KS*
byʾxʾl "eat!" (Pers *bekᵛor*), cf. Chist *bioxol* "id.," PG *okhōl-* "to
eat" (*sic* Ivanow, 1920, p. 291: not *okyōl*); < Aram *āxal* "ate."
Abd *axlamoq* "to eat" may derive via medieval JLtr from Aram
ptc. ʾ*axl-*, cf. Shir *ōxel-* "to eat" < Heb ptc. ʾ*ōxel-*.

Other Aramaic verbs shared by *KS* and the JLtr and gentile argots of the twentieth century are:

KS br kym "get up! arise!" (Pers *bar-ḵiz-*). PG, Kav, Ju *kim-* "get up"; Ar *barkim*; Ju *bur kim, dar kim* "get going." Gol *kām-* "stand up, exist"; Neh causative *kāmun-* "to put in a state, cause"; Her *kem-*, Neh *dar kām-* "sit down"; Mus Luti *kemeed*, Mus Tošmāl *keemed*, LG Osof, LG Fars *kemeed* "went" < Aram *q-w-m*, with forms *qām* and *qīm* "to arise, put in place." (Lazard's speculative derivation of *kām-* from the Indic Gypsy word seen in Ju *kam* "work" [< Sanskrit *karman-*] must now be discarded.[27])

KS *brsydn (unpointed) for prsydn "to eat" (Pers *ḵ*ᵛ*ordan*). Ham, Gol, Isf *peris-*, *piris-*, *pris-* "to eat." In the Kurdish argot LuJ, *pirüs* "food, eating" (= Pers *ḵ*ᵛ*oreš*, Kurd *xwârešt*), notably a noun like the etymon, Aram ptc. *pārīs* (f. *pərīsā*) "broken (bread) for distribution or blessing." LuJ has also *düywen* "ghee" (Pers rowḡan/ruḡan, Kurd řun) *dūhan Aram dōḥan "oil (other than olive oil)," and zâyra "barley" (Pers jow, Kurd jüywa), cf. *KS* sʾryʾ... (last letters illegible), Aram sə'āryā (śə'āryā) "barley" (cf. Gol sa'ur, Khom sa'uri Heb śə'ōrā, pl. śə'ōrīm "barley"), PG zabul, zaul "barley" may have u for ō < ā, cf. PG mezūl below.

Other traces of Aramaic, not evidenced in later JLtr are:

KS hʾzydn "to show" (Pers *nemudan*) < Aram *ḥazzey* "to make see, to show." From the Aram root *ḥ-z-y*; Mag has *mi-azi* "you see," *bi-az* "look!".[28] For the loss of *ḥ-, cf. Sheikh Momedi (Mag) *ādur* "begging" below.

KS hrʾšydn "play a flute" (Pers *ney zadan*) < Aram *ḥ-r-š* "to enchant, hypnotize," in reference to snake-charming, or < Aram *ḥ-r-š*, in view of the following brklh ṭrwšydn "to play (lit. "strike") a lute" (Pers *barbaṭ zadan*, see below), bṭrwš "beat! strike!" (Pers *bezan*) < Aram *ṭ-r-š* "to batter" (*KS* <ṭ-> probably via Arabic *ṭ-r-š* "to deafen," which also occurs in Aramaic).

Jewish Culture in the Muslim Argot Vocabulary

The Jewish cultural background of the Aramaic components of the
KS is dramatically clear from the outset of the latter, the first line of
which, beginning the chapter on names pertinent to Islam, has
rhmʾnʾ "God" (Pers *kodā*) < Aram *raḥmānā* "The Merciful One,"
usual for "God" in Jewish Aramaic texts; kmʾr "John the Baptist"
(Pers *Yaḥyā*) < Aram *kəmārā* "priest of a pagan temple"; and hwyʾkʾr
(Pers *Musâ*), lit. "snake-handler" from Aram *ḥiwyā* "snake" + Pers -*kār*
(see below) in allusion to Moses's curative brazen/copper and/or the
contest with Pharaoh's sorcerers.

Talmudic Aramaic usage is reflected in *KS* nhwr "eye" (Pers *čašm*)
and separately *nhwr* "blind" (Pers *kur*). Ju *nuhur* and SamL *nuhŭr*
are again both "eye" and "blind"; in PG and PD *nuhur* (AG *nhūr*),
Mus Luti, Mus Tošmāl, LG Osof, LG Fars, LG Kermān *náhur*
means "eye," versus Ar, Mag, Sogut, and Abd *nuhur* "blind." From
argot came Pers *nohur* and Tajik dialectal *nuhūr* "sight, eye." The
Talmud has *nəhōrā* "light (of the eyes)," and, as euphemism for
"blind," *saggī nəhōrā* "having much 'light'" (Syriac *saggī nuhrā*,
with phonological differences). The Talmudic phrase survives in
Yeshiva Yiddish. *KS* also has nhwr tykynh "victory," lit. "(day)
light-making," a kind of etymological calque for the additional
glosses Arabic *fajr al-manṣur* "the victor's dawn, victory" (Pers
piruzi). Earlier explanations of the argot word as from Arab *nūr*
"light" are wrong.

Aram *gālūt* "(the Jewish) Exile" > Gol *gālut* "(in) misery,
miserable" (*gālut-and* "the are in misery") point to *KS* kʾlwt as *gālūt
(still a noun, obj. of nwnd- "give" in an unglossed verse) as confirmed
by Djougi *galout* "bad" (see below), SamL *gohlut*, Abd *gaulud, golud*,
Ju and Ar *gohlud* "ill, sick."

The aforementioned *KS* hwyʾkʾr "Moses" separately recurs
glossed as Pers *mārān-gir* "grasper of snakes" in the section on
professions, the first of which is *knʾw (ms. kyʾw) = *gnʾw
"thief" (Pers *dozd*), cf. Chist *ganav*, Ju *ginop*, Abd *genou*, Ar *ginau*,
ginop, PG *genew* < Aram (and Heb) *gannāβ* "thief," whence Gol
qannō "id."

Our hwy'k'r represents a compound of *ḥiwyā* "snake" plus Pers
-*kār* "doer"; cf. the rhyming Pers *daryākār* "seaman." Another
Aramaeo-Persian compound is dm'krd "red" (Pers *sork̠*) < "made of
blood" (Aram *dammā* = Heb *dam* "blood," whence Bor *dam* "red").
The uncompounded hwy' "snake" occurs in the section on animal
names, after another Aramaeo-Persian form, dhb'b' "scorpion" (Pers
gazdom) *"golden-legged," with dhb' from Aram *dəhaβā* "gold" and -
b' = -*pā* "foot, leg"; this describes Iran's most conspicuous scorpion,
Odontobuthus doriae.

KS mylh (Pers *harza* "idle talk, gossip") < Aram *milleh* in
Talmudic usage both "his word"; cf. *millē* "words" and "gossip." For
-*h* = -*ēh* *"his," see below.

Other words with Aramaic background in the *KS* section on
animals are klb' and tn'ɣwl. The first, klb' "dog" (Pers *sag*), cf. Ju
kalpak, PG *kalpik* etc. "id.," is equatable with Aram *kalbā* "dog,"
which, via comparison with Arabic *kalb* "dog," gave rise to an argotic
-*ā* attached to Arabic words: *KS* qlb' "heart," bṭn' "belly," etc.; thus
KS forms like yd' "hand" are ambiguous in origin.

KS tn'ɣwl (ɣ unpointed) "hen, chicken" (Pers *morḡ*), cf. Abd and
Ar *tanoɣul, tanaɣul* "id." < Aram. *tarnəḡōl* {tarnəɣōl} "rooster,"
whence Bor *tarnegul* "id."; the notable *tanā- of the *KS* and Gypsy
forms versus Aram *tarnə*- will be discussed below.

For "lion" (Pers *šir*) *KS* has klb' mlk'n "dog-render," and for
"hawk" (Pers *bāz*) *KS* has tn'ɣwl mlk'n "chicken decapitator,"
structurally Persian participles, i.e. Persian compound participles
based on Aram *m-l-q*, ptc. *malq*- "to lop the head off a bird, tear apart
with the claws"; further below.

Other Early Aramaisms Preserved in Muslim Argot

KS has many other nouns from Aramaic that must have been
extant in medieval JLtr, although few survive in modern JLtr.
Examples are:

KS *s'wth (ms. s'wnh) "old (man)" (Pers *pir*), cf. Ju *sovut*, PG
sobut, Ar *sout* "old man" < Aram *sāβūt* replacing *sēβūt* "old

age" via *sāβā, sāβtā* "old woman"; for *-ūt-* Bor *hevalut* "bad" <
Heb *hevalūt* "vanity."

KS rhm³ "lover" (Pers *ʿāšeq*) < Aram *raḥamā* "id."

KS šyd³ "insane" (Pers *divāna*, from *div* "demon") > Pers *šeydā*
"crazy" < Aram *šēdā* "demon"; cf. Shir *šed(d)-* "to catch disease."
KS škr³ "lie" (Pers *dorūḡ*) < Aram *šiqrā* "id." Cf. Heb *šeqer*
"lie," which entered various Jewish languages, e.g. Judeo-
Isfahani and Yiddish.

KS m³hwz "city" (Pers *šahr*), cf. SamL *muhûz*, Ju *muγuz*
"town" < Aram *māḥōzā* "city."

KS also uses m³hwz in a series of argot terms for various cities
of Iran and Central Asia. Very interestingly, Herat (hryw)
appears to be called m³hwz hr[³?]t ls³nk "the city of Herat
speech"; *ls³n³ elsewhere < Arabic *lisān* "tongue" (Pers *zabān*).
Assuming the apparent hrt *ls³nk has -k = diminutive *-ak*,
then "Herat *argot." Alternatively, the -k could be a copyist's
error for the ³ of ls³n³. In either event, the phrase thus refers to
the (*Jewish?) argot of Herat, or that city's distinctive Persian
dialect.

KS dkh (*sic* twice; not dlh = Ju *dela*, below) "house"
(Pers *kāna*). Cf. Ju *dak* "locality, community," cf. Ju *dak-i mo*
"one of our people"; Ju *indak* *"this place; here"; *undak* "that
place; there." Cf. also Ju *gdok* "where?" < *kudok* "what
place?"; Shir *dāqim* "place" (*"my place," cf. Shir *qutim*
"myself" [below], or conceivably *"this place," cf. Mid. Pers
im "this"), *idāqim* "here." In addition, Kav and Mag have
duka "house." Toward an etymological solution, note further
Her *indof* "here," Mash *kondāf* "where" (< *kudōf* via *indāf*).
These may derive from Aram *daf* "framing plank, column on
page" > *"locus" (cf. German *Rahmen* "frame, milieu,
scope"). With Ju and Mag *duka* < early JLtr *dūq* < Aram
dūx "place," one can see contaminations *daf/*dāf and *dūx*
(> *dūq) giving rise to *dax > *daq > *dak, and *dāx >
*dāq > *dāk (> *dāq). The phonetic affinity between x and f
would have had a role; cf. German *Luft* < *luxt*; Pers *joft*
"paired" < *yuxta-*.

The change of /x/ to early JLtr /q/ to *KS* k is also reflected by Pers *ḵ*ᵛ*od* "oneself," Shir *qutim* "myself," *qutit* "thyself," *qutiš* "himself," cf. *KS* kwdʾwndm "myself" (Pers *man* "I"), *kwdʾwndt "thyself" (Pers *to* "thou"), and kwdʾwndš "himself" (Pers *ū* "he"). Pers *ḵodāvand* "lord, possessor, authority" suggests the possibility that "self" in "thyself, himself" underwent an argot expansion to "thy lordship, his lordship," whence "myself" = "milordship," giving inflated forms for "I, thou, he." For */x/ > */q/, see also below on *KS* ʾbyk, Shir *abeq* < Heb *ʾaβīx(ā)*.

Forms from Aramaic Possessive Nouns

Like the still-extant JLtr, *KS* reflects Aramaic nouns taken over independently (like Middle Iranian Aramaeograms) as non-possessive forms with what were originally various personal possessive endings. This applies in *KS* particularly to body parts (cf. Khom *ragle* "foot" < Aram *ragleh* "his foot," like Pahlavi LGLH = "foot"). Along forms with additional -*h* < Aram -*eh* "his" are *KS* hrh "rump, behind" (Pers *kun*) < Aram *hor*; lkth "finger" (Pers *angošt*), cf. Aram *l-q-ṭ* "pick up," and (reflecting Aram -*ī* "my") *KS* dkny "beard" (Pers *riš*), cf. PG *dagnā*, *degño* "mouth, beard, lips, teeth," AG *daqnā* "mouth."

Without reflection of Aram possessive suffix, *KS* hʾr (Pers *gu* [*sic* for *guh*]), Central Asiatic argots *hor* < Aram *hārē* "feces"; and kʾkʾ "tooth" (Pers *dandān*), cf. Ju *kokon* "face," PG *kōkīdan* "to laugh" < Aram *kakkā* "(molar) tooth."[29]

KS rjyʾjh "nose" (Pers *bini*) is probably < Aram *rehā* "breath" plus Persian suffix -*ča*. Cf. ryhʾny "fragrance, odor" (Pers *bu*) < Aram *rēhānē* "fragrance." *KS* hwtrʾ < Aram *huṭrā* "stick" glossed Pers *dār-e vey* "its beam," referring to the preceding entry myʾn tnk (?) probably = Pers *miān-tang* "having a narrow middle" (glossed Pers *sollam* "ladder").

As Ivanow suspected,[30] *KS* br is both associative and privative. The associative meaning is found in Aram *bar* "son, someone or something exemplifying a part/implement." *KS* brkʾlʾ "lute" (Pers *barbaṭ* or *barboṭ*), spelled brkʾlh before ṭrwš- "beat, play" (see above). Probably < Aram *bar qālā* *"(implement) having a voice"; for formation, cf. Aram *bar ṭawāy* "utensil under a roast," *bar lōʾā* "board securing an animal's jaw," and for the meaning, cf. Flamenco Caló argot *sonanta* "guitar." The next entry has brkʾlʾ dyɣʾ "false (or Turkish) lute," glossed as Pers jnk, i.e. *čang* "harp."

KS br < Aram *bar* "without" (cf. Pahlavi Aramaeogram BRH = *bē* "without") is found with yet another Aram noun in brmyʾ "thirsty" (Pers *tešna*, miscopied as *fetna* "sedition"), where -myʾ compares with PG, PD *moi*, Ju *mayō*, *mayob*, etc., Chist *mai* "water," cf. PG *mionew*, AG *mianu* "water," Mus Luti, Tošmāl *meyow*, Mus Čāli *meyab*, LG Fars *meyow*, all from Aram *mayyā* "water." Preceding brmyʾ is br hrsyt "hungry" (Pers *gorosna*), with *KS* hrsyt "bread" (Pers *nān*) = Central Asiatic Gypsy argots *harsīt* (< Arab *harīsa?*).

A rare instance of a correspondence of a *KS* and JLtr noun: *KS* klʾh "stone" for *glʾlh correlates with JLtr glʾlh (= Heb *even*)[31] "stone, rock" < Aram *gəlālā*, *gəlāltā* "stone, rock." Despite the gloss, the *KS* copyist may have read *kolāh* "hat" under the influence of words for headdresses and garments some lines earlier.

The Gypsy etc. argots of Iran and Central Asia also preserve traces of Aramaic verbs not in *KS*, some of which have equivalents in JLtr: for "give," Ju *hob-/how-* and SamL *hob-/hov-* straightforwardly correlate with Shir *av-* and Bor *ab-* (with *h*-loss) from Aram (also Heb) *hav* "give."

In the same semantic field, Kav *zamon-* "to give" compares with Shir *za(w)n-*, Isf *dam-*, Teh *dev-* < Aram *zabben* (caus. of *zəvan* "buy"), all "to sell." Formally the comparison is enhanced by the possibility, noted by Yarshater,[32] that the JLtr final merged with the Iranian causative marker (-*ān-* > -*on-/-un-*). For semantics, cf. Russian *davat'* "to give": *pro-davat'* "to sell," and English "I'll *give* it to you for five dollars."

Ju *ošin-* "to take (up)" is closest to Her *ošin-*, cf. Gol *(dar) ašun-* "to take," Kash *der ašan-*, Gol *dar āšne* "take!" Neh *be-m-āš-i* "I brought, took." Gol *mi-āšun-am* (stem *āšun-*) "I put right, set, fix, prepare, make, render" from *āš-un* "to put right, set, fix, prepare, make, render" points to the stem *āš-* < Aram ʾ-*š*-*š*: ʾ*iššeš* "founded, made firm," cf. *nitʾošeš* "was confirmed," *uššā* "fortification." Here note Ju *ošišt-*, past stem to *ošin-* (*ošišt-* assimilated < *aš-ist-*, past stem -*ist-?*).

Words of Aramaic origin not in *KS* or *JLtr* still preserved in the Pers argots are PG *tub-*, Chist *tup-*, Ju *tuvok* "to sit," *tuvol-* "to seat" from Aram *tūβ* "sit!"

To PG *sak*, *seg*, *sig*, Ju *sak-* "to observe" < Aram *sakkē* "observing" may be added *be-sok* "observe (carefully)" in the mainstream general colloquial of Isfahan,[33] a trace of the earlier Isfahani Loterā'i.

PG *tubur-* "to break," Shirazi/Kāzeruni Gypsy ironmonger argot *tavar* ~ *tobor-* "to hit,"[34] Ju *tarb-*, *tarv-* "to beat" (influence of Arabic *ḍ-r-b* "beat"?) < Aram *tabber* "to smash" find correlation in Abu Dolaf's Arabic *tatbīr*.[35]

Ju *umor-*, *umošt-* (SamL *ůmor-*, *ůmošt-*) "to say" (constructed like Tajik *gumor-*, *gumošt-* "arrange") < *omor-*; AG *bī-āmār* "say" < Aram *'āmar* "said" (vocalism like Ju *oxol-* "eat" from Aram *āxal*; cf. below Ju *otor* < *otar* "bazaar").

Alongside the above verbs are attested nouns of ultimate JLtr Aram provenance; some interesting for their semantic development from Talmudic usage are Chist *parzal* "knife" < Aram *parzel* "iron, iron implement or tool," Ju *givor* = Tajik *bosmačī* (Russian *basmač* "guerilla brigand fighter against early Russian Soviets in Central Asia") < Aram *gibbārā* "hero." Cf. Mus Mehtar *geevar* (= *givār*) "man," which would be a cross of the Aram word for "hero" with the word seen in Ju *γavrik*, *havrik* "man" < Aram *gaβrā* "man"; cf. Mus Sāzanda *gaveh* "man." Ju *havrik*, variant of *γavrik*, may be due to the influence of the word represented by Aram/Heb *ḥaβer* "friend, associate." Cf. above on *KS nhwr* etc. "blind."

For PG "*mezūl(?)*" "fortune-telling" < *mezōl*[36] is < Aram *mazzāla* (Bab Amoraic Mishnaic *mazzāl*) "fortune."[37]

Words of everyday economy include Abd *otar*, *otor*, Ju *otor* "bazaar, town" < Aram *'ātar* "place, town, market"; PG, PD *parak* "cow" < Aram *par(ā)* "bovine, cow"; and Chist *turun(k)* "bull," AG *tirang* "bovine" (Pers *gāv*); Ju *ozaxtor* "calf" (*"young bull," cf. LuJ and PD *āzak* "child" [< Middle Pers *zahāg?*]) < Aram *tōr*, pl. *tōrān* "bull."

Chist *katuna* "clothing" < Aram *kittūnā* "shirt, clothing" (*KS* tnwdh = Pers *pirāhan* "shirt" may be miscopying of *ktwnh).

Old Integration of Hebrew Words from Jewish Culture

The above large number of Aramaisms in the gentile argots, with and without correspondences in twentieth-century JLtr, confirms the etymology of Loterā'i etc. = non-Toraic = Aramaic, in reference to the chief source of the vocabulary. However, Loterā'i had, even in its medieval phase, a number of Hebrew words as Jewish *Kulturwörter.*

For twentieth-century JLtr, the agreement in Hebraisms shown between the JLtr of Iran and Herat (on the medieval distinction of which speech cf. below on the numerals) in Shir *melāxā:* Her *maloxo* "work, action, affair" and Go *lašun:* Her *lošun* "speech" (< "tongue") suggests a fairly early common origin; thus also Mash, Yazd *lex-:* Her *le(y)x-* "to go," cf., in the exclusionary Jewish Neo-Aram of northwestern Iraq, *līx* "leave quickly!, scram!" Bor *noma,* Isf *"nouma"* (nwm'), *nummâ* "moon"[38] may be explained from Heb *lɔβānā*[b], via well-paralleled assimilations and contractions, whose result points to early adaptation. Gol *tanāim,* Bor *tanāyim* (*sic*) "hen" is explainable as a metaphoric development, referring to the hen's putative deference to the rooster, from Heb *tɔnāyīm* "wedding arrangements," an early sacral-ritual entry. The words in fact have Yiddish equivalents: *mɔloxɔ, lošn,* and *leyx-lɔxo* (a *topos* from Genesis 1.12, and name of a Sabbath lection, Genesis 1.12–17.27) and *tnoyim* ("marriage contract"). Other Hebraisms may have been part of JLtr before the desuetude of Aramaic speech among Iranian Jews (cf. the occurrence of Hebrew in early Jewish documents of Afghanistan). Note also forms like Judeo-Kashani *melōx-e hamōvet,* Judeo-Isfahani *melax movat* = Yiddish *malax ha-moves* "Angel of Death."

KS attests the Hebraisms bysh "egg" (Pers *kāya-ye morḡ*) < Heb *bēṣā*[b] "id."; n'r (miswritten n'z) "boy" (Pers *ḡolām*) < Heb *na'ar* "id."; and hz'n "caller, reciter, singer" (Pers *k*ʿ*ānda* [for **k*ʿ*ānanda*]) < Heb *ḥazzān* "(synagogal) announcer, precentor, cantor."

Interestingly, *KS* kymwlw "camel" (Pers *oštor*), also in br kymwlw "camel driver" (with br < associative Aram *bar,* cf. e.g. *bar ḥaylā* "soldier") and kymwlw mlk'n *"camel-render" (Aram *malq-,* see above) = "elephant" (Pers *pil*); whereas Aram *gaml-* is irrelevant here, kymwlw = */gimōlō/ < Heb *gɔmallō* "his camel," cf. Gol *gamelli* < Heb *gɔmallī* "my camel," with a different possessive suffix.

For *gym-, cf. Early Judeo-Persian *nym'z* < *namāz* "prayer" and *nymyk* < *name(h)k* "salt" (in a *tafsir* of Ezekiel).

KS ʾbyk "father" compares with Shir *abeq* "father" < Heb *ʾaβīx(ā)* "thy father" versus Khom *ābi* "father" < Heb "my father"; cf. the variation underlying possessive suffixes in the word for "camel."

SamL *dela* "house, door," Ju, Abd, Ar *dela, dila*, Luli *dila* "house, tent," AG *dila* "room, tent" may derive from Heb *delet* "door," as does Bor *delét* "door." Possibly via reanalysis as *dela-t* *"thy door," or, if from early Heb pronunciation, *deleθ* giving *deleh* when Old Pers θ went to Mid. Pers *h*, resulting finally in *dela*. For semantics, cf. Pers and Tajik *dar* "door, gate, court"?

PG *nidu, nodo, nedeo*, LG Osof and Kermān *nedow* "woman, wife" seem to presuppose *nidō*, which could derive from Heb (> Aram) *niddā*ᵇ "menstruation, menstruant," if KS and manuscripts of Asadi's *Loḡāt-e fors* dnh "woman" (Pers *zan*), Abd *dana*, PG/PD *danew, denew, dinki*, and LuJ *dānu*, Mus Mehtar *danow*, Mus Sāzanda *duneh*, Mus Torbat-e Jām *danow*, LG Fars *danow* represent a taboo metathesis < *nidā, *nidō*. Influence of Arabic *danab* "tail" is possible (cf. vulgar English slang "tail" for "woman as sexual object," e.g., "chase tail"), cf. Abd *danap*, PG/PD *deneb*, Ju *danam*, Kav *danap*, etc. "woman."

Both Aramaic and Hebrew were alternative sources of older JLtr, as reflected by the names of numerals. Aram *ḥad* "one" gave KS hʾdk "one," PG *ḥōt* "a unit"; counting suffix -*ḥōd*, -*ḥōt* (= Pers *tā*); so also AG *(ḥ)āt, (ḥ)od, (ḥ)ot*. The latter forms compare with *-ḥat- < Aram *ḥad* in Her *tɔreynatak* "two" < Aram *tɔrey(n)* "two" + *ḥat* + -*ak*; the segmentation *tɔrey-natak* gave the Her numerative -*natak*. For "two" Heb *šɔnayim, šɔney* is reflected by KS šym < *šnym, SD *šann* (Bosworth, 1976, vol. 2, p. 313); cf. Shir *šane*, Bor *šené*. KS has slws = *šlwš < Heb *šālōš* "three," cf. Shir *šalošā*, but KS has štʾ from Aram *šittā* "six," and ʾmʾ < late Aram *ʾɔmmā* "thousand."

Evidence for a Jewish Underworld Component in the Old Muslim Argots

The actual involvement of a Jewish underworld in the early formation of the Muslim argot is confirmed by the data of the tenth-century Banu Sāsān *qaṣida* (AD), together with later data. Aram *hādōr* "circle" and *hādōrā* "peddler, beggar" (both from the root *h-d-r* "to go around") are involved in the first example: AD h'δwr/ h'dwr "the circle [of fortunetellers and their shills operating in a street assemblage] about which people congregate."[39] *KS* h'dwr "job" (Pers *kār*) may refer to this charlatanry, or professional begging, like PG *khōdur,* SamL, Ar, Abd *hodur,* etc., "beggar," SamL *hodūri* "begging"; cf. Mag *ādur* "peddling," the chief occupation of the Sheikh Momadi (Moḥammadi) itinerants of Afghanistan;[40] loss of *h-* as in Mag *az-* "look, see" (above, *s.v. KS* h'zydn).

AD *barkakk* is "street dentist"[41] < Aram *bar* (see above on *KS* br kymwlw) + *kakkā* "(molar) tooth," whence *KS* k'k' "tooth" (see above). Privative *bar* (cf. *KS* brmy' above) is seen in AD brkwš "one pretending deafness"[42] = *KS* br kwš, where kwš = Pers *guš* "ear."

AD *maysarāni* (verb *maysara*) "someone who begs, pretending to have fought the infidel on the frontier,"[43] *KS* mysr "fighter for the faith" (Pers *ġāzi*), < Aram *mēyṣar* "border," *mēyṣarānā* "pertaining to the frontier."

In the expected field of obscenities are *hurr* "rump," *KS* hrh (Pers *kun*) and kyδ "penis",[44] *KS* kyt = *gyt *"penis" (Pers dnd *dand* "rib," probably misreading of *kyr = *kir* "penis," near other words pertaining to the abdomen and genitalia; cf. Ju *git* "penis, male," Aram *gīd* "vein, tendon, penis").

The foregoing correlations of the AD with *KS* again show the Jewish Aramaic of the Muslim argot, already in the tenth century.

Note also Bosworth, 1976, vol. 2, p. 210, on AD verse 187, where travelers who go from place to place to lay out rugs are equated with *al-mašāṭiḥ,* this derivable from Aram *mišṭāḥā* "land where something (e.g., a fishing-net) is spread out to dry"; cf. Bosworth, 1976, vol. 2, p. 279, with a comparable Hebrew root and derivative. The Arabic *ḥ* indicates a direct borrowing from the Aramaic, as against the *h* of *hurr* "rump," whose *h* is due to Persian Jewish intermediation.

Bosworth tried to make a case for the presence of Jews in the Banu Sāsān,[45] arguing from both *a priori* considerations and scant textual testimonia, which he notes are uncertain as evidence. The correctness of his overall case is now confirmed by the linguistic evidence presented here.

Tenth-Century Astarābād and the Early Diffusion of Jewish Jargon: Evidence from Early Twentieth-Century "Djougi"

It is in the tenth century (the period of Abu Dolaf), we recall, that the term lwtr³ first occurs with regard to Astarābād, without Jewish reference. That this area was indeed instrumental in the entry of the Jewish exclusionary vocabulary into gentile argot is shown by de Morgan's linguistic material of "Djougi" Gypsies of Astarābād,[46] the city in which Lō/uterā(²i) is first attested by the Ḥodud al-ʿĀlam in the tenth century. It is likely that, at least in part, this "Djougi" group described by de Morgan as impoverished migratory tent dwellers, who seasonally migrate outwards from Astarābād and return there, at least in part represent the group from which are descended the identically named Jugi Gypsies of Tajikistan, as indicated by such unique correspondences as Djougi "homoachtan," Jugi umoštan (ůmoštan), umor- (ůmor-), cf. AG āmār- "to say" < Aram āmar-. The vocabulary of Djougi, as given by de Morgan, has close equivalents to other Gypsy argots of Iran and Central Asia in general:

From Indic: mônes "man"; djévéd "woman, wife"; lô "iron"; pounó "water"; bohót- "big"; vagal "goat"; gôrá "horse"; gérà "donkey"; bedjalonen "to light something up"; etc.

From Arabic: khashpouk "stick of wood"; ghèlil "small," cf. kölèl "child"; nárák "fire"; etc.

From Iranian: dakhlodj "girl"; takhnoï "knife"; süthaï "charcoal" (probably a Caspian reflex of suxta- "burned," cf. Djougi southa = Tajik argots suta "black," but note KS swd³ < Arabic); and hedjonddan "to make" (= PG ajon-,[47]).

From Aramaic/Hebrew: dakhana "good"; modakhî "bad" (mo- < Pers "not"); nouhour "eye"; hakhaliden "to eat"; miokholî "thou eatest"; bekimin "to go"; hamoachtan "to speak, say" (see above);

galout "bad"; *daghno* "mouth"; *-hot/-hod* numerative suffix; and *dela* "house."

Now, in addition to these forms in the last paragraph which are found throughout the Central Asiatic argots, Djougi has words from Aram/Hebrew not found in the other Muslim argots. These are: *pichto* "easy," cf. Aram *pəšiṭā* "id."; *moda ana* "ewe" (Pers *māda* "female" + Aram *ʿānā* "sheep"); *nomárát* "night" (< *(a)rāt* "night, evening" < Indic + disambiguating *noma* = Bor, Isf *noma*, *nu (m)mā* < Hebrew *ləβānā*, discussed above); and also:

Djougi *thünoï* "hen" (cf. *tunoï* "egg," probably parallel to Pers *tokm-e morḡ* "seed of chicken" = "egg," cf. Pers *tokm* "seed; egg; testicle"). This *t(h)ünoï* would represent something like /tɔno'ï/ < */tanāʾī/, which, with the common denasalization after long vowels, compares with Gol *tanāim*, Bor *tanā(y)īm* (*sic*; confirmed by Professor Yarshater in a letter of 2011)."Hen," whose Hebrew origin is discussed below, KS tnʾγwl (Pers *morḡ*), Abd and Ar *tanaγul* "chicken" emerges as a cross of **tarneγul*, cf. Bor *tarnegul* < Aram *tarnəgōl* {tarnɔγōl} "rooster," and *tanā(y)i(m)* "hen," whose antiquity in gentile argot is reflected by Djougi.

With the addition to the foregoing of Djougi *hedjonndan*, which has correspondences in PG of northern Iran (with and without causative *-on-*), cf. Shir *āj-* and Her *huj-* from fossilized Old Iranian, we have confirmation for the antiquity of the argot in Astarābād, for which the term lwtrʾ(y) is attested in the tenth century. These data also confirm the Jewish origin of lwtr(ʾ)(y) as both term and speech, referred to in early Persian sources.

The Role of Deylam in the Early Diffusion

As for the passage of the exclusionary Judeo-Iranian speech into non-Jewish argot, specifically in Astarābād in the tenth century, the latter city was variously connected with Deylam during this unstable period, which gave rise to two dynasties of Deylami origin, the Ziyarids and more importantly the Shiʿite Buyids, whose power soon extended over most of Iran, setting the scene for peregrinations of Abu Dolaf al-Yanbuʿi and his patronage among the Buyids. In this context it is relevant that *KS* refers to Deylam as mlkyʾ = Aram *malkayyē* "the kings," cf. *KS* mlkʾ, glossed as Pers *amir*. Furthermore, a Deylami locus of the spread of the argot may be confirmed by *KS* dʾ = Pers *deh* "village," if this represents the Māzandarāni pronunciation *də* (of which Habib Borjian has informed me). *KS* mʾhwz mlkʾn "city of amirs" = "Ray" seems also to reflect Buyid realia. The role of a Jewish underworld—noted above for the tenth-century period of Abu Dolaf on linguistic grounds—may well have been furthered in post-Buyid Deylam via the activities of Ḥasan Ṣabbāḥ, among whose fighters were three communities of tough rapacious Jews (thus Benjamin of Tudela). It could be expected that such groups settled in cities as a prestigious part of the Iranian underworld.

Jews and Argots, East and West

The sociological scenario for the beginnings of gentilization of Loterāʾi would have been the emergence of a large Iranian underworld, culminating in the tenth century in the Caspian area, of which Jews were a part. Whereas such Jews inherited a vocabulary meant originally to exclude non-Jews (the core of which speech persisted in this function among respectable Jews), for Jews of the Iranian lower class (including poor tradesmen and laborers), this vocabulary was intended to exclude the solid citizens, police, gentry, and rulers. For the non-Jewish underworld, their Jewish colleagues offered a readymade exclusionary vocabulary whose acquisition was useful. This vocabulary was then transmitted to other marginal groups, particularly Gypsies, and is still partially attested. A very similar development took place independently in the fifteenth– sixteenth century rise of Gaunersprache/Rotwelsch (Rotwälsch), with its large Jewish vocabulary, among gentile beggars and scoundrels of the German-speaking area. Indeed, Oranskï (pp. 44–5) notes a brief series of gentile Iranian argot words of Jewish etymology, and on p. 46 with fn. 37 adduces Ju *oxol-*: Rotwelsch *acheln* "to eat." Note further such correlations with early sixteenth century R(otwelsch) as Chist *ganavidan*, etc., R *genffen* "to steal"; Ju *γavrik*, etc., R *gaver* "man"; and KS *bysh* "egg," R *betzam* "eggs."

Early Jewish Loterā'i Reflected in the Scope of the Persian Vocabulary

Early Persian poetry and lexica contain a number of words of Jewish Aramaic origin via our Muslim argot. These include the aforementioned lwtr' words in Suzani's poems, dx "fair," zyf "vile"; words noted as used by the **sāsiān* (mss. 'sy'n): s'bwth, ṣ'bwth "old woman," dnh "woman"; words redolent of the underworld: *ḥār* "feces" and hrh "rump"; the important word h'dwry "member of a class of intrepid beggars"; and words that still survive: nhwr (old vocalism *nuhōr*, cf. Aram *nəhōr(ā)*) and Tajik *nuhūr* "sight, eye"; and *šeydā* "crazy, wild, infatuated, lovesick, enamored" (in Persian literature). The Aramaic provenance of such words seems indicated in the two tags "suri" for the argot verses in the final portion of the KS. This term is to be taken as the equivalent of *suryāni* (*"Syrian"), which was the usual term for the Aramaic language among Arabic-speaking Jews and others. Already in the Hellenistic period the similar Greek words *Syriakē* and *syristí* were used by Hellenistic Jews for "Aramaic" (the latter word > **swrystyn* in the Palestinian Talmud, fourth–fifth centuries CE). Syriac does not come into consideration; although Syriac is similar to the Babylonian Jewish Aramaic source of the argot, it is in fact distinguishable by words like Syriac *nuhrā* versus Aram *nəhōrā* "eyesight," Syriac *gīd* "tendon, vein," but Aram also "penis," a Jewish usage reflected in the Muslim argot.

Conclusion

Loterā'i may now be seen as not only a long-extant Judeo-Iranian speech, but a speech that exerted a remarkable influence on the course of Persian sociolects and Persian in general, with a history that

illuminates the history of interethnic relationships and class in the
Middle East and Central Asia.

Addendum

Dr. Habib Borjian (e-mail, May 5, 2014) reports the interviewing
of a 70-year-old informant in New York, a Jew who spent his
early youth in Kabul and remembers some words and phrases
from the then already disappearing exclusionary Kabuli Jewish
speech of his childhood, which he called Loterā'i. The three verbs
in the data trasmitted by Dr. Borjian are all found in the above
data from Iran and Herat (the last also KS) and are respectively from
early Iranian, Hebrew, and Aramaic: ruč- "look," lex- "go," and
tikin- "to make."

Notes

1 I thank Mahmoud Omidsalar for his invaluable remarks on KS; and for helpful
   provision of suggestions and bibliographic materials toward the preparation of
   this article, Habib Borjian, Ken Blady, Agnes Korn, Tatiana Oranskaia, Ludwig
   Paul, Nahid Pirnazar, Houman Sarshar, Dan Shapira, Don Stilo, and Ehsan
   Yarshater. This article is dedicated to Professor Yarshater.

2 Ehsan Yarshater, "The Hybrid Language of the Jewish Community of Persia,"
   JAOS, 97:1 (1977), pp. 1–7; abridged in Encyclopaedia Iranica 15, pp. 156–60.

3 V. Ivanow, "Further Notes on Gypsies in Persia," Journal {and Proceedings} of the
   Asiatic Society of Bengal, NS/16 (1920), pp. 281–91.

4 Ehsan Yarshater, "The Dialect of Borujerd Jews," in L. Meyer and E. Haerinck
   (eds), Miscellanea in Honorem Louis Vanden Berghe (Ghent, 1989), pp. 1029–46.

5 Yarshater, 1977.

6 Hanina Mizrahi, Yehudey Paras (Tel Aviv, 1959), pp. 121–3.

7 Gilbert Lazard, "Note sur le jargon des juifs d'Iran," JA, 266 (1978), pp. 251–55.

8 W. Ivanow, "On the Language of the Gypsies of Qainat (in Eastern Persia),"
   Journal {and Proceedings} of the Asiatic Society of Bengal, NS/10 (1914),
   pp. 438–53; and Ivanow, 1920.

9 W. Ivanow, "Jargon of Persian Mendicant Darwishes," Journal {and Proceedings}
   of the Asiatic Society of Bengal, NS/23 (1927), pp. 243–5.

10 J. de Morgan, Mission scientifique en Perse V. Études linguistiques (Paris, 1904),
   pp. 304–6.

11 M. Moghaddam, Guyeshhā-ye Vafs o Āshtiān o Tafresh (Tehran (Irānkuda 11),
   c.1960), pp. 142–52.

12　Sekandar Amanolahi and Edward Norbeck, "A Note on the Secret Language of the Traditional Musicians of Iran," *Journal of the Gypsy Lore Society*, Ser. 4, 1/4 (1978), pp. 283–6.

13　Ibid.

14　Anna Leonidovna Troitskaya, "Abdoltili—tsekha artistov i muzykantov Srednei Azii," *Sovetskoe Vostokovedenie*, 5 (1948), pp. 251–4.

15　I. M. Oranskii, *Tadzhikoyazychnie etnograficheskie gruppy Gissarskoi doliny Srednaya Aziy, Etnolingvisticheskoe issledovanie* (Moscow, 1983).

16　Jadwiga Pstrusińska, *O tajnych językach Afganistanu i ich użytownikach* [On the secret languages of Afghanistan] (Cracow, 2004), p. 71–3; see pp. 105–7 for comparisons of Mag with other Gypsy argots of Central Asia.

17　Edition and commentaries in: C. E. Bosworth, *The Mediaeval Islamic Underworld, the Banū Sāsān in Arabic Society and Literature*, 2 vols (Leiden, 1976).

18　Edition and commentaries in ibid.

19　Gholām-Hosayn Karimi, "Lwtr-e Jāberi," *Majalleh-ye zabānshenāsi*, 7:2 (1990), p. 66–8. Cf. Ludwig Paul, "Die Geheimsprache von Kahak (Tafreš)," *Orientalia Suecana*, 48 (1999), pp. 105–14.

20　Datum from Dan Shapira.

21　Yarshater, 1977, pp. 4–5.

22　Mizrahi, p. 123.

23　Troitskaya, p. 264.

24　Bosworth, 1976, vol. 2, p. 303.

25　Mizrahi, p. 123.

26　Ayub Ebrāhimi, *Esfahān nesf-e Jahān. Farhang-e vāžahā va estelāḥāt-e maḥalli-e Esfahān* (2nd edn, Los Angeles, 2006), p. 15.

27　Lazard, p. 254.

28　Jadwiga Pstrusińska, *O tajnych językach Afganistanu i ich użytownikach* [On the secret languages of Afghanistan] (Cracow, 2004), p. 71.

29　Troitskaya wrongly cites a Syriac "kokha," which led others to attribute Syriac as a component of our Gypsy argot vocabulary. See Troitskaya, p. 254.

30　V. Ivanow, "An Old Gypsy-Darwish Jargon," *Journal [and Proceedings] of the Asiatic Society of Bengal*, NS/18, (1922) [1923], p. 378.

31　Mizrahi, p. 123.

32　Yarshater, 1977.

33　Datum from Habib Borjian.

34　Datum from Don Stilo.

35　See Bosworth, 1976, vol. 2, p. 308.

36　Ivanow, 1914, p. 452, and, for the vowel of the second syllable, pp. 445–6.

37　Note Ivanow, 1920, p. 282, on Persian Gypsies not being fortunetellers; Jews were known until recent times in the Near East as practitioners of occult sciences.

38　Respectively Ebrāhimi, p. 51 and Irān Kalbāsi, *Guyesh-e kalimiān-e Esfahān* (Tehran, 1994), p. 229. The latter glossed as Pers *māh* [*borj*], i.e. "moon as month"; neither entry designates the word as Loterāʾi.

39 See Bosworth, 1976, vol. 2, pp. 240–1, with a different Semitic etymology.
40 Petrusińska, p. 48, with literature.
41 Bosworth, 1976, vol. 1, pp. 90, 146, 148, 161.
42 Ibid., pp. 161, 175.
43 Bosworth, 1976, vol. 1, p. 175; vol. 2, pp. 194, 224.
44 Bosworth, 1976, vol. 2, pp. 192, 218–19.
45 C.E. Bosworth, "Jewish Elements in the Banū Sāsān," *Bibliotheca Orientalis*, 33 (1974), pp. 289–94.
46 De Morgan, pp. 304–6.
47 Ivanow, 1914, p. 454 with pp. 447–8 on the suffix: cf. above on Shir *aj-*, Her *huj-*.

CHAPTER 3

THE INTELLECTUAL PARAMETERS OF THE JUDEO-PERSIAN TREATISE *HOVOT RAFA'EL* BY EL'AZAR HAYIM B. MOLLA ELIYAHU (NINETEENTH CENTURY)

Vera B. Moreen and David Yeroushalmi

Introduction

The intellectual world of pre-modern Iranian Jews is still largely ensconced in numerous, little-studied Judeo-Persian manuscripts. While the exploration of their contributions to and participation in the creation of belles-lettres is well on its way,[1] we know little about the levels of religious and philosophical knowledge among the elite. The scarcity of texts that could shed light on this theme is only apparent, for we have not yet thoroughly searched and researched the Judeo-Persian manuscript collections in the Western world let alone those that continue to be unavailable, hidden either in private hands or in Iran. In the meantime, texts that can diminish this large lacuna need to be thoroughly investigated. One such text is the *resāleh* [Pers., treatise] *Hovot Rafa'el* (henceforth *HR*; Heb. The Duties of Raphael) by Molla El'azar Hayim b. ha-Dayyan Eliyahu b. El'azar written sometime during the second half of the nineteenth century. The product of a complicated and controversial personality, this treatise sheds some light on the religious and polemical concerns of a learned and pious individual confronted by both internal (communal) and external pressures.

In his edition of Rabbi Judah ben El'azar (Riba)'s *Hovot Yehudah*,[2] Amnon Netzer identifies El'azar Hayim as "a scholar from Hamadan, who lived in Teheran, probably during the second half of the nineteenth century."[3] Netzer's interest in this personage is limited to noting that, to his (Netzer's) knowledge, El'azar Hayim is the only person whose mention of *Hovot Yehudah* has come down to us; but he does not provide a manuscript source for El'azar Hayim's essay. Our combined efforts have unearthed considerably more information about this author; information that lifts the veil off the allusive language of the *resāleh* considerably.

Molla El'azar: Biographical Notes

Molla El'azar Hayim was the son of Molla [*dayyan*; Heb., communal judge] Eliyahu b. El'azar, the learned and influential chief rabbi and spiritual leader of the Jewish community of Hamadan between the 1840s and 1860s. Biographical information about him as well as his intellectual profile, including his professional career in Hamadan and Baghdad (where he reportedly died), can be gleaned from diverse and at times conflicting written and oral sources related to the author and his family, as well as to the Jewish community of Hamadan during the first and second halves of the nineteenth century. Born and raised in a rabbinic family in the old-established Jewish community of Hamadan, Molla El'azar, known also by his similar-sounding Persian name of Lalezar [Pers., garden of tulips], also acquired training as a pre-modern physician [Pers., *hakim*]. In this respect he pursued a career that was common among many male members of the better-educated and rabbinic families in several other Jewish communities of Iran—among them those of Yazd, Kashan, Tehran, Golpaygan and Khansar—between the sixteenth and twentieth centuries. Due to his highly respected ancestry, and on account of his abilities and considerable charisma, Molla El'azar was appointed head of the Jewish community of Hamadan some time in the 1850s.[4] Conflicts, interpersonal rivalries, and jealousies in the community, however, led to serious complaints and charges against him. Some members of the community accused him of misappropriating and embezzling communal taxes. As a result, he was summoned to Tehran in the late summer of 1865 and was jailed under harsh conditions. Subsequently, after a long ordeal, the details of which are documented in the report of Charles Alison, the British Minister Plenipotentiary at Tehran, he was released by the authorities in January 1866 and allowed to return to his native city. These details include a long list of physical and psychological hardships endured by Molla El'azar after his departure from Hamadan. Apparently, a number of Jews from Hamadan and Tehran, as well as several government officials and influential figures in Tehran, were involved in intrigues and extortions connected with Molla El'azar's case and detention in Tehran. On his way to Tehran, he was arrested by some footmen hired and bribed by his detractors. They brought Molla El'azar to Tehran with great violence and extorted a large sum of money from him in order to stop them maltreating him. Though set free for a few days, he was then imprisoned, chained, and tortured. In his own words, "Once every hour they put a chain of twenty *mann*s[5] on my neck [. . .]; they ill-treated me in various ways and took twenty *toman*s from me." When news of his father's death reached him in prison, Molla El'azar was not allowed to return to Hamadan.[6] Released again, he was granted a meeting with Mohammad Khan Qajar Sepahsalar, Naser al-Din Shah's (r. 1848–96) grand vizier, following which he was referred to a court of law. His opponents, however, never showed up at court. In order to issue a judgment in his favor, the judge demanded that Molla El'azar pay him the exorbitant sum of 200 *toman*s as a "gift" [*pishkash*].[7] Unable to produce such a large sum, Molla El'azar found sanctuary [*bast*] in the grand vizier's stable where he remained under harsh conditions, experiencing continuous harassment, threats, and extortionary demands until his final release and return to Hamadan.[8] Once there, he did not succeed in regaining his prestige and authority, and left his native community. He moved to Baghdad, where he is said to have set up a medical practice. He died in Baghdad in 1881,[9] or, according to another source, in 1887.[10]

We lack concrete information concerning Molla El'azar's date of birth, his early education, and subsequent professional and scholarly activities. However, from what is known about his family, and particularly on the basis of documentation regarding the primary and advanced stages of the educational system in the Jewish community of Hamadan during the first half of the nineteenth century, we may be confident that he received a thorough education in the traditional branches of Jewish law, liturgy, and literature. Furthermore, he was evidently familiar with the various genres and works of Judeo-Persian literature. Based on the books and manuscripts found in his library, some of which were reportedly sold to outsiders after his death, Molla El'azar possessed a considerable number of Judeo-Persian works, including some elegantly illuminated manuscripts of works by the fourteenth-century Judeo-Persian poet Shāhin.[11]

More is known about Molla El'azar's father, that is Molla Eliyahu b. El'azar, than about his son. He undoubtedly supervised the education and upbringing of his son and was known both in Hamadan and outside the city for his erudition and religious authority. References to Molla Eliyahu's broad knowledge and acumen are found in the writings of several European visitors and Christian missionaries, particularly those belonging to the British evangelical institution known as the London Society for Promoting Christianity amongst the Jews. The German Jew Henry A. Stern, a convert to Christianity, visited the Jewish community of Hamadan in the spring of 1845 and was present in the Great Synagogue on an occasion when Molla Eliyahu translated long passages from Hebrew into Persian for his congregants. He referred to Molla Eliyahu thus: "He is the most learned Jew in Persia, and is greatly respected both by Jews and Moslems."[12] On another occasion, upon his arrival in Hamadan on March 7, 1852, Stern noted, "I went direct to the house of Chacham [Heb., sage] Eliyahu, the Chief Rabbi, a man of considerable learning and great influence."[13] Similarly, the well-known Jewish Austrian ethnographer and professor of medicine Jacob Eduard Polak, who visited the Jewish community of Hamadan several times during the 1850s, spoke highly of Molla El'azar's father. Polak, who among his other writings about the Jews of Iran devoted a number of articles to the Jewish community of Hamadan in the mid-nineteenth century, referred to Molla Eliyahu in German as *ein gelehrter Jude* (a learned Jew).[14]

Molla Eliyahu's uncontested prominence and influence in the religious and communal lives of Hamadan's Jews are equally evident in the extant writings of the Jews of Hamadan themselves. The learned rabbi, scholar, and educator Menahem Shemuel Halevy (b. Hamadan, 1884; d. Jerusalem, 1940),[15] the scion of an old rabbinic family of Hamadan intimately involved in the educational and cultural life of its Jewish community until his immigration to Palestine in 1923, devoted a rather long passage to Molla Eliyahu's erudition and high moral standing in the eyes of Jews and Muslims alike.[16] Molla Eliyahu's learning and command of Hebrew and Jewish sources are also evident in the surviving letters he wrote in the 1860s. For example in a long petition, a cry for assistance he wrote to the famous philanthropist Sir Moses Montefiore (d. 1885) and the Jewish philanthropic organizations of Britain and France on September 14, 1864, we come across Molla Eliyahu's solid command of rabbinic Hebrew and his thorough familiarity with the conventions of rabbinic prose, biblical sources, and pre-modern Jewish literature.[17] This petition, written in Hebrew rabbinic style and in rhymed prose, as well as a relatively large body of other Hebrew letters, poems, and documents written by rabbis and the better-educated members of the Jewish community of Hamadan (where the author of our treatise was raised and educated) attest to the considerably high standards of Jewish and Judeo-Persian education and literacy among the leading rabbinic families and well-to-do Jewish merchants and professionals of Hamadan in Molla El'azar's lifetime.[18]

As far as the immediate cultural and intellectual surroundings of Molla El'azar are concerned, we possess quite rich and detailed information. Interestingly, one of our main written sources regarding the contemporary educational system, curriculum, and the advanced stages of Jewish learning in Hamadan is also connected to the

activities of Molla Eliyahu, his father. It was supplied by Rabbi
Nissim Bar Selomah (Nissim ben Solomon), an emissary on behalf of
Molla Eliyahu and the Jewish community of Hamadan, and
published in *The Jewish Chronicle* of London in the summer of 1850.[19]
Molla Eliyahu sent Rabbi Nissim to London and from there to
Montreal, Canada, in order to inform the leaders of European Jewry
about the hardships and needs of Iranian Jewry and, in particular, in
the hope of obtaining their assistance for the Jewish community of
Hamadan. Based on the information provided by this indirect means,
eight informative articles were written by Dr. Abraham de Sola, the
Chief Rabbi of the Spanish and Portuguese congregation of Montreal,
related to various aspects of life among the Jews of Hamadan,
including their religious lives and synagogues, their dwellings,
customs, professions, relations with Muslim neighbors, and more.
Rabbi Nissim also provided much relevant information about the
various stages and contents of primary, intermediate, and advanced
education in the community.[20] Among other facts and details that
shed light on Molla El'azar's likely course of studies, we learn of the
existence of a Jewish Yeshiva, or Talmudic college and academy, in
Hamadan. Its curriculum included the study of *Shulhan Arukh*,
the authoritative code of Jewish law by Rabbi Joseph Caro (d. 1575);
the first three books of Maimonides' (d. 1204) *Yad Ha-Hazaka*
commonly known as *Mishneh Torah*; tractates of both the Jerusalem
and Babylonian Talmuds; the popular book of ethics known as *'Eyn
Ya'acov* (a collection of aggadic passages and ethical exhortations
composed by the Spanish scholar Jacob b. Solomon ibn Habib,
d. 1515/6); and more.[21]

As to Molla El'azar's familiarity with Persian and Islamic sources
and the manner and channels through which he acquired his attested
command of the Persian and Arabic languages, here again we lack
direct information and must thus rely on inference and
circumstantial evidence. While knowledge of the Persian-Arabic
script and familiarity with Persian and Arabic writings in their
original forms was rather rare among the majority of Iranian Jews
until the beginning of the twentieth century, Judeo-Persian texts
testify that small circles of Persian-speaking Jews in various cities and

towns (including Golpaygan and Khansar) read and wrote the Persian script and were proficient in classical Persian throughout the Middle Ages. They may be presumed to have been exclusively males belonging mostly to the families of rabbis, physicians, and well-to-do merchants who possessed and used Persian and Arabic books and manuscripts.[22] According to the evidence at our disposal, there were several such educated individuals in the Jewish community of Hamadan, particularly during the second half of the nineteenth century. One of the direct and instructive references to the cultural and intellectual profile of the better-educated Jews of Hamadan during Molla El'azar's lifetime is found in the writings of another educated rabbi of Hamadan who, as far as we can tell, was about the same age, or perhaps just a few years younger than Molla El'azar. Born and raised in the Jewish community of Hamadan some time during the early nineteenth century, Molla and Hakham Bakhaj Ben Yehezghel also belonged to an old rabbinic family. At some point (*circa* mid-nineteenth century) he moved to Tehran, where he was appointed (around 1870) chief rabbi and dayyan of the growing Jewish community of the capital, a position he retained until his death, *c.*1876.[23] Molla Bakhaj conducted a rather extensive correspondence with the Jewish leaders and communal organizations of Western Europe, chief among them the Alliance Israélite Universelle of Paris.[24] In one of his letters, while referring to his own educational background and familiarity with classical Persian, Molla Bakhaj relates that having been born and raised in the Jewish community of Hamadan he is proficient in classical Persian and its literary sources.[25] References to close and amicable ties and relations between the Jews of Hamadan and some members of the Shi'ite clergy and merchants in Hamadan between the 1860s and 1870s can also be found in the various historical sources of the period. For example, the Christian missionary Jacob Lotka, who conducted evangelical work among the Jews of Hamadan during the 1870s, reported in 1882 that "some six years ago [that is, in 1876] a party of influential Jews and Moslems [in Hamadan] used to gather for the purpose of discussing diverse topics of learning."[26] Such contacts may explain, in part, the manner in which Jews, including Molla El'azar, could have acquired and expanded their knowledge of Persian and Arabic-Islamic literary and religio-theological sources. Quite revealingly, in the affidavit that Molla El'azar submitted to the British Legation in Tehran in connection with his arrest and imprisonment in the city, he points to his extensive friendly ties and relations with "Ulama [Muslim religious scholars] and with merchants and respectable Musulmans of Hamadan."[27]

Much like Molla Bakhaj, the Hamadan-born chief rabbi of Tehran, Molla El'azar appears to have belonged to a rather small but growing group of educated Jews in Hamadan and Tehran during the 1840s and later, individuals who manifested a high degree of openness toward the growing influence of European culture and education in nineteenth-century Iran. Already in the 1850s there were some among the rabbinic families of Hamadan who sent their sons to Paris to study medicine.[28] This trend was the result, on the one hand, of the growing contact between local Jews and the agents and representatives of European and Western consular, commercial, and missionary establishments in Hamadan and in Iran's other major cities and commercial centers. On the other hand, the Jews' receptiveness toward ideas and stimulants of cultural change were closely linked with socio-religious trends and movements at work within the broader Iranian Shi'ite society. Chief among these trends and having a direct impact on Molla El'azar's nuclear and extended family, were the Bábi and Baha'i reformist and messianic currents in Hamadan. The Bábi movement and its offshoot, the Baha'i faith, attracted and transformed a significant number of Jewish individuals and families in Hamadan in the early 1850s. Out of an estimated Jewish population of 800 households (roughly 4,000 souls) counted in 1879, some 150 families had embraced the Baha'i faith.[29] Among them were Molla El'azar's eldest son, Hakim [physician] Agha Jan (d.1880), as well as his youngest son, Hakim Elyas.[30] Other members of Molla El'azar's extended family who reportedly joined the Baha'i faith included some of the descendants of his two sisters, that is the daughters of Molla Eliyahu.[31]

Molla El'azar's receptiveness toward the new channels and ideas associated with Western cultural influence in nineteenth-century Iran is also evident in his acquisition of the French language. Although at this stage we do not know how and by what exact methods he did so, there is evidence that he was familiar with and was acknowledged for his proficiency in French. The renowned French writer, thinker, and diplomat Comte Arthur de Gobineau (d. 1882), who lived and served in Iran during the years 1855–8, pointed out that Molla Lalezar (El'azar) had assisted him in translating from French into Persian the acclaimed philosophical treatise *Discours de la méthode* of the French mathematician and philosopher Descartes (d. 1650).[32]

Hovot Rafa'el: Contents, Style, Polemics

Molla El'azar's treatise takes its name from a work, *HR*, to which it serves as an introduction. A manuscript of *HR* is yet to surface, and its author (a certain Rabbi Rafa'el) and contents are so far unknown. Molla El'azar relates that he was commissioned to write his *resāleh* by a number of individuals, whom he names but who remain unidentified, and upon whose generosity he bestows profuse blessings.[33] His primary reason for writing this introduction was to advocate the need to inculcate and spread correct religious and philosophical beliefs among his coreligionists in order to enable them to attain to Resurrection, teach them to refute and resist erroneous beliefs and, very likely, various pressures to convert. Molla El'azar opines toward the end of the essay that *HR* was the best work to promote such beliefs for the reason to be mentioned below. However, he also appears to have had some other, pronouncedly polemical aims, as we shall see.

The 23-page treatise (ff. 71r–82r) lacks a title in ms. 1445 of the Jewish Theological Seminary of America (New York) and is missing part of the very end of the last sentence containing an imprecation against anyone rejecting the contents of *HR*, the text of which was supposed to follow Molla El'azar's introduction. Although foliated consecutively, a catchword indicates a lacuna following fol. 78v and, without having (yet) seen other copies, we are unable to determine what part of the treatise may have been, in our view, deliberately removed. Most folios have 20 lines and the calligraphy is highly legible. Some water damage and a certain amount of erratic spelling typical of most Judeo-Persian manuscripts present a few deciphering problems.

It is necessary to present first a brief synopsis of Molla El'azar's arguments and then proceed to a brief discussion of his aims and sources. At first glance, the *resāleh* gives the impression of being a long meditation on death. It is that and more. In accordance with conventional Jewish and Muslim beliefs, Molla El'azar maintains that God endowed man with intelligence as the "supreme agent" of creation in order to help him find the "right path" to Him. Satan was "planted" in this arrangement as a tester of mankind. Although all religions lead to God, one should persevere upon one's own religious path in order to prepare for the final meeting with God after death. Molla El'azar dwells at length both on the inevitability and on the positive aspects of death. Since the hour of death cannot be known, man's striving must be both continuous and joyful. Although one should strive on the path of one's own religion, one should not shun learning and wisdom coming from the sages of the "nations of the world" [Heb., *ummot ha-'olam*]. Even though some Jewish sages have opposed doing so, the majority have always accepted truth and wisdom coming from sources outside Judaism. Moreover, Jews ought to become acquainted with other religions, including various heretical views, in order to better refute them and, most likely, repulse attempts at conversion. Above all, Jews must have a thorough understanding of the fundamental principles [Heb., *'iqqarim*] of their faith and distinguish them clearly from the branches, or derived secondary truths [Heb., *'anaf(im)*]. Molla El'azar does not review the extensive literature on *'iqqarim* and mentions only that important philosophers have tried to establish them. He specifies that Maimonides claimed there were 13; Hasdai Crescas (d. 1410/1) reduced them to six; Yosef Albo (d. probably 1444) to three; and Messer David b. Judah Leon (d. 1526?) to four; this last being the view that R. Yehudah b. El'azar, the author of *Hovot Yehudah*, also espoused.[34] In Molla El'azar's view, however, Rabbi Rafa'el, the author of *Ets ha-hayim derekh ha-hayim* [Heb., The tree of life/The way of life] and presumably also of *HR*, held the most correct view with regard to *'iqqarim*. He reduced them to one, namely, *Torat Moshe emet* [Heb., the Torah of Moshe is truth/true]. Molla El'azar agrees with the author of *HR* and maintains that this is the supreme fundamental principle of Judaism; everything else derives from and is therefore secondary to it.[35]

This synopsis provides greater coherence to the *resāleh* than it really possesses. In accordance with the flowery rhetoric of late Persian prose and in order to display his erudition, Molla El'azar's treatise is studded with anecdotes and brief, not always accurate references to religious and secular, Jewish and Muslim sources. Not surprisingly, he refers most frequently to the Hebrew Bible (nine times); the mishnaic ethical tractate Pirke Avot [Heb., The chapters of the fathers] (once); the Babylonian Talmud (three times); the Palestinian Talmud (once); Maimonides' treatise *Shemona Perakim* [Heb., eight chapters] (once); and various midrashic compilations, such as Bereshit Rabba and Pirke d'Rabbi Eliezer (once, each). In addition to the philosophers mentioned above, Molla El'azar makes cursory references to the Jewish philosophers Saadia Gaon (d. 942), Isaac Abravanel (d. 1508), Azariah dei Rossi (d. 1578), and R. Abraham Azoulay (d. 1569). His use of Muslim sources is rather intriguing. He cites the Koran verbatim four times[36] and not quite verbatim twice more.[37] In most of these instances he does so in conjunction with Jewish sources emphasizing that the two religions are in agreement with regard to the concept of the inevitability of death. Referring to Koranic verses respectfully, Molla El'azar calls them "noble verse" [Ar., *aya sharifa*], employing Muslim terminology and clearly according Muslim scripture sacred status. This is in sharp contrast to an anonymous Judeo-Persian text and Yehudah b. El'azar's *Hovot Yehudah*, both of which quote the Koran a few times but always for polemical purposes.[38] Molla El'azar was fond of the great Persian poet Rumi (d. 1273) and quotes two fairly long passages and one short verse from the *Masnavi*.[39] The first quotation comes from the story of Eblis's (Devil) dialogue with the caliph Mu'awiya (r. 661–80), in which Eblis points out that he was divinely appointed to be "the test of lion and cur," that is, to separate the spiritually adept from ordinary humans. His second quotation is the well-known passage describing the soul's ascent from the inorganic to the human state, culminating in the question: "When have I become less by dying?" The single verse he quotes from the *Masnavi* is taken from the story of the dispute between four grape sellers, each of whom describes his produce differently. In a thoroughly Sufi vein, Rumi states: "People's difference[s of opinion] come from the Name;" that is, different perceptions of the divine do not alter His essential Oneness and are inherent in it. In the same spirit, Molla El'azar quotes some verses by Mirza Ebrahim Jawhar: "Those who circumambulate the Kaba or Somnat / Whether they call on the Eternal or on [al-] Lāt / They call upon the Friend, for Who is there other / Than the Friend? What other *tughrā* exists / Except his?"[40]

Molla El'azar quotes "the poet," three times, most likely referring to Sadi (d. 1291?).[41] He even quotes respectfully a saying of Ali (d. 661), the first Shi'ite Imam, probably from *Nahj al-balagha*,[42] and refers to him by the well-known Muslim honorific, *amir al-mu'menin* [Ar., commander of the faithful]. The context of the saying is difficult to determine, as it occurs right after the lacuna. The author refers to the "Shaykh *al-Milal*," who we assume is al-Shahrestani (d. 1153), the author of the famous compendium on religions and sects *Ketāb al-melal wa al-nehāl* [Ar., The book of religions and systems of thought]. He also refers to a work called *Ādāb-e filsufiyān* [Pers., The manners of philosophers], which we have yet to identify.

The longest narrative in the *resāleh* (ff. 74r–76v) revolves around the death of Eskandar (Alexander the Great) and his mother's mourning over his death. Molla El'azar's retelling is based primarily on *Eghbāl-nāmeh*, the second of Nezami's (d. 1209) epic romances and based on the life of Alexander (itself a reworking of Pseudo-Calisthenes, a Greek Alexander romance), as well as on Ferdowsi's (d. 1020) account in the *Shāh-nāmeh*.[43] Like a good preacher (the tone, if not the structure, of the *resāleh* is reminiscent of a Hebrew homily [*derashah*]), and probably adding small details of his own, Molla El'azar chose to emphasize the concept of the leveling nature of death by recounting the popular story that when Alexander was placed in his golden coffin, a pupil of Aristotle pulled out his hand in order to show all present that the mighty ruler was unable to take with him any of his precious possessions. Similarly, Molla El'azar deplores the irrationality of excessive mourning given that *"everything will perish save His Face,"*[44] and that death is the transition to a higher form of being in the presence of God. He illustrates this point with another famous anecdote about the letter of consolation that Eskandar sent his mother urging her not to mourn him excessively because everything in nature "passes on" and all men experience this grief. He tells her to invite guests to dinner and permit only those who have not experienced grief to partake from it. On doing so, she finds that no one can participate in the feast for no one has been exempted from sorrow, and she thus comes to realize the profound wisdom of her son.

Molla El'azar makes passing mention of some of the Greek sages, Aristotle, Hypocrates, and Pythagoras, as well as the great Muslim philosophers Ibn Sina (d. 1037), al-Ghazali (d. 1111), Ibn Rushd (d. 1198), and al-Farabi (d. 951).[45]

Clearly, his use and awareness of such a variety of sources indicate Molla El'azar's ecumenical outlook and erudition while also revealing, in particular, the depth of his acculturation. One would be inclined to see a degree of Sufi influence in his penchant to extol "passing away," denigrate the physical world, and quote from Sufi literary sources, were it not for the fact that he refers to Sufis twice, specifically and pejoratively. The first time, he includes them in the category of people who do not believe in or have erroneous beliefs about Resurrection.[46] He refers to them a second time while polemicizing that Jews should accept correct beliefs from whatever source, even from a "Ben Taddal," the fictitious name of a foolish babbler in Talmudic vocabulary, whom he identifies with a *Sufi va divāneh* [Pers., the Sufi and the madman].[47] Thus, Molla El'azar's ascetic outlook is probably as much the product of Jewish sources, beginning with Ecclesiastes (which he quotes four times), as it is of the pervasive Sufi ethos of most post-Mongol Persian poetry. Moreover, Molla El'azar's apparent ecumenical outlook is somewhat undercut by his insistence that Jews need to hold correct beliefs and become acquainted with the views of their detractors in order to refute them,[48] which suggests that his coreligionists were subjected to Shi'ite, Baha'i and, less likely but more inviting, Sufi pressures. This view also contradicts Molla El'azar's statement to the effect that all religions lead to God, even as it accords with his view that one ought, nevertheless, to walk in the path of one's forefathers.

Molla El'azar's treatise has a serious polemical undertone, which may well have been its primary intent. He rails against narrow-mindedness, against contemporary Jews who refuse any outside knowledge from their (non-Jewish) environment, and who may thus not be able to arrive at a correct understanding of their own faith. He also deems arriving at correct tenets crucial to the future encounter with God after death. He strongly believes that such correct beliefs must be introduced to children.[49] Here we probably have a hint at what may have been omitted from the text, for the last sentence before the lacuna mentions that he, Molla El'azar, went from Hamadan to Tehran and found that (Heb.) "*on account of our numerous sins*, when a child is taken to school, to the extent that the commentary of the Torah [...]." Then the sentence stops abruptly, interrupted by the lacuna. More than likely what followed was a criticism of the state of Jewish education in Tehran, perhaps in comparison with Hamadan. In light of Molla El'azar's erudition and involvement in Jewish education in Hamadan, it is fascinating that precisely this section, whose contents we can as yet only guess at, is missing while the rest of the *resāleh* has been preserved.

Molla El'azar's *resāleh*, though eloquent, is not original. Its full importance will not be understood definitively until more copies are found that could fill the lacuna of the JTS ms. As it stands, this treatise is, nevertheless, a good example of the learning parameters of a nineteenth-century religious Iranian Jew, definitely an intellectual by the standards of his day. His articulate polished rhetoric and his familiarity with quite a number of Jewish and Muslim sources show Molla El'azar to have been passionate about defending Judaism, even as he was thoroughly integrated in his Iranian environment. That Jewish tradition was under assault in Iran in his day is sadly demonstrated by the fate of his offspring and relatives who abandoned their ancestral faith.[50] Above all, this short *resāleh*, even in its incomplete form, demonstrates that in the absence of more definite historical texts there are numerous unexplored Judeo-Persian manuscripts that provide considerable information aiding the recovery of the intellectual world of pre-modern Iranian Jewry.

Notes

1 For general overviews and textual examples, see: Amnon Netzer, *Montakhab-e ash'ār-e fārsi az āsār-e yahudiān-e Irān* (Tehran, 1973); and Vera Basch Moreen, *In Queen Esther's Garden: An Anthology of Judeo-Persian Literature* (New Haven and London, 2000).

2 A. Netzer, *Hobot Yehudah le-Rabbi Yehudah ben El'azar* (Jerusalem, 1995); pp. 11–12, 13, ii, v.

3 Netzer, *Hobot Yehudah*, pp. ii, v, 1–12.

4 See Hanina Mizrahi, *Yehude Paras* (Tel Aviv, 1959), pp. 143–4.

5 140 lbs.

6 See Molla El'azar's statement to the British Legation in Tehran from November 1865 in the documents of the Foreign Office (hereafter FO) 60/296.

7 The monthly wages of a skilled laborer in Tehran at that time was about 3 *tomans*.

8 See the report of Charles Alison, no. 17 (January 31, 1866), to the British Foreign Office, in FO 60/296. Cf. A. Netzer, "Montefiore ve-yehude Paras," *Pe'amim*, 20 (1984), pp. 57–8. On the circumstances of Molla El'azar's imprisonment and release, see *Hamagid* of Lyck (Prussia), 10:13 (1866), p. 100, particularly the report of Rabbi Shelomo Hosin, author and communal activist in the Jewish community of Baghdad, in *Hamagid*, 10:13 (1866), p. 364.

9 The information about Molla El'azar's emigration to Baghdad, his medical practice there, and the date of his death in 1881, was provided to us by Dr. Jamshid Javid, M.D., of Old Tappan, New Jersey. Dr. Javid is a great-grandson of Molla El'azar's sister. We would like to thank him for the information he kindly provided about Molla El'azar and his other family members.

10 See Arsalan Geula, *Iranian Bahá'is from Jewish Background: A Portrait of an Emerging Bahá'i Community* (Claremont, 2007), p. 77.

11 Mizrahi, *Yehude Paras*, p. 144.

12 See H. A. Stern's report of May 1845 in *Jewish Intelligence and Monthly Account of the Proceedings of the London Society for Promoting Christianity amongst the Jews* (December 1845), p. 412.

13 *Jewish Intelligence* (August 1852), p. 291. For additional references to Molla Eliyahu's high standing in the European Jewish press of the 1850s, see particularly *The Jewish Chronicle, London*, old series, 6:33 (1850), pp. 262–3.

14 J. E. Polak, *Persien, das Land und Seine Bewohner* (Leipzig, 1865), p. 21. For further allusions by Polak to Molla Eliyahu's erudition and breadth of knowledge, see his article in Hebrew translation in *Hamagid*, 48 (1862), p. 383.

15 Regarding him and for other useful information about the religious and cultural lives of the Jews of Hamadan during the nineteenth and twentieth centuries, see Giora Fuzailov, *Hakhmehem shel yehude Paras ve-Afganistan* (Jerusalem, 1996), pp. 123–44.

16 See Shemuel Menahem Halevy, *Masevet Ester ve-Mordekhay* (Jerusalem, 1932), pp. 6–7.

17 For the text of this long letter, which was originally dispatched to Isaac Luria, the headmaster of the Alliance boys' school in Baghdad, and which was subsequently published in two consecutive issues of *Hamagid* of Lyck, see *Hamagid*, 9:3 (1865), p. 20. For an English translation, annotation, and discussion of the petition, see David Yeroushalmi, *The Jews of Iran in the Nineteenth Century: Aspects of History, Community and Culture* (Leiden & Boston, 2009), pp. 274–8.

18 For representative samples of such Hebrew writings and documents from the pen of Jews from Hamadan in the second half of the nineteenth century, see, for example, archival file 311 at the Ben Zvi Institute, Jerusalem.

19 Regarding Rabbi Nissim and his mission on behalf of the Jewish community of Hamadan, see Daniel Tsadik, *Between Foreigners and Shi'is: Nineteenth-Century Iran and Its Jewish Minority* (Stanford, 2007), pp. 38–9, 49, 149–50. For additional information, see Yeroushalmi, *The Jews of Iran*, pp. 125–7, 151.

20 *The Jewish Chronicle*, old series, 6 (1850), pp. 167–8, 252–3, 262–3, 346–7, 354–5, 362–3, 370–1, 379–80.

21 *The Jewish Chronicle*, old series, 6:46 (1850), pp. 262–3.

22 For the Persian and Arabic manuscript library of one Jewish family of physicians from Golpaygan between the seventeenth and twentieth century, see the Rahmian Collection in the Manuscript Department of the Jewish National and University Library, Jerusalem. For the contents of numerous other manuscripts in circulation among Iranian Jews, see Amnon Netzer, *Osar kitve ha-yad shel yehude Paras be-makhon Ben Sevi* (Jerusalem, 1985); and Vera B. Moreen, *Catalog of the Judeo-Persian Manuscripts of the Jewish Theological Seminary of America* (Leiden & Boston, 2014). For a sample page from one such medical manuscript, see Houman Sarshar (ed.), *Esther's Children: A Portrait of Iranian Jews* (Los Angeles, 2002), pp. 79, 286.

23 See Habib Levy, *Tārikh-e Yahud-e Irān*, 3 vols (Tehran, 1956–60), vol. 3, p. 642.

24 For further information and discussion about this rabbi and his illuminating letters, see Yeroushalmi, *The Jews of Iran*, pp. 242–9 and 290–1. Cf., Tsadik, *Between Foreigners*, pp. 76, 85, 196, 227, 240.

25 See his handwritten Hebrew letter of 26 Tammuz 5635 (July 29 1875), in the Archives of the Alliance Israélite Universelle, Paris, file IRAN, IIC.6. No. 9847.

26 See J. Lotka's report, "Recent Conversions of Jews in Hamadan," at the Dept. C. M. J. d. 52/3, document no. 7, the Bodleian Library, Oxford University.

27 See the document entitled "Translation: Details of the Case of the Jew Lalazar, November 1865," in FO 60/296 folio 5.

28 Fuzailov, *Hakhmehem*, p. 123.

29 Ephraim Newmark, *Masa' be-eres ha-qedem* (Jerusalem, 1947), p. 81.

30 Geula, *Iranian Bahá'is*, especially pp. 85–9.

31 Based on information provided by Dr. Javid (see above, n. 9).

32 See Comte Joseph Arthur de Gobineau, *Les Religions et philosophies dans l'Asie Centrale* (3rd edn, Paris, 1866), p. 101.

33 Ff. 81v–82r.

34 Ff. 80v–81r. Netzer, *Hovot Yehudah*, pp. 74–5 (nos. 43–6).

35 Fol. 81r.

36 Surahs 1:6 (fol. 71r), 3:185 (72v), 10:49 and 7:34 (fol. 73r).

37 See fols. 75r and 76v.

38 Vera B. Moreen, "Polemical Use of the Qur'ān in Two Judeo-Persian Texts," in Shaked S. and Netzer A. (eds), *Irano-Judaica*, vol. 5: *Studies Relating to Jewish Contacts with Persian Culture Throughout the Ages* (Jerusalem, 1999), pp. 203–13.

39 See R. A. Nicholson, *Mathnawi-yi Ma'nawi* (Leiden, 1933–5); *The Mathnawi of Jalaluddin Rumi* (London, 1977) repr., vol. 2, ll. 2673–9 (fol. 71v); and ll. 3901–7 (fol. 75r).

40 Fol. 71v. "Lāt" refers to a pre-Islamic female deity (Sura 53:19–23) and *tughrā* is a royal signature usually appended to official letters. These verses may well come from the pen of Mirza Ebrahim Jawhari, also known as Mohammad Bagher Jawhari (d. *c*.1836/7), a skilled and popular poet and writer. His best-known work, *Tufān al-buka'* (Storm of weeping), was printed several times in the course of the nineteenth century but we were unable to find this quotation in it. For sources on Jawhari, see Mohammad Ali Modarres (Tabrizi), *Ketāb-e Rayhanat al-adab* (Tehran, 1945), vol. 1, p. 286. Cf. Ali Akbar Dekhoda, *Loghat-nameh* (Tehran, 1993–4) [new ed.], vol. 5, p. 6953.

41 Ff. 71r, 73r, 73v.

42 Fol. 79r.

43 See *Eghbāl-nāmeh* in *Kolliyāt-e khamseh-ye Nezāmi-ye Ganjavi* (Tehran, 1972), especially pp. 1316–20; *Sunset of Empire: Stories from the Shahnameh of Ferdowsi*, tr. Dick Davis (Washington, 2004), vol. 3, pp. 113–18; *The Greek Alexander Romance*, tr. Richard Stoneman (London, 1991), pp. 156–7.

44 Surah 28:88.

45 Ff. 79r–79v.

46 Fol. 78v.

47 Ff. 78v, 79v; Babylonian Talmud, *Hulin* 134a.

48 Fol. 81r.

49 Ibid.

50 See above, pp. 56–7.

CHAPTER 4

TWO WARS, TWO CITIES, TWO RELIGIONS: THE JEWS OF MASHHAD AND THE HERAT WARS

Haideh Sahim

The Jews of Mashhad are unique, for they have a history unlike any other Jewish community in Iran. Settled by force of events in a place that was hostile to them, they managed to persevere in spite of all odds in one of the darkest periods of Iranian social and religious history. A small minority within the systematically marginalized Jewish community of Iran, they battled persecution until some found freedom, only to lose it to war, bias, and greed. They were accused of hostility to Islam, apostasy and treason against their homeland. Caught between two cities, two wars, and two religions, they truly became the casualty of circumstances beyond their control.

This essay recounts the unique story of the Mashhadi Jews: their arrival in Mashhad, the attack on them by a Shi'ite mob and the mass conversion to Islam they undertook to save their lives, their emigration to the nearby city of Herat, their forced return and finally release from captivity after British intervention and the paying of a ransom. The role played by the Mashhadi Jews, victims caught in the middle of two wars Iran waged to retake Herat, raises many issues important for the history of Iran in the nineteenth century. The question of identity and citizenship, religious conversion and persecution, and pressure placed on the Tehran government by the British to ameliorate the situation are also reflected in the plight of Jewish communities in other parts of Iran. This paper, based on all currently available sources, attempts to clarify and evaluate previous accounts of this episode and highlight the ambiguities of historical interpretation.

According to the oral history of Mashhadi Jews, in the mid-eighteenth century[1] 40 prominent Jewish families from Qazvin were relocated by Nāder Shah (r. 1736–47) and sent to the fortress of Kalāt, known as *Kalāt-e Nāderi*, northeast of Mashhad. By then some Jews had arrived in Kalāt, and others were still en route in Mashhad and Sabzevar. Eventually, almost all families settled in Mashhad, but that city, having the most important Shi'ite shrine in Iran,[2] was not very welcoming. After the death of Nāder Shah, who was assassinated in 1747 and opposed clerical influence, once again the Iranian clergy regained their power and life became more difficult for the non-Muslims, in particular those living in Mashhad. The Jews finally managed to buy some land in a neighborhood called *Eydgāh*, near the city, and established their own community.[3]

Due to its location on the trade routes to Herat, India, Central Asia and Russia, Mashhad was a gateway of commerce. The Mashhadi Jews took advantage of this location and the network of Jewish merchants in other cities and, in spite of persecutions and restrictions imposed on them, they were soon trading widely and became prosperous. The Jews brought their expertise in manufacturing and weaving silk from Gilan, their original homeland. Shortly after this, a number of Mashhadi Jews moved to Bukhara, and a small number of Jewish families moved to Herat.[4]

The Jews' networks and connections soon helped them achieve a special status and, in addition to their successful trade, they provided loans and, reportedly, information to the British agents in the area.[5] Due to the threat of robbers and particularly the danger from Turkman bandits, these agents did not dare carry large sums of money. Jewish merchants, particularly the Mashhadi ones, advanced them funds wherever and whenever they needed it, which made the British quite reliant on them. The British preferred the services of the

Jews and Afghans to Armenians, who had closer cultural and religious ties with the Russians, who sabotaged the British market.[6] At the same time, having close ties with the British was beneficial to the Jews, since they could expect protection from them. This was not true of their rivals, the Russians, who had anti-Semitic policies, nor was the Shi'ite government of Iran particularly sympathetic to them. The symbiotic relation between the Jews and the British later became a cause for misery for the former.

The First Herat War

From the early years of the Qajar dynasty (1779–1925), Iran had tried to reclaim Herat, a city then nominally part of what became the loose entity of Afghanistan. Iran's aim, as always, was to retake this city that it had historically governed. This was a goal that was particularly dear due to Iran's humiliating loss of territories in the northwest and in Central Asia. The first attempt (1832–3) by Abbās Mirzā, the crown prince of Fath-Ali Shah (r. 1797–1834), ended suddenly because of his death in 1833. During the reign of Fath-Ali Shah's grandson, Mohammad Shah (r. 1834–48), Iran became a pawn in the hands of the British and Russians. The shah was very pro-Russian, as was his prime minister, Hāj Mirzā Āghāsi.[7] The shah was weak, but had full trust in Hāj Mirzā Āghāsi, who for 13 years was the real ruler of Iran.[8] Encouraged by the Russians, and supported by the clergy who declared *jihād* against the Sunni Afghans, in the summer of 1837 Iran set out to conquer and annex Herat,[9] which it considered its own territory, and besieged it for about a year. The British meanwhile, ever fearful of Russia's intentions, wanted to maintain Afghanistan as a buffer between Russia and India.

In an effort to force the shah to withdraw from Herat, the British invaded Kharg Island in the Persian Gulf on June 19, 1838. In September, having failed to take Herat, Iran finally retreated. Khurasan in particular was affected by this war, and its mismanagement added to the problem. In addition, famine had driven thousands of Heratis to take refuge in Mashhad.[10] In February 1839, Mohammad Shah camped near Mashhad.[11] The *jihād* had failed; Iran had retreated, probably having stranded a number of its soldiers to fend for themselves.[12]

Things came to a head during the Persian New Year in March 1839. On March 21, the shah ordered a day of mourning instead of the usual celebration.[13] On March 25, the British landing in Bushehr (Bushire) turned into a minor military conflict.[14] On March 27, a day after the anniversary of the martyrdom of Husayn, the third Shi'ite emam, the Jewish community of Mashhad was attacked.

Mashhadi Jewish traditions recount that on March 27, 1839, a Jewish woman who had a sore or sphacelus on her hand was told by "all doctors"[15] to wash it in the warm blood of a newly slaughtered dog, a treatment that was not very unusual in traditional Eastern medicine. When she did that and the Muslim neighbors saw the discarded corpse, they assumed that the Jews had done this to ridicule their mourning. Some British travelers of the period indicate that the clergy's constant incitement of people against the Jews in previous years had a major impact on what ensued.[16] Others think that refusing to pay a *sayyid* extortion money in return for protection was the real cause.[17] Another pretext may have been that the Muslims, who were angry after the loss of Herat and the failed *jihād*, associated the Jews with the detested, victorious British.[18] The burden of having to board and provide for the garrison of unruly soldiers had also strained the people.[19] Whatever the reason—hardship, war, soldiers running amok, religious prejudice, or possible commercial rivalry[20]—the result was a catastrophe for the Jews of this city.

On the ominous day of March 27, a mob stormed the streets, looted and killed many Jews, and destroyed their houses and buildings. Men, women and children, whoever was able, ran to the synagogues. Dilmānīān is of the opinion that the Muslims of Mashhad had asked the *emām jom'eh* for a *fatwā* to attack or kill the Jews, but that he postponed this until after the mourning period, probably to quiet the mob.[21] The Jews, not fully aware of exactly what was brewing in the city, went to their houses, hid behind their closed doors and made no attempt to appeal to the authorities for protection. Finally before noon on Wednesday, the 11th of Moharram,[22] a day after *Āshurā*, the mob attacked the Jewish quarter,[23] possibly with the approval of the *emām jom'eh*.[24] It seems that the mob may have consisted mainly of soldiers of the garrison that had camped in Mashhad en route home from the Herat war.[25] Hungry and angry, the soldiers, who had not been paid for a long time, took whatever they could in food and clothing, and killed some of the inhabitants. Despite a reputation for being just, Āsef al-Dowleh,[26] the governor, made no attempt to prevent or contain the tumult. There were rumors he may have even promoted this event, given his hatred for Jews and Armenians.[27]

The attacks were brutal, with much property destroyed and 36 Jews slaughtered. With the approval of the elders of the community, 27 Jewish men went to the *emām jom'eh* to stop a total annihilation of the city's Jewish population.[28] They converted to Islam in his presence, and asked him to stop the looting and killing, so that they could convert the rest of the community.[29] And they did. From this day on, the converted Jews were called *Jadid al-Islām*, meaning "new Muslims," or *Jadid*.

Orders were given to stop the attack, and peace was restored. To further calm the crowd, the *emām jom'eh* took wives from the Jews[30] and he ordered that since these people were now Muslims, their properties should be returned.[31] Only a fraction of what was looted, however, was regained. One such item was a large quantity of silk, the owner of which had been killed. By order of the *emām jom'eh*, the silk was sold and the funds were used to buy a plot for a cemetery. That this group was in need of a separate cemetery is in itself significant. It is not known whether this segregation was because they were not accepted as real Muslims, and hence could not be allowed to defile the Muslim cemetery, or it was the Jews who did not want to bury their dead in a non-Jewish cemetery contrary to their customs and rituals. While sources are silent on the particulars, we do know that the new converts took pains, such as burying their dead late in the day, to ensure proper Jewish burial rituals.

The event became known as *Allāh-dād* (lit. "God given" or "God's judgment"). While for the Muslims this indicated divine justice in the sense of a triumph for Islam, for the Jews it was interpreted as God's judgment and subsequent punishment for their sins.

After *Allāh-dād*

According to Jewish sources, most Jews, while grateful that their lives were spared, could not conceive of being anything but Jews. From this day on the Jews of Mashhad, the Crypto-Jews of Iran, led a double life, outwardly Muslim and secretly Jewish. A few became sincere Muslims and remained so. Most others, however, went to mosques and publicly observed the Muslim holidays, but at home they secretly gathered through hidden passages that connected their houses, prayed together, and observed Jewish rituals. They betrothed their children in early childhood, so they would not have to accept the hand of outsiders. They would buy bread during Passover, but would not eat it. What happened to these people in Mashhad and the details of how they coped with their lives is beyond the scope of this paper.[32] Suffice it to say that they were watched daily by their Muslim neighbors to make sure that they had not strayed and returned to Judaism, in which case their blood could have been shed. There are indications that the Muslim authorities were aware that the *Jadids* secretly practiced Judaism.[33] In spite of such hardship, they stayed Jewish and observed all aspects of Jewish life, until they gradually moved to Tehran after World War II, where they could openly practice their faith.

The response of Mohammad Shah to these events was much delayed. It was not until October that he sent his minister of foreign affairs, Mirzā Mas'ud,[34] to Mashhad to investigate and return the stolen goods to the Jews.[35] It is quite possible that the *emām jom'eh*'s order to return the goods may have been inspired by this order. Judging by the outcome, one can only assume that either the shah lost interest or his orders could not be carried out in light of his conflict with governor, Āsef al-Dowleh.

Departure from Mashhad

After *Allāh-dād*, some *Jadids* who could not tolerate the constant pressure of a dual life and preferred to openly practice Judaism gradually left Mashhad. A very large group—some 200 families[36]—settled in Herat,[37] where they joined the Herati Jews who were largely of Mashhadi origin.[38] Another 100 families went to other places in Khurasan or cities in Afghanistan and Central Asia, specifically Bukhara, where the Sunni majority was more tolerant of Jews.

For those who left Mashhad, the departure came at a cost. In the nineteenth century, travel from one city to another usually required a permit. Governors were not very eager to have their population reduced and lose taxpayers. According to the French traveler Joseph Pierre Ferrier, the *Jadid al-Islām* were forbidden to leave Mashhad and would have been fined if caught.[39] It is plausible to assume that to obtain permission to go to another city, especially in significant numbers, they had to bribe the *emām jom'eh* and other functionaries,[40] particularly considering that the government had already lost the *jizya* that the new converts had had to pay as Jews.

What was the position of the Iranian government? The Iranian prime minister said the Jews had "renounced the Mussulman religion and for having done so, they were sentenced to be put to death, in accordance with the Mahommedan Law."[41] In that case, they would have had to leave as soon as they could. To escape this fate, they joined caravans leaving Iran in disguise and secretly and gradually moved to Herat and Baghdad.[42]

Those who stayed in Mashhad did not find total acceptance, and they continued to live in *Eydgāh*, the old Jewish quarter or *mahalleh*. The separate cemetery, the seeming lack of or limited Persian education (as documented in their Muslim marriage contracts where the *Jadids* have signed their names in the Hebrew alphabet rather than Persian), the separate neighborhoods, etc., are all indicators that the *Jadids* were still kept at arm's length and not fully assimilated. These factors demonstrate that while these new Muslims were not treated as badly as non-Muslims, they were certainly treated as second-class citizens. Indeed, we see evidence of this in later correspondence between the British and the Iranian governments.

While the Jews in Mashhad struggled with the issue of hostility in their environment and tried to live and work the best they could, those who had emigrated to the mostly Sunni Herat and other cities in Afghanistan and Central Asia lived openly as Jews, built synagogues, and moved about freely without much problem—even though they had to live in special areas and pay *jizya*—and prospered for the next 20 years.

Jewish and non-Jewish sources vary on the details of the *Allāh-dād* events. Understandably, there are very few contemporary Jewish sources available. However, the Mashhadis have been quite resolute in preserving this story orally and making sure their children remember it and pass it on. Of the few Mashhadi histories that remain only one is from an eyewitness, who was a child at the time. These histories focus on the event from the anti-Semitic perspective. Almost all the primary histories written by non-Jewish Iranians have remained silent about this event, and the rare non-Jewish sources that mention it do so briefly, almost all quoting foreign sources.[43] Pirnazar attributes this disregard on the one hand to the diminished value of human life because of war, famine, poverty, prejudice and superstition, and, on the other hand, a general lack of attention to the deprived and discriminated-against groups of society, such as women and ethnic and religious minorities, because of the institutionalization of the culture of bias.[44] In the unfortunate absence of access to the archives in Iran, particularly those of the Iranian Ministry of Foreign Affairs and the Shrine of Emam Reza, all accounts have to be based on foreign sources, mainly the British missionary accounts and British diplomatic archives, which mostly give outsiders' perspectives and illuminate some other underlying causes.

Jews in Herat

The Afghans were mostly Sunnis and, therefore, more tolerant of non-Muslims than Shi'ites. In any case, Herat had a large Shi'ite community, as well. Ephraim Neumark, a Polish traveler to the area in the 1880s, says, "The Afghani hates the Persian (the Shi'ite) and loves the Jew, takes pity on him and treats him as a brother; ... he [*sic*] does not become angry at seeing a Jew drink wine; the Jew will not defile him..."[45] Indeed, the issue of *najāsa* (religious impurity), which exists in Shi'ism, was one of the main reasons non-Muslims were so mistreated in Shi'ite Iran.

Mashhadi emigrants soon joined the network of Jewish merchants doing business between Iran, Afghanistan, India, and Central Asia. Jews were engaged in money changing, winemaking, and production of liquor. They traded in grains, carpets, raw cotton, cotton and silk fabrics, jewelry, dried fruits, wool, precious stones, furs (a field which at the time they exclusively controlled) and other commodities.[46] The diversity of the population of Afghanistan gave the Jews the advantage of brokering transactions between various groups, and they also served as agents for commercial companies. The relative freedom that they enjoyed in Herat, the presence of the British, and their connections gave them a special status.

The Mashhadi Jews' connection with the British and their financial services to them was at times misconstrued as providing information and later became a source of much misery. Since as merchants they did move around and were in constant contact with associates all over that area, they could supply the British with information about the movements of the Russians. Due to the hardship they suffered at the hands of the Iranians and the rampant anti-Semitism that existed in Russia at the time, it is not surprising that the Jews supported the British influence in Herat. In fact, in most instances of persecution that continued to occur throughout Iran during the rest of the nineteenth and earlier part of the twentieth century, it was British officials who would come to their aid, albeit sometimes because of pressure from their own influential Jewish subjects. For the Jews, the reoccupation of Herat by the Shi'ite Iranians or the increased influence of the Russians—or even the prospect of it—was probably tantamount to a new nightmare of persecution and hardship, which they would want to avoid.

Renewed Struggle over Herat

Unfortunately for the Mashhadi Jews, the city they had chosen to settle in, Herat, was 20 years later once again at the center of international interest, and the "Great Game" (the contest between Britain and Russia for influence in Central Asia) was heating up.[47] The British position was clear: Afghanistan had to be maintained as a buffer between Russia and India. They sought to exclude the Iranians from Herat, fearing that if the shah retook the city it would serve as an opening for Russian influence and thereby pose a threat to British interests in India. To carry out this policy Britain waged the First Anglo-Afghan War from 1838–42, which was prompted by the Persian attack on Herat (supposedly due to Russian advice) in 1837. Britain aimed to remove the ruler of Kabul, Dost Mohammad Khān, and replace him with the more pliable Shah Shojāʿ, but the project ended in disaster as the British faced armed resistance by 1841 and British forces were massacred during their retreat to India in January 1842. Shortly after this Shah Shojāʿ was assassinated.

The former ruler, Dost Mohammad Khān, was restored to power and signed a peace treaty with British India in March 1855.[48] He also resumed his quest to unify the country, conquering Qandahar in December 1855. Once established there, Nāser al-Din Shah feared it would not be long before he took Herat and became determined to beat him to it.

In February 1856, Iran sent an army against Herat, as Britain withdrew its representatives from Tehran due to a personal quarrel involving its minister. Taking advantage of local unrest, the Iranian army under Hosām al-Saltaneh[49] besieged Herat and entered the city on September 26, 1856,[50] after a seven-month siege.[51] The Iranian troops raped, looted, and massacred the Heratis.[52]

In order to pressure the shah to withdraw, Britain once again sent a fleet from India to the Persian Gulf in November 1856, where they invaded Kharg Island and Bushehr (Bushire) in December 1856.[53] Britain subsequently bombarded Mohammareh (present-day Khorramshahr) to further pressure Iran.[54] In the end the shah was prepared to leave Herat in return for peace with Britain, even though there were some in Iran, including Hosām al-Saltaneh, who thought Iran had a good chance of victory because of British preoccupation in India.[55] Finally, on March 4, 1857, a peace treaty was signed between the two in Paris. Britain agreed to leave Iranian territory in a short time and release the Iranian captives, and Iran agreed to evacuate Herat and relinquish its claim to the city and any other part of Afghanistan. Thus, Herat was separated from Iran forever.[56]

Expulsion to Mashhad

The Jewish emigrants from Mashhad found themselves in the middle of this international imbroglio and suffered greatly because of it. Before the news of the British invasion of Iran reached Herat, officers of the Iranian army arrested a Jew. On him, they found a letter addressed to the British representative in Qandahar signed by Jews living in Herat. It contained complaints about the conduct of the Iranians at the time of the occupation. The officers, cognizant of the connection between the Jews and the British and ever apprehensive about the power of the latter, assumed, though wrongly, that the order of withdrawal from Herat was in response to this complaint of the Jews. The man was hanged, and the incident served as proof of the Jews' support of the enemy.[57]

Prime Minister Āghā-Khān Nuri[58] very quickly ordered Hosām al-Saltaneh, the commander of the Iranian army—who advocated the continuation of the siege—to evacuate Herat and return to Mashhad with a group of Herati immigrants (*mohājer*) who were "entirely Shi'ites".[59] The true composition of this group is not known, and it is not clear whether the prime minister was referring to the Jews in particular or he had some other people in mind, e.g. other Shi'ites living in Herat. There were some Jamshidis and Hezarehs (Hazaras) who were also taken captive, but the available documents do not discuss them together with the Jews.

When the Iranian army initiated its withdrawal in September 1857, they rounded up the "entire Jewish community" of Herat (about 5,000 individuals)[60] and incarcerated them in a place called Mosallā.[61] The Iranians had also captured groups of Qizilbāsh and some Turkmans, in addition to the groups mentioned, but it does not seem that they were placed together with the Jews or that their fates were similar. The Herati Shi'ites apparently had gone to Hosām al-Saltaneh and complained about the Jews, saying that they sold horseshoes and nails, and gunpowder and lead for guns to the Heratis, with the clear implication that these were to be used against the Iranians. (There were a few Jewish merchants who did indeed engage in such trade, according to one source, but the maximum volume of their trade was 100 *tomans*.)[62] There is no doubt that this group, who had fled their tormentors at great financial, psychological and physical cost, wanted to remain in Herat, free from the influence of Iran and closer to the British.

In an undated petition from the captive Jews to Mr. Murray,[63] (around January 1858) they write:

> When the Persian army proceeded to Herat and besieged that place, we (also) found ourselves for a time besieged and distressed until (the town) fell into their possession. After a lapse of three months an order was given that in three days, the Jewish community should be removed from Herat. A body of Ferashes and soldiers was despatched to the Jewish quarter—it was in the middle of winter—and by beating with sticks, drove all the men, women and children out of the town to the Musalla. Their houses were plundered and destroyed. Those who were able, removed some of their furniture into rooms in Caravanserais. Four synagogues were sacked; about 120 Volumes of the Pentateuch, each worth from 20 to 30 Tomanns,[64] and about two thousand printed books were all carried off, together with carpets and candlesticks. When brought to the Musalla, we were numbered about one thousand persons [*sic*]. After our removal from thence, we were seventeen days on the journey. Some of us perished from cold, and some from starvation. We thus diminished in number, until we arrived at the Robat Baba Koodret, outside of Meshed.[65]

Amid mass looting, almost all of the Herati Jews' property and money was seized. Dr. Jakob Polak, the personal physician of Nāser al-Din Shah, writes that the looters searched the houses of Jews for gems, in particular a precious stone known as *Saqa*,[66] as well as other valuables. Interestingly, some seem to have managed to salvage some of their property, as is evident from the petition above. However, there is no indication whether or not they could reclaim it later. As will be seen below, it seems that a number of the captives must have had some valuables with them upon their departure, since they were forced to pay for transportation.

The captives included all the Jews of Herat, both those who had resided there previously and those who had come from Mashhad after the *Allāh-dād*. After three or four days the Jews were rounded up— possibly by the order of the Iranian prime minister[67]—to be removed from the city on February 13, 1857,[68] in the cold and snow of winter. They were beaten and led in chains alongside the army on foot to Mashhad. During this trip of about 17 days, many of the sick and weak died of hunger, thirst, lack of proper clothing and, above all, the cold weather.

And several people abandoned their religion on the way because of the great suffering ... for the oppressors administered everyday cruel punishment they inflicted upon us. [*sic*] And for the renting of the camels that brought us from Herat, the camels were the property of the king, and most of those who rode them were poor and miserable, and they [the soldiers] imposed the rental fee on the rest of the people. And on the other hand, there was, God forbid, sickness and epidemics, and many souls died.[69]

In Mashhad

On March 5, 1857 the caravan of captives arrived in Mashhad, and they were imprisoned in Baba Qodrat Rebat, a dilapidated caravanserai outside the city walls, supposedly so that they would not defile the holy city. Very soon the Shi'ites of Herat were given permission to return, but the Jews remained "under the surveillance of Sentries."[70] Jewish sources state that Ahmad Shah, the Iranian-nominated ruler of Herat, was not in favor of their return to Herat, supposedly because of the lack of food and meager earnings available there at that time.[71] While this may have been true, it hardly seems plausible that a ruler would exclude a group of prominent merchants whose income, not to mention *jizya*, would have greatly benefited him and the commerce of Herat. It is evident that this was a political move to appease the Iranian government.

Not until August 1857 did the British get involved and start corresponding with the Iranian government regarding the Jewish captives. Around this time when the British Commissioner to Herat, Col. Taylor,[72] was in Mashhad with some other officers on his way to Herat, the captive Jews were very harshly prevented from entering the town to see him. Two or three, therefore, contrived to meet with the Indian Hāji Sayyid Husayn, known as the The Doctor, and told him their story. He conveyed the account to Taylor, who sent for some of the Jews in Mashhad and "completely informed himself of our situation."[73] Taylor reports that on September 20 he heard that they were in such a miserable state of hunger that he bought two mule-loads of bread and his servants delivered them to the captive Jews.[74]

Prince Hosām al-Saltaneh was so touched (or maybe embarrassed) when he heard that Taylor had done this that he ordered Ghavām al-Dowleh,[75] his deputy (*pishkār*), to make sure that the captives were properly fed. The Iranians were quite intimidated by the power of the British and would probably not dare contradict a British official. Since the condition of the Jews did not improve and food continued to be scarce, one can assume that Ghavām al-Dowleh ignored the order. His solution was to allow the captive Jews to go and beg in the city, as they had done before the arrival of Taylor, when it was stopped.[76] They could, however, only stand at the gates and beg from passersby.[77] Soldiers were stationed at the gates to prevent them from leaving. They were often beaten and bastinadoed. Some tried to subsist by making a meager living working as water carriers, which paid a very low wage, but they faced severe persecution.[78] Money was regularly extorted from them; for example, ten *shāhis*[79] to allow them to go to the town for the day (this was later reduced to two *shāhis*). When nothing more remained to be taken, they left the Jews alone.[80]

A few months later, while still captive, another petition was presented by the Jews to one Malek Mohammad Beg, in Hebrew and

Persian, with the hope that it would reach Taylor. In it the Jews claimed that they had been in captivity for nine months.[81] The petition also claimed that 1,000 people were brought to the Musallā. Leaving Herat they were 300 families (about 1,500 to 1,800 individuals), but now they were only 900 souls.[82] Some had died on the road, but life in Mashhad was not any better.

In total they were detained in Mashhad for two years, under the most dire conditions, without adequate provisions, clothing, heat, medication, and bathing facilities in an area much too small for 1,000 people.

British Intervention

In cases when the Iranian authorities would not address injustices, it was common in the nineteenth century for both Jews and Muslims to appeal to representatives of foreign countries, especially the British. Fortunately, in this instance, the British took it upon themselves early on to mediate on the Jews' behalf. The large volume of correspondence, at a time when the relationship between the two countries was strained, is an indicator of this effort. Murray was one who sincerely tried to free these captives, but the inability to send agents to the location worked against him. He repeatedly reported to the British foreign ministry the unjustifiably cruel treatment of the captive Jews and strongly advised the Iranian government to release them as many more might die if no steps were taken soon.[83]

A letter to the famous British Jewish philanthropist, Sir Moses Montefiore,[84] dated March 19, 1858, states that some 300 to 400 had died, while the earlier petition to Mr. Murray gives the number as 150—either case showing the rapid rate of mortality. Fear of revealing their own subterfuge prevented the *Jadids* of Mashhad from openly helping the captives. Nonetheless, they did as much as they could in secret.[85]

A question arises as to why this group was kept captive for such a long time. They were not in possession of significant wealth. Was their detention revenge for the loss of Herat? This, too, does not seem plausible, as nothing much was gained. The strongest reason seems to be that the governor was of the belief that the Jews had a very precious stone and he wanted it.

The British repeatedly invoked Iran's responsibility as a signatory of the Treaty of Paris to release the Jews. It should be noted that Article 4 of the Treaty of Paris stipulated:

> His Majesty the Shah of Persia engages, immediately on the exchange of the ratifications of this Treaty, to publish a full and complete amnesty, absolving all Persian subjects who may have in any way been compromised by their intercourse with the British forces during the war from any responsibility for their conduct in that respect, so that no person, of whatever degree, shall be exposed to vexation, persecution, or punishment on that account.[86]

The provisions of this treaty certainly applied to the Jews. The Iranian government claimed that it had adhered to the articles of the treaty regarding the evacuation of Herat, and had notified all Afghans residing in Khurasan, Tehran, and elsewhere "under whatever circumstance" that they were free to leave the country or remain in Iran.[87] As we shall see later, however, the Iranian authorities were determined to exclude the captive Jews. Once again, the Jews fell into a dark hole due to the ambiguity of their identity, and became scapegoats for the defeat of Iran, as well as hostages to the discrimination and prejudices that they had fled from.

Iranian or Afghan?

Two issues were at the center of the arguments about the status of these captives: their nationality and their religion. The subject of nationality was a very difficult one to ascertain. There was no registration in either Iran or Afghanistan, and neither government issued passports. In the absence of documentation, proving citizenship would come down to the word of one person against the other. The issue of citizenship, as it appears here, had never come up in previous treaties, and neither the Treaty of Gulistan (1813) nor the Treaty of Turkmanchai (1828) defines nationality.[88] It is only later in 1894, in a draft of bylaws for a treaty between Iran and the Ottomans, that we see the matter of citizenship (*tābe'iyat*) mentioned, and only in reference to the migrating tribes.[89] The dual national and religious identity of this group now became a major point of contention. The Jews, having lived in Herat for such a long period, considered themselves Heratis. They themselves declared, "We were, are, and wish to be subjects of Herat."[90] This was sufficient for the British. Indeed, by this time some of them had lived in that city for generations. In the opinion of the Iranian prime minister, however, the Herati Jews had originated in Iran and were thus Iranian subjects. In an earlier meeting with the British diplomats, the prime minister had even maintained that Herat "never had any people of that [Jewish] persuasion."[91] They were all or nearly all fugitives from Mashhad, and, as such, the subjects of the shah, and in fact few, if any, of them, were bona fide Heratis.[92] Besides, they were also accused of having emigrated against the wishes of the shah.[93] Taylor found these claims "greatly exaggerated." Of the 300 families brought from Herat, two thirds "never saw Mashhad in their lives," he wrote, "and of the remainder, not more than one half was originally resident in this city."[94]

The official explanation of the prime minister, Mirzā Āghā Khān Nuri, E'temād al-Dowleh, was that after the tumult in 1839, in which the Jews embraced Islam to save their lives, a number of them renounced Islam, and for having done so they were sentenced to death in accordance with Islamic law. It should be considered here that these Jews were converted by force—which according to the same Islamic law is not permitted[95]—and reverted to Judaism after they left Iran. Therefore the Jews' conversion should have been null and void. This said, there have been incidents in Iran when Jews were forced to convert and afterwards the local governor, realizing the loss of *jizya*'s effect on his income, asked—and even forced—them; to revert to Judaism.[96]

It was clear, the prime minister continued, that "the above Jews and those now residing in Meshed as Mahommedans, are all nearly related to each other and many of them members of the same family; How [*sic*] can it be that one brother should be a native of Meshed,

and another a native of Herat?" he asked Mr. Murray, the British
minister.[97] This, however, is not an unusual phenomenon in the
Middle East, where families, clans and tribes are often divided by
artificial borders. As Iranian subjects, Prime Minister Nuri did not
see any contradiction in keeping them in Mashhad, though the
British rightfully maintained that this action was in defiance of
Articles 3 and 4 of the Treaty of Paris, by which the two governments
pledged that all the captives would be immediately freed and that
there would be a blanket amnesty.

In his conversation with the authorities, Murray indicated that
even if these Jews were natives of Iran, it was the government-
sanctioned "fanatism and violence of Mohamedan persecution" that
forced them to flee to safety.[98] In the same line he strongly
confronted the Iranian prime minister, saying that all his
explanations given in their previous correspondence were simply
pretexts given to "palliate the cruelty they have been guilty of
doing." He also pointed out that although these Jews might be of
some use in the bazaar of Herat, they were of no use as miserable
prisoners guarded by sentries.[99]

To clarify their citizenship, Murray suggested that each and every
one of these captives should be interviewed by representatives of both
sides to verify their nationality. The prime minister rejected this on
two grounds. One, that it would be a very cumbersome and almost
interminable job; and, two, "the Persian Ministers would feel loathe
to submit to the humiliation of appearing at a tribunal, and pleading
against these Jewish subjects, who are the most abject of the subjects
of the Persian Government."[100] Murray does not fail to remind the
prime minister of the damage the news of plundered homes and
synagogues would do to the international image of Iran. As the Jews,
though a race "without a home and nation," he said, have relations in
all parts of the world, it would not be long before "the tale of their
sufferings is noised abroad."[101]

To his credit, however, the prime minister did make an effort to
learn more about matters of citizenship. In a query to the British
minister, he requested clarification about what in Europe constituted
a right to protection or being a subject of a country in order to

"prevent future embarrassment and to facilitate the settlement of matters." It is not certain whether this was a genuine effort to resolve the matter or a maneuver to prolong the procedure and to divert attention. The British minister's response, which came after consultation with Britain's minister of foreign affairs, did not seem to give a definite and direct answer to the question. A clear and direct response would have been helpful to the Jews.[102] The British, at the same time, tried very hard to at least establish that a larger number of the captives were bona fide Heratis.[103]

The captives' religion was also a matter of debate. A small group had immigrated to Herat before the *Allāh-dād* and had always lived as Jews. Almost all the rest were those who had left after the *Allāh-dād*, when they were forced to convert to Islam. There they had returned to Judaism, and in Herat, as well as some parts of Central Asia and among the Turkmans with whom they traded extensively, they were known as Jews.

Their special treatment is also controversial and raises many questions. Captives were normally sold as slaves or used as servants, yet none of these Jews is known to have been sold or put into service. Of course, the pious Shi'ite would avoid contact with impure infidel servants. Also, non-Muslim captives were normally forced to convert, but, surprisingly, there is no such indication here. It could be that the Herati Jews, who were mostly *Jadid al-Islāms* of Mashhad, were still perceived by others as Muslims. A *Jewish Chronicle* article confirms that some prisoners became water carriers.[104] As Jews, they would be considered *najis*, and no Shi'ite would have taken water from them. Another issue was that the captives' dead were not even allowed to be buried in the *Jadid* cemetery, but outside of town in a place called Askariyeh, a military camp.[105] Whether their treatment was because of policy or the residents were convinced that they were Jews remains unclear. Until documents in Iran become available, it is not possible to shed light on this issue.

Surprisingly, in the long and detailed correspondence between Iranian officials and the British minister or other members of the embassy, not once did they refer to them as Muslims, *Jadids* or *Jadid al-Islāms*. Both sides refer to them as "the Jews" or the "Jewish

captives," even when arguing that they were converted to Islam.[106]
Even while maintaining that they were in fact Muslims, the Iranian
prime minister refers to them in a humiliating language that was
very common in this period in reference to Jews, and, for example,
uses expressions like "low and miserable Jews," "the most abject of
the subjects of the Iranian government," and "a few miserable
Jews,"[107] among others—an indication of the strong, prevalent, anti-
Semitism in Iran at every level.

Ransom

The issue of ransom now became the key to the release of the Jewish
hostages. An account given by Ghavām al-Dowleh, the deputy
governor (*pishkār*), conveyed that after the removal of the Jews to
Mashhad, the *mollās* went through a mock trial and sentenced the
entire group to death (probably on charges of apostasy), "but as the
same law permits a money fine in lieu of every punishment, so
were these unfortunate Jews allowed to purchase their lives for the
sum of 100,000 *tomans*."[108] These proceedings, Ghavām added, had
received the approval of the shah.[109] Pending the payment of this
amount, they would be subjected to abuse, Ghavām al-Dowleh
warned. None of the Jewish sources confirm this version, raising
suspicion that the story was concocted to give the British the
impression of legitimacy and that the matter had gone through
proper legal procedure.

The captives, of course, had their property looted in Herat and did
not have access to their possessions left there. There are indications
that a small number had either liquid assets or access to funds in
Mashhad. However, considering the outcome of the events and the
dire condition of this group, the number of these individuals must
have been very few. Later, this ransom was reduced to 70,000 *tomans*,
which still exceeded the wealth of all the *Jadids* in Mashhad.[110]
Ghavām al-Dowleh then "boasted" to the British that because of the
inability of the Jews to pay, he persuaded his government to reduce it
to 25,000 *tomans*.[111] Ghavām al-Dowleh also said that the orders that
he had received from time to time from the prime minister only

mentioned the Afghan prisoners and not the Jews, so he could not set the Jews free.[112]

Taylor pointed out to Ghavām al-Dowleh that Article 8 of the Treaty of Paris stipulated the release of "*all prisoners*" taken during the war, and these Jews came under that category, so by refusing to release the Jews, Iran was in direct violation of the treaty. He also stressed that they had to be released "*without ransom*" according to said treaty.[113]

As mentioned above, the British referred to articles of the Treaty of Paris, which provided for the release of prisoners of war and of hostages and captives detained on political grounds. According to Lord Palmerston,[114] while the treaty may not have exactly covered these people, it did not authorize the Iranian government to violate all principles of humanity either. He also emphasized that demands for ransom for those who were unjustifiably captured and carried to Iran were not acceptable to the British government. Palmerston seems quite sympathetic to the cause of these captives.[115]

Murray was very concerned about the condition of these captives and pointed out to the prime minister the "inhumanity and absurdity" of extorting "a ransom of 25,000 *toman*s from 300 wretched families whose property was confiscated in Herat, whose baggage was plundered on the long march to Mashhad, and who are in a state of misery from insufficient clothing and food, whilst they are persecuted exercising any vocation whereby they might support themselves and their families."[116]

It appears that the Iranians' obstinacy wore out the British. On August 27, 1857 the Earl of Clarendon instructed Murray to order Taylor to "discontinue all official demands on behalf of the Jewish Prisoners from Herat, but to continue his personal and official endeavors to ameliorate their miserable condition, and if possible to persuade the local authorities to release those who are bona fide citizens of Herat...." In response Murray rather strongly objected that had these been Europeans—Russians, for example—the request for their release without ransom would have been considered justified.[117]

In spite of all the attempts of the British—and Murray, in particular—it seems that they knew their efforts were falling on deaf ears. Lord Clarendon suggested to Murray that the best policy was to wait and watch the progress of events.[118]

The Aftermath

Despairing of assistance from the British, the prisoners sent letters to their brethren in Tehran to be forwarded to the king or other monarchs who might help. They appealed to Governor Hosām al-Saltaneh, too, but he neglected to forward their appeal to the shah. His final verdict was that they could pay or perish.[119] It is plausible to assume that he may not have wanted the king—or probably his courtiers—to know about the ransom. There is a possibility that he may have confiscated what was left of the Jews' property after the Iranian army's looting of Herat. Appeals to the Jewish community of Tehran were not effective either, since the government had asked them to pay war tax and *they* were threatened with expulsion. The Tehran Jewish community did, however, manage to bring the situation to the attention of their European co-religionists.[120]

When their efforts through local authorities failed, the British appealed directly to the prime minister, who declared that the condition of the Jews in Mashhad was satisfactory. The Russians never intervened in favor of Jews, and they were interested in maintaining close ties to the Qajar rulers. The French ambassador was following a convenient policy of non-intervention.

Finally, and in spite of the possible risks, two Jewish emissaries from Mashhad arrived in Tehran, appeared before the shah, presented their grievances and received an order for the captives' freedom.[121] We do not know if the shah was aware of the situation before this audience. In later incidents of persecution, as in Hamadan, Nāser al-Din Shah took a strong position in the Jews' favor, albeit again under pressure from the British.[122]

Ghavām al-Dowleh—at this time the acting governor—refused to carry out the shah's order, still insisting on the payment of the ransom.[123] This was indeed daring and insubordinate, and showed the weakness of the central government or the lack of interest of the shah. Earlier on, Taylor indicated in his report that he had good reason to know that Ghavām al-Dowleh was "trying to extort a handsome douceur as the price of their liberty."[124] Another source quoting the *Jewish Chronicle* gives another version. In December 1857 the Jews of Tehran wrote to Sir Moses Montefiore and gave him an account of the hunger, disease, and death of 300 to 400 in the camp. They also informed him that the Iranian government was demanding a ransom of 15,000 *toman*s (£7,500, by their account). The captives had sold everything, including their religious books (which may have made their way to Tehran as waste paper), and had only been able to pay half of this amount,[125] probably, as Livi states, thanks to the Mashhadi *Jadids*.[126] With the intervention of the *Jadids* of Mashhad, and after more than half of them died in the two years of captivity, the amount was finally reduced to 7,000 *toman*s. This "discount" may have been granted because a large number of the Jews had in fact died, yet the governor still insisted that they could either bring this money or die.[127]

In light of these final demands, it seems that these people could be considered hostages to be milked for ransom, eclipsing earlier issues of nationality or religion.

Previously Mr. Doria[128] had written to Farrokh Khān,[129] saying that two months before (that is, in November) he had seen the shah and asked him to intervene on behalf of the Herati Jews in Mashhad from whom the Ghavām al-Dowleh had extorted 1,500 *toman*s. The shah assured him that no such extortion had taken place. Doria, however, insisted that he had received convincing proof that the sum of 1,500 *toman*s had been extorted from 121 families of Herat Jews, in addition to 1,500 from those Jewish families that the Iranian government "asserts belong to Meshed," for a total of 3,000 *toman*s, which is much less than the other sources have reported.[130] The British agent later wrote that the amount in question was no more than 700 *toman*s collected from the Mashhadi Jews and 700 *toman*s from the Heratis.[131] It is not clear whether the later figures were part of the ransom or additional money extorted from the Jews.

By April 1858, Murray, frustrated, wrote that there were only two ways that the surviving captive Jews could be released: either the

British government must demand it as a matter of right or the stipulations of the Treaty of Paris, or else a sufficient amount must be raised from some quarter to satisfy the avaricious demands of the Iranian authorities, as appeals to the humanity of the latter would be fruitless.[132]

In the end, it was only money that set them free. Faraj-Allāh Livi writes that once the governor reduced the ransom to 7,000 *tomans* the heads of the *Jadid* community of Mashhad finally managed to collect and pay this amount.[133] Finally the Jews were released, and by December 20, 1858 the Mashhad community made arrangements to send them back to Herat.[134] The ruler of Herat was even willing to send "a sufficient escort to the frontier to ensure their safe transit."[135] It is not known why the ruler was willing to provide an escort. It could have been because of pressure from the British or because he wanted to gain favors from them. It is also possible that the absence of the Jews was felt in Herat's markets. Azaria Levy indicates that Hosām al-Saltaneh was removed prior to the release of the prisoners.[136] The documents at hand do not elucidate who actually received the ransom.

Conclusion

Caught between two wars, two cities, two religions and two governments, the story of the Jews of Mashhad raises more questions than it answers. At the center of this account lies the definition of citizenship and identity, as well as religious persecution and survival strategies in Qajar Iran. After 20 years of living in Herat, should these Jews have been considered Herati or still Mashhadi? Should they have been considered Iranians or Afghans? Muslim or Jewish? At a time when there was no formal citizenship, where did the Herati Jews belong? Did their wishes matter in this? There is no precedent of similar incidents in Iran and therefore the Iranian authorities had no previous case on which to base their policy. Nor, it seems, had the British faced a similar incident before. The unavailability of Persian documents has kept certain aspects of this incident in the dark.

Another added problem is the underlying, endemic anti-Semitism that existed in Iran in general, and in a religious city like Mashhad in particular. Such sentiments probably led the main parties involved—for example, Hosām al-Saltaneh and Ghavām al-Dowleh, not to mention the *emām jom'eh* of 1839—to feel little remorse for persecuting the Jews and failing to make serious efforts to ameliorate their situation.

Another factor complicating the situation was the many parties involved, few of whom seem to have been in agreement and most of whom had their own political and financial agenda: the Iranian government, the local authorities, the Jews—both Herati and Mashhadi—the British and last, but not least, the local Herati rulers.

The weakness of the central government and the seemingly limited power of the shah over local governors and authorities at this time hurt the Jews tremendously, and efforts of the shah do not seem to have been significant or effective. Had it not been for the British, the captive Jews might have suffered an even worse fate.

The story of converting Jews to Islam is nothing new. Iranian social history is tormented by incidents of persecution of minorities under inconsequential, and often false, pretexts since the early Safavid period. Although it is not mentioned in this case, the issue of the poll tax (*jizya*) may have been a factor. It was no longer collected after the Jews had converted, and the treasury of Khurasan must have been affected, so the revenue from the commercial activities of the *Jadids* must have been considerable enough to cover the loss. A question raised here is why the *Jadids* were allowed to leave in the first place. Was it anti-Semitism or the greed and corruption of the local authorities, which was widespread in Qajar Iran? Which authority allowed such a source of revenue to be lost? Exactly who was paid? And what was the amount of the bribe? While we do know that the clergy may have welcomed the departure of the infidels, some sources mention that the high clergy were also on the receiving end of bribes. It is also possible that the elevated status of the Jews and their success in commerce were not well received by the Muslim merchants and they may have been instrumental in forcing their rivals out of the city, as happened in other cities. We cannot be sure whether the effort to persecute them was solely religious-based or whether it included commercial rivalry as well.

Both the Mashhadi and Herati Jews suffered because of their multiple identities. The former's new identity was not well accepted, and the latter's old one was rejected by the Iranians, while it is the British, the foreigners, who were more sympathetic to their identity both as Jews and as Heratis.

In the above incident we see the Jews as moving between different worlds, both in terms of nationality and of religion, not to mention foreign affairs (constantly appealing to outsiders to intervene on their behalf), while managing to persevere and preserve their unique identity. This is not an unusual phenomenon for a group or groups under constant pressure, as they have to emphasize the most salient of their identities at any one time and play the side that would benefit or protect them to survive. In other words, they had to use others, as the others used them. Possessing a dual identity and being forced to leave one's homeland and emigrate, as a necessity for survival, is nothing new today. In a world of conflict, countries are full of refugees. For this unfortunate group, however, their dual identity proved hazardous at every step. The question of the identity felt by this group of *Jadid al-Islāms* is worthy of further investigation and needs more space than this chapter allows.

In the end, once again, this became another story of persecution, greed and corruption of authorities in the Qajar era, one that, as with other similar incidents, has been omitted from contemporary Iranian histories.

Notes

1 The date varies from 1730 to 1760 in different sources. Since Nāder died in 1747, it may be that some dates refer to the arrival of various segments of this group in their destination, Kalāt, or in Mashhad.
2 The eighth Shi'ite Emam, Ali b. Musā b. Ja'far, known as Musā al-Rezā, was poisoned and died in this city—hence its original name, Mashhad al-Rezā, the place of martyrdom of Rezā.
3 Ya'qub Dilmāniān in *Tārikh-e yahudiān-e Mashhad: az vorud beh Mashhad dar zamān-e Nāder Shāh-e Afshār elā mohājerat az Mashhad* (New York, 1995), p. 18.

4 Azaria Levy, "Evidence and Documents Concerning the History of the Jews of Mashad," in *The Jews of Mashad* (new edn, Jerusalem, 2006), p. 3.

5 A. Levy, "Evidence", p. 4. Much has been made of the role of the Mashhadi Jews in providing intelligence to the British. Levy's claim that, as agents— and in fact representatives—of the British, they were involved in providing information, has been misunderstood as espionage against Iran. It is very unlikely that they were able to provide sensitive information, as they were not allowed in the inner circles of the political and military elite or access to privileged information.

6 Laurence Lockhart, *Nadir Shah: A Critical Study Based Mainly Upon Contemporary Sources* (London, 1938; repr. Jalandhar, India, 1993), p. 288.

7 Hāj Mirzā Abbās Iravāni, known as Hāj Mirzā Āghāsi (1784–1849), began as the tutor of then Mohammad Mirzā and was the prime minister of Mohammad Shah for 14 years. He had great influence on the shah. In spite of his long term in office, he is known to have been ignorant of government. (Mehdi Bāmdād, *Sharh-e hāl-e rejāl-e Irān: dar qarn-e 12 va 13 va 14 hejri*, vol. 2 (Tehran, 1992), pp. 203–9).

8 Jamileh Ruhzendeh, *Gozari bar tārikh-e ravābet-e siāsi-ye Irān va Afghānestān* (Tehran, 2005), p. 69.

9 Vanessa Martin, *The Qajar Pact: Bargaining, Protest and the State in Nineteenth-Century Persia* (London, 2005), p. 35.

10 FO 60/65, Justin Sheil to Viscount Palmerston, February 20, 1839. Sheil does admit that the figure may have been exaggerated.

11 A. Levy, "Evidence", p. 6.

12 Mehrdad Amanat, *Jewish Identities in Iran: Resistance and Conversion to Islam and the Baha'i Faith* (London, 2011), p. 51.

13 A. Levy, "Evidence", p. 6. The Iranian New Year, Nowruz, in this year fell on the 5th of the month of Moharram, a period of mourning for Shi'ite Muslims. The fact that the shah issued an order for the cancellation of celebrations is an indication of the gloomy atmosphere of the time.

14 A British fleet invaded Bushehr, but they and the British Residency left this city for Kharg Island on the 30th (Martin, *Qajar Pact*, p. 37). For a fuller version see J. B. Kelly, "The Egyptian and Persian Crises 1837–1841," in *Britain and the Persian Gulf 1795–1880* (Oxford, 1968), esp. pp. 308–11.

15 Faraj-Allāh Nasr-Allāhof, "Livi", in *Gusheh-hā-yi az tārikh-e jāme'eh-ye mā* (New York, 1987), p. 8.

16 T. S. R. OFlynn, "Western Christian presence in the North Caucasus, Circaucasus, Transcaucasus and Persia, c.1770s-1870s" [working title], Chapter 6 (forthcoming). I am most grateful to Dr. OFlynn, who so generously permitted me to cite his valuable work before its publication.

17 Dilmāniān, *Tārikh*, pp. 22–3.

18 Daniel Tsadik, *Between Foreigners and Shi'is: Nineteenth-Century Iran and its Jewish Minority* (Stanford, CA, 2007), p. 35.

19 Mehrdad Amanat, *Identities*, p. 51.

20 J. P. Ferrier, *Caravan Journeys and Wanderings in Persia, Afghanistan, Turkistan and Beloochistan* (London, 1856), p. 122.

21 Dilmāniān, *Tārikh*, p. 23

22 The sources are contradictory regarding the date of this event. A. Levy gives the date as the 27th ("Evidence", p. 6). Patai, quoting an account given in 1839 by one Jadidi Samad Āghā ben Yosef Dilmāni [*sic*], mentions that the event took place on "the Great Sabbath" before Passover on 12th Nissan. While 12th Nissan corresponds with March 27, it was not a Saturday, but a Wednesday (see Raphael Patai in *Jadīd al-Islām: The Jewish "New Muslims" of Meshhed* (Detroit, 1997), p. 57). Dilmāniān, quoting J. Wolff, mentions the year 1838 and the day of the killing of the dog as Saturday 8th or Sunday 9th Moharram and the attack on "Saturday" 13th Moharram (*Tārikh*, pp. 22, 23), which corresponds to March 29, which was a Friday and a day before Passover. Livi, whose dates are usually very reliable, also gives 12th Nissan, 27th March (*Gusheh-hā*, p. 9). Habib Levi, quoting Eugène Flandin, the French orientalist and politician, mentions the date as 13 Nissan 5599, corresponding to March 29, 1839 (Habib Levi, *Tārikh-e yahud-e Irān*, vol. 3, 2nd printing (Los Angeles, 1984), p. 589). It is possible, as in other cases, that the attack continued for several days, hence the contradictions.

23 Dilmāniān, *Tārikh*, p. 23.

24 Livi writes that a large group of Muslims went to the *emām jom'eh* and testified that the Jews had killed a dog in mockery of Husayn's martyrdom, and that the *emām jom'eh* consequently ordered the looting and massacre of the Jews (*Gusheh-hā*, p. 9). Another source, however, claims that the *emām jom'eh* warned his Jewish friends of the imminent danger (Amanat, *Identities*, p. 53). The veracity of this assertion needs further investigation.

25 Ferrier, *Caravan Journeys*, p. 122. Dilmāniān mentions that the soldiers arrived after the mob had dispersed (*Tārikh*, p. 24).

26 Allāhyār Khān, Āsef al-Dowleh was the maternal uncle of Mohammad Shah and son-in-law of Fath-Ali Shah. He was the prime minister of the latter for three years. (Bāmdād, *Sharh-e hāl*, vol. 1, pp. 154–8).

27 Ferrier, *Caravan Journeys*, p. 122.

28 This number varies between 31 and 52, depending on sources.

29 Livi, *Gusheh-hā*, p. 9. Livi's comment that they were supposed to convert them *gradually* is contrary to the Mashhadi oral tradition, which maintains that the entire community was converted in one day. It is possible that the conversion happened quickly.

30 Livi says he married four Jewish girls (*Gusheh-hā*, p. 10). Dilmāniān recounts that six girls were kidnapped and the *emām jom'eh* ordered one to be brought for him, whom he married (*Tārikh*, pp. 24–5). Patai says he married two (*Jadīd al-Islām*, p. 58). Col. Taylor, chief commissioner to Herat, writes that girls were seized, forcibly converted, and married off to the leading men of the city. The *emām jom'eh* married three of them (IOR/PS/L/9/158, Taylor to Murray, October 26, 1857).

31 Patai, *Jadīd al-Islām*, p. 58.

32 For more information on the *Allāh-dād* see: Dilmānian, *Tārikh*, pp. 21–5; Habib Levi, *Tārikh-e yahud*, vol. 3, pp. 589–93; Livi, *Gusheh-hā*, pp. 8–15; Raphael Patai, *Jadīd al-Islām*, pp. 51–64; Azaria Levy, "Evidence"; Jāleh Pirnazar, "Yahudiān-e Jadid al-Eslām-e Mashhad", *Iran-Nameh*, 19:1–2, (1379–80), pp. 41–59; and Mehrdad Amanat, *Identities*, pp. 47–59.

33 Joseph Wolff, *Narrative of a Mission to Bukhara in the Years 1843–1845* (London, 1845), p. 396.

34 Hāj Mirzā Mas'ud Garmrudi Ishlighi (1790–1848) was appointed minister of foreign affairs in 1835, and in the same year married Ziā al-Saltaneh, the favorite daughter of Fath-Ali Shah. She was of a Jewish mother and Mohammad Shah's aunt (Bāmdād, *Sharh-e hāl*, vol. 4, pp. 75–8).

35 A. Levy, "Evidence", p. 7.

36 There is a problem with calculating demographic figures at this time. One issue is the different figures given by the various sources. The main problem is that some give the population as the number of families and some as the number of people, which may very well only include men. The problem with family/household figures is the estimation of the number living in each house or the number of family members. Western scholars calculate each family or household with five members, which is extremely small for the Middle East, particularly in this period, since most families had more than three children and many lived with extended families.

37 Albert Kaganovich, *The Mashhadi Jews (Djedids) in Central Asia*, Anor 14 (Berlin, 2007), pp. 2–3. For a detailed discussion of the Mashhadi and Herati population, see pp. 1–8.

38 A. Levy, "Evidence," p. 3.

39 Ferrier, *Caravan Journeys*, p. 153.

40 A. Levy, "Evidence," p. 11; Patai, *Jadīd al-Islām*, p. 72.

41 FO 60/229, Sadr Azam [Nuri] to Murray (translation), January 7, 1858.

42 FO 60/229, Sadr Azam to Murray (translation), January 7, 1858.

43 For example, Mohammad Hasan Khān Mohaddam, Sani' al-Dowleh, E'temād al-Saltaneh, quotes J. P. Ferrier that there are "six hundred Jews in this city [Mashhad] who have accepted Islam to save their lives," and adds, "Here Monsieur Ferrier recounts some fabricated stories that the Jews have told him." (Mohammad Hasan Khān Mohaddam, Sani' al-Dowleh, E'temād al-Saltaneh, *Matla' al-Shams: Tārikh-e arz-e aghdas va Mashhad-e moghaddas*, ed. Teimur Borhān-Limudehi [lithograph] (Tehran, 1983), p. 320).

44 Pirnazar, "Yahudiān," p. 42.

45 Azaria Levy, "The Expulsion of the Jews of Mashad from Herat," in *The Jews of Mashad* (new edn, Jerusalem, 2006), p. 3, quoting Neumark.

46 A. Levy, "Expulsion," p. 5; Kaganovich, *Mashhadi Jews*, pp. 47–51.

47 The situation in Herat is covered in detail in David Charles Champagne, "The Afghan–Iranian Conflict over Herat Province and European Intervention 1796–1863: A Reinterpretation", Ph.D. dissertation, University of Texas at

Austin, 1981, pp. 162–461; also see Shannon Caroline Stack, "Herat: A Political and Social Study", Ph.D. dissertation, UCLA, 1975, pp. 335–467; and J. B. Kelly, "The Persian War, 1856–1857," in *Britain and the Persian Gulf 1795–1880* (Oxford, 1991), pp. 452–99.

48 For the text of the treaty see "Treaty of Perpetual Peace and Friendship: British India and the Amir of Kabul, 30 March 1855" in Hurewitz (ed.), *The Middle East and North Africa*, vol. 1 (New Haven, CT, 1975), p. 310.

49 Soltān Morād Mirzā, Hosām al-Saltaneh (d. 1883) was the grandson of Fath-Ali Shah. He was appointed governor of Khurasan several times. He was the commander of the Iranian army in the Herat war and adamantly against surrendering Herat (Bāmdād, *Sharh-e hāl*, vol. 2, pp. 104–10).

50 There is some controversy about the exact date of Iran's conquest of Herat. Ruhzendeh writes that it happened on September 26 (*Gozar*, p. 98), Stack gives October 24 as the date ("Herat," p. 454), and Kelly believes it was on October 26 (*Britain and the Persian Gulf*, p. 475).

51 Ruhzendeh, *Gozar*, pp. 96–8.

52 A. Levy, "Expulsion," p. 8.

53 Kelly, *Britain and the Persian Gulf*, pp. 472–3.

54 Ibid., pp. 494–5.

55 Mahmud Mahmud, *Tārikh-e ravābet-e siyāsi-ye Irān va Engelis dar qarn-e nuzdahom-e milādi* (Tehran, 1988), p. 717; and Ruhzendeh, *Gozar*, p. 104.

56 "Treaty of Peace (Paris): Great Britain and Persia, 4 March 1857," in Hurewitz, *The Middle East and North Africa*, vol. 1, pp. 341–3.

57 Dilmāniān, *Tārikh*, pp. 38–9.

58 Mirzā Nasr-Allāh Khān Nuri, known as Mirzā Āghā-Khān Nuri, E'temād al-Dowleh (1807–65) started his career in the service of Āsef al-Dowleh. He was appointed as the minister of the army. He was very conniving, ambitious and vengeful. In 1852 he gave up his British citizenship to become prime minister for seven years. Nuri was instrumental in the death of Amir Kabir (Bāmdād, *Sharh-e hāl*, vol. 4, pp. 363–79).

59 Mahmud, *Tārikh-e Ravābet*, pp. 717–8.

60 A. Levy, "Expulsion," p. 9. The exact number of the Jews of Herat is difficult to ascertain. His figure is based on statistics given by other sources. A petition by the Jews mentions the number of the captives as 1,000 (FO 60/229, Translation of the petition of the Captive Jews in Meshed to Murray, undated, *c.* January 1858).

61 The Mosallā is a Timurid compound built in 1417 comprising the mausoleums of Gowharshād (the wife of Shāhrokh, the Timurid ruler) and the Sufi poet and politician, Amir Ali-Shir Navā'i, and a *madrasa* (religious school). In 1885, fearing a Russian attack on Herat, the British dynamited most of the complex to have a clear line of fire for their artillery. The invasion never took place.

62 Livi, *Gusheh-hā*, pp. 32–3. This was about £45 at the time and about $5,000 based on the value of silver in September 2012.

63 Sir Charles Augustus Murray (1806–95) was the British ambassador to the court of Nāser al-Din Shah from 1854 through 1859, except for a short break.

64 Worth approximately $1,000 to $1,500, based on the value of silver in September 2012.

65 FO 60/229, Translation of the petition of the Captive Jews in Meshed to Murray, undated, c. January 1858.

66 Ha-Maggid, 48 (18 Kislev, 5623/December 1862), p. 383.

67 A. Levy, "Expulsion," p. 10.

68 Once again, there is disagreement on the date of this event and it is given as January, February or March. In any case, it seems that the Jews were incarcerated for some time before they were moved.

69 R. Mattityahu Garji, as quoted in Patai, Jadīd al-Islām, p. 73. Another document of the same period also recounts the hardship of the trip and mentions that some were thrown from the camels into the river (IOR/PS/L/9/158, Taylor to Murray, October 26, 1857).

70 IOR/PS/L/9/158, Taylor to Murray, September 17, 1857.

71 A. Levy, "Expulsion," p. 14.

72 Robert Lewis Taylor started as a captain in the 18th Bombay Native Infantry and became a major by the time he went to Persia. Later he was promoted to colonel and made the British chief commissioner to Herat.

73 FO 60/229, Translation of the petition of the Captive Jews in Meshed to Murray, undated, c. January 1858.

74 IOR/PS/L/9/158, Taylor to Murray, September 24, 1857.

75 Mirzā Mohammad Mostowfi, Ghavām al-Dowleh (d. March 1873) started his career as deputy (pishkār) to the governor of Azarbayjan. In 1855, when Āghā-Khān Nuri was recalled from the custodianship of the Shrine of Emām Rezā, he was appointed the deputy of Khurasan. In the absence of Hosām al-Saltaneh, he ruled Khurasan (Bāmdād, Sharh-e hāl, vol. 3, pp. 267–72).

76 IOR/PS/L/9/158, Taylor to Murray, September 24, 1857. Taylor says that the begging was stopped when he arrived and resumed after his meeting with the prince.

77 Dilmāniān, Tārikh, p. 39. He says that normally when captives were taken they were either put to forced labor, and their food and clothing were provided, or they were left somewhere to work for a living.

78 A. Levy, "Expulsion," p. 12. It is surprising that they attempted this job. In Shi'ite Iran the concept of najāsa would prevent non-Muslims from touching, in particular, water or any liquid that a Muslim would touch or consume, as water in particular was believed to be the greatest transmitter of this alleged religious impurity.

79 Each shāhi is about 25 cents, based on the value of silver in September 2012.

80 FO 60/229, Translation of the petition of the Captive Jews in Meshed to Murray, undated, c. January 1858.

81 FO 60/229, Translation of the petition of the Captive Jews in Meshed to Murray, undated, c. January 1858.

82 There is great difference in numbers given by various sources. It is fair to assume the number provided by the captives is more accurate, since it is not as high as the others, while a higher number would have strengthened their case.

83 FO 60/229, Murray to Lord Clarendon, January 13, 1858.

84 Moses Haim Montefiore (1784–1885), Italian-born British financier, banker and philanthropist, is probably the most famous Jew of nineteenth-century England. He was the president of the Board of Deputies of the British Jews for 37 years and served as the Sheriff of London from 1837–8. He donated large sums to Jewish causes and actively intervened to alleviate the problems of Jews in Iran.

85 For information about the condition of the captive Jews see FO 60/229, Translation of the petition of the Captive Jews in Meshed to Murray, undated, c. January 1858; Patai, Jadīd al-Islām, pp. 72–3; Dilmāniān, Tārikh, p. 39; Livi, Gusheh-hā, pp. 33–4; A. Levy, "Expulsion," pp. 12–3, among others.

86 For the full English text of the Treaty of Paris (1857) see Hurewitz, The Middle East and North Africa, pp. 341–3; for the Persian text see Mahmud, Ravābet, pp. 695–700.

87 IOR/PS/L/9/158, Sadr Azam to Murray, August 1, 1857 (Zu'l-hajja 10, 1273).

88 For the text of these two treaties see Hurewitz, The Middle East and North Africa, pp. 198 and 234, respectively.

89 "Dastur al-amal-hā-ye kārgozāri-ye mahāmm-e khārejec-ye Āzarbāijān," in Iraj Afshar (ed.), Daftar-e tārikh, vol. 2 (Tehran, 1384/2005), p. 326. I am grateful to Dr. Kiumars Ghereghlou for bringing this to my attention.

90 FO 60/229, Translation of the petition of the Captive Jews in Meshed to Murray, undated, c. January 1858.

91 IOR/PS/L/9/158, Taylor to Murray, August 16, 1857.

92 FO 60/232, Murray to the Earl of Malmsbury, July 31, 1858.

93 A. Levy, "Expulsion," p. 10.

94 IOR/PS/L/9/158, Taylor to Murray, September 24, 1857.

95 Qur'an, sura al-Baqara, verse 256.

96 Vera Basch Moreen, Iranian Jewry's Hour of Peril and Heroism (New York, 1987), pp. 101–2, among others.

97 FO 60/230, Sadr Azam to Murray (translation), January 7, 1858.

98 FO 60/228, Palmerston to Murray, January 16, 1858.

99 FO 60/229, Murray to Sadr Azim [sic], January 18, 1858.

100 FO 60/228, Sadr Azam to Murray (translation), February 22, 1858 (Rajab 7, 1274).

101 FO 60/229, Murray to the Sadr Azim [sic], January 18, 1858.

102 For the prime minister's query, see FO 60/229, Sadr Azam to Murray, February 23, 1858 (Rajab 8, 1274); for responses see FO 60/229, Murray to the Sadr Azam, February 1858, undated, after the 23rd and FO 60/228, Foreign Office (no signature) to Murray, May 29, 1858.

103 IOR/L/PS/9/159, Murray to Sadr Azam, January 3, 1858.

104 A. Levy, "Expulsion," p. 12, quoting a letter from the Jews dated May 12, 1857, published in *Jewish Chronicle*, March 19, 1858.

105 A. Levy, "Expulsion," p. 13. Dilmāniān, *Tārikh*, p. 39, writes that they were buried *behind* Askariyeh.

106 FO 60/229, Sadr Azam to Murray (translation), January 7, 1858, for example.

107 FO 60/229 Sadr Azam to Murray (translation), February 22, 1858 (7 Rajab 1274); FO 60/230 Sadr Azam to Murray, March 7, 1858.

108 This was about £45,000 at the time and about $5,000,000, based on the value of silver in September 2012.

109 IOR/PS/L/9/158, Taylor to Murray, September 24, 1857.

110 Livi, *Gusheh-hā*, p. 34.

111 He also claimed that the instructions came from the prime minister. The British documents do not corroborate this, but it may very well have been true.

112 IOR/PS/L/9/158, Taylor to Murray, September 24, 1857.

113 Ibid.

114 Henry John Temple, 3rd Viscount Palmerston (1784–1865) was foreign secretary from 1846 until 1851, and served as prime minister from 1855 to 1858. He is known as the chief architect of British foreign policy in the mid-nineteenth century.

115 FO 60/228, Palmerston to Murray, January 16, 1858.

116 IOR/PS/L/9/158, Murray to the Earl of Clarendon, October 5, 1857.

117 Ibid.

118 FO 60/228, Clarendon to Murray, January 1858.

119 Livi, *Gusheh-hā*, p. 34; Dilmāniān, *Tārikh*, p. 39.

120 A. Levy, "Expulsion," p. 15.

121 Dilmāniān, *Tārikh*, p. 39. He does not provide a date.

122 For the case of Hamadan Jews and the infamous tumult caused by Akhund Mollā Abd-Allāh, see Haideh Sahim, "Jews of Iran in the Qajar Period: Persecution and perseverance," in Robert Gleave (ed.), *Religion and Society in Qajar Iran* (London, 2005), pp. 293–310.

123 A. Levy, "Expulsion," p. 17.

124 IOR/PS/L/9/158, Taylor to Murray, September 24, 1857 (Report from camp at Meshed).

125 A. Levy, "Expulsion," pp. 15–16.

126 Livi, *Gusheh-hā*, pp. 34–5. Livi says they collected and paid 7,000 *toman*s.

127 Livi, *Gusheh-hā*, p. 34.

128 William Doria, later Sir, was the British Chargé d'Affaires from 1858 to 1859.

129 Farrokh Khān Kāshi, also known by the titles Vazir Hozur, Amin al-Molk, and Amin al-Dowleh (d. 1871), started in the service of Fath-Ali Shah and became one of his trusted servants. After the conquest of Herat, Farrokh Khān went to Paris, and signed the peace treaty with Britain on March 4, 1857, according to which Iran gave up all rights to Herat and Afghanistan. In 1858 he was appointed minister for foreign affairs (Bāmdād, *Sharh-e hāl*, vol. 3, pp. 80–5).

130 FO 60/238, Doria to the Minister of Foreign Affairs (translation), January 20, 1859.

131 FO 60/239, Agent at Meshed (extract), August 7, 1859.

132 FO 60/231, Murray to the Earl of Malmsbury, April 30, 1858.

133 Livi, *Gusheh-hā*, p. 35.

134 Livi, *Gusheh-hā*, p. 35. He says that they were released on Shevat 25, 5619 (January 30, 1858), after two years and ten days, and that gradually by 15 Tevet 5619 (December 20, 1858) they [all] arrived in Herat.

135 IOR/PS/L/9/158, Taylor to Murray, October 26, 1857 (from Herat).

136 Nuri, the prime minister, and Hosām al-Saltaneh were both deposed on Muharram 20, 1275 (August 30, 1858).

CHAPTER 5

THE ORIGINS OF THE DECORATED KETUBBAH IN IRAN AND AFGHANISTAN

Shalom Sabar

The Decorated Ketubbah in Muslim Countries

The sources of the most elaborate decorated ketubbahs from earlier centuries are Italy and the European Sephardic communities, as is well known. A careful and comprehensive examination of the entire corpus of decorated ketubbahs from all areas of the Diaspora extant in public libraries, museums, and many private collections throughout the world, however, reveals a lesser-known fact: the practice of decorating ketubbahs was much more widespread among Jews living in Muslim countries. While in Italy and Holland the wealthier members of the community commissioned talented folk artists to decorate ketubbahs tastefully and lavishly for their sons and daughters, in many communities in the Muslim world the decorated ketubbah was used at all levels of Jewish society. Moreover, as we will see below, the practice appears to have originated in the Jewish regions of Muslim lands, whence it evidently reached Muslim Spain in the Middle Ages, and from there to Italy and the Sephardic Diaspora after the Expulsion of 1492. In addition, changes in religious practice and daily life in the modern era led to the decline of the custom in Europe in the early nineteenth century, while in Muslim lands Jews continued to decorate their ketubbahs even in the early twentieth century, and in some places until the mass immigration to Israel after the establishment of the State.[1]

In the decoration of ketubbahs and their physical appearance, there are a number of distinctions between those from Muslim lands and those from Western Europe. The first is the material on which the ketubbah was written. In Italy and in some Sephardic communities (including the Sephardic community of Morocco, for example) it was customary to use parchment, while in most Muslim countries—at least in the last generations—they commonly preferred large sheets of paper. Another distinction is the calligraphy. While Italian Jewish calligraphers used a square script throughout the ketubbah, their Sephardic counterparts and those in most of the communities in Muslim countries wrote the main text of the ketubbah in cursive rabbinic script, and generally used the more exquisite square lettering only for the verses of the blessings written within the ornamental frame. With regards to the imagery, the most notable difference is that the Jewish artists in Muslim lands followed the dominant restriction of Islamic society against producing representational images in religious art and thus refrained (in all fields of the visual arts) from depicting the human figure.[2] Consequently, their ketubbahs have no Biblical narrative pictures, heroes, allegorical or mythological figures, wedding scenes, portraits of the bride and groom and the like, which were all commonplace in ketubbahs from Baroque Italy and Western Sephardic communities. Other typical European Jewish motifs, such as depictions of Jerusalem and the holy places, the Temple and its utensils, the signs of the Twelve Tribes of Israel, and other Jewish symbols appear only rarely in some ketubbahs from Muslim countries.[3]

Instead of all of these motifs, Jewish scribes and artists in Muslim countries limited themselves by and large to the use of floral and geometric decorations, with which they would fill the entire background of the ketubbah. Architectural elements and faunal representations were also common motifs in ketubbahs produced in places such as India and Iran. In further contrast to European ketubbahs, the images in those from Muslim lands were in most cases drawn directly onto the paper, generally without outlines, in predominantly strong and bright watercolors.[4] European ketubbah artists, on the other hand, sometimes used tempera and gouache, and at times additionally employed copper plates to print large decorative borders. Due to these differences in material and technique, the brighter colors and often more elaborate free-hand ornamentation of ketubbahs from Muslim lands produce in part a more striking visual impression. Finally, despite the limitations and creative restrictions under which folk artists in Muslim communities operated—or perhaps because of them—the decorative elements in their work provide valuable insights into the ways of life, artistic tastes, and daily and religious customs of their Jewish patrons, particularly in Iran and its sister communities.

The most important center for decorating ketubbahs outside Italy was the greater Iranian region, which includes Afghanistan and Bukhara. The practice was so widespread that the different Jewish communities in this area, like those in Baroque Italy, developed characteristic motifs and decorative styles specific to each of the major Jewish artistic centers within the region: primarily Tehran, Hamadan, Isfahan, Sanandaj (or Senna), Yazd, Mashhad, Herat, and Bukhara.[5] Indeed, ketubbahs from Afghanistan have attracted relatively considerable attention in the literature.[6] Despite the great wealth of the material and the large number of artifacts that have survived from the other centers, however, no comprehensive artistic or cultural examination of Iranian ketubbahs has been undertaken to date. In this article I intend to discuss only some basic questions that have not been treated in the existing body of scholarship.

The Beginning of Ketubbah Decoration in the Greater Iranian Sphere

We do not know when the Jewish communities of the greater Iranian region began to decorate their ketubbahs. The earliest examples known to date come from Iran proper, and they date back to the seventeenth century. There are two ketubbahs from 1647, one from Isfahan and the

Figure 5.1   Ketubbah, Isfahan, 1647. The Jewish Museum, New York, no. F3901.

other from the Kurdish community of Maragheh in northwestern Iran (Lake Urmia region).[7] Excluding the Kurdish ketubbah, the one from Isfahan is the earliest known surviving document of its kind from Iran (*Figure 5.1*). As was the practice in Isfahan and other towns in Iran and Afghanistan in later centuries, this ketubbah was written on a large sheet of paper (81.3 × 61 cm). The scribe and decorator used high-quality paper, of the kind used for exquisite Persian manuscripts in the seventeenth century. Undoubtedly, the quality of the paper facilitated the preservation of this early document.[8]

To decorate this early ketubbah the artist used silver and gold colors, and a repeated block-print floral pattern that fills the frame tightly. Although the use of gold and silver was not common in later Iranian ketubbahs, decorating the sheet with a recurrent block print of one kind or another is known from the nineteenth century, mainly from Hamadan.[9] Furthermore, in addition to verses that remain common in contemporary times, the verses inscribed in the internal and external frames include selections that were not common in later generations. The former include popular and beloved biblical verses that refer to marriage at the city gate, the jewelry of the bride and groom, finding a suitable match, and blessings for fertility and longevity. These verses are inscribed in the external frame (Ruth 4:11; Isaiah 61:9–10, 62:5; Proverbs 5:18, 18:22) and in part of the internal frame (Psalms 128:3–6). Less common, however, are the verses of "Woman of Valor" (Proverbs 31:10–12),[10] which were also rarely used in Italy despite their suitability for a document pertaining to the wedding ceremony and raising a family.

The combination of well-known elements with less familiar ones suggests that this early ketubbah from Isfahan was not a random or unique specimen. The ketubbah was created during a particularly difficult time for the Jews of Iran, a time of debilitating decrees and extreme persecution under the despotic rule of Shah Abbas II (r. 1642–66).[11] Moreover, this period in Isfahan is also marked by a flourishing in the production of illustrated Judeo-Persian manuscripts replete with figurative miniatures.[12] Although it is difficult to prove a connection between the miniatures and ketubbah decoration,[13] it is clear that despite the persecutions artistic creation thrived among the Jews of Isfahan at that time. While the socio-cultural background of this phenomenon needs further research, it is not implausible that the harsh conditions actually drove contemporary Jews to deepen their inner cultural activities and artistic creativity, which provided a sanctuary from the horrific realities of daily life.[14] Accordingly, the attractively decorated ketubbah continued to be a central symbol of the new union, establishing a new house in Israel, and inner reinforcement of the community's hopes for security and steadfastness.

Figure 5.2   Ketubbah, Isfahan, 1763. Gross Family Collection, Tel Aviv.

The next two oldest known surviving examples of ketubbahs from Iran date back to 1763 (*Figure 5.2*) and 1781.[15] These contracts contain elements that link them both to early ketubbahs and to those that were created at a later date in the area of Iranian culture. For example, in the 1763 ketubbah the verses of "A Woman of Valor" are inscribed, and in the one from 1781 a recurrent floral block print is used in the exterior frame. Moreover both ketubbahs, like the earlier specimen from 1647, conform to the same design: an elongated rectangular sheet of paper consisting of two central "windows," the upper one containing verses of blessing and the lower one the text of the ketubbah itself; the windows are surrounded by an ornamental frame, around which (in the exterior border of the sheet) are inscribed verses of blessing in very large Hebrew letters. This is the basic design of the ketubbahs from nineteenth-century Afghanistan, as will be discussed below.

The Connection to the Middle Ages and to Ketubbahs from the Genizah

The earliest known decorated ketubbahs come from the Cairo Genizah, comprising a collection of about two dozen fragments created in the Eretz Israel–Egypt region from the end of the tenth century onwards.[16] Providing for a bride's dowry was an expensive ordeal at the time, as it often included a wide range of items such as rare and ornate textiles, jewelry, varied items of apparel, house wares, bedding, furniture, and the bride's personal wardrobe.[17] The items were publically displayed and evaluated by expert appraisers, and their description and total value in local currency were recorded in detail in many ketubbahs,[18] as was the custom in Muslim countries until modern times.

Besides listing the details of the dowry, it was customary to recite the contents of the ketubbah before the couple and the guests;[19] a custom that increased the social importance of the ketubbah within the wedding ceremony. The widely opened document that was read aloud with much joy and pride before the respected guests, highlighting the wealth and social status of the wedded families, apparently called for even more elaborate decorations that would further impress those present at the festivity. Consequently, it became customary to decorate the ketubbah, although not with the richness we know from Italian and Iranian ketubbahs in later generations (*Figures 5.3 and 5.4*).[20] The most popular decorative feature in the

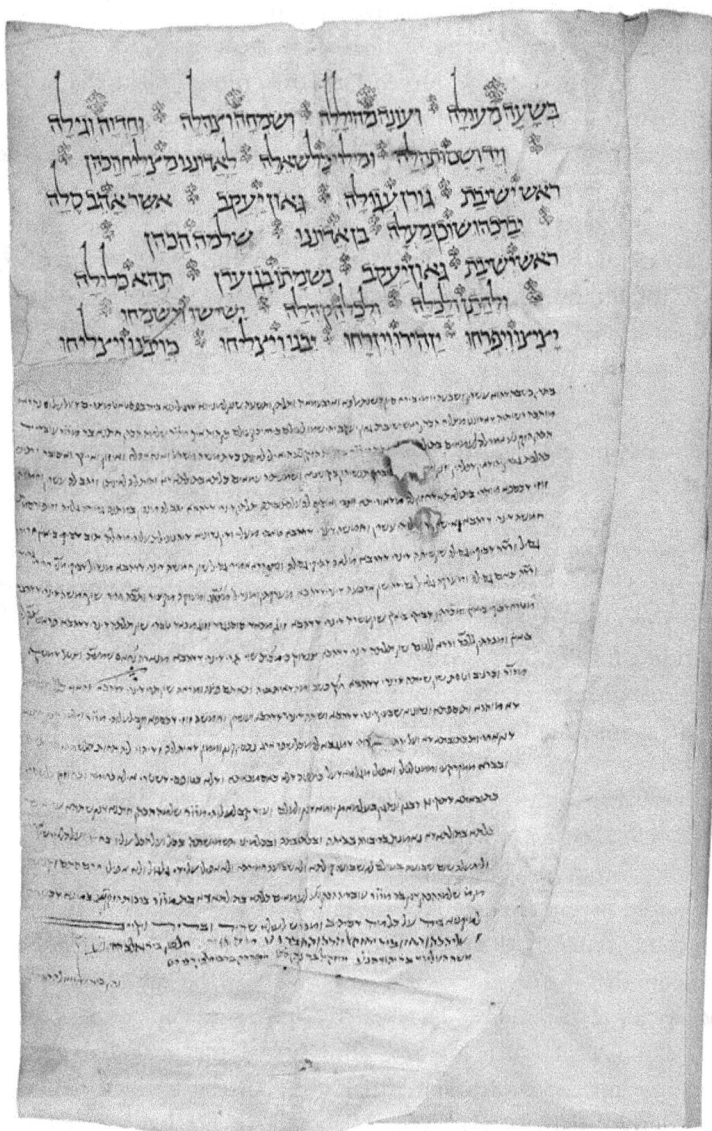

Figure 5.3 Ketubbah, Fustat, 1128. Oxford, Bodleian Library, MS Heb. a 3, fol. 40r.

Figure 5.4   Ketubbah fragment, Egypt(?), twelfth century. Cambridge University Library, MS. T-S K10.4.

ketubbah fragments from the Genizah was micrographic ornamentation—i.e., the use of tiny Hebrew letters to create geometric patterns and floral decorations (*Figure 5.4*).[21] Likewise, architectural elements such as an arch or a pair of arches were used in a number of examples, a decorative feature that developed both in the East and in the West, acquiring various meanings in different regions—i.e., the association of the arches with the act of setting up house, or the interpretation of the arch as a passageway signifying the couple's "passage" into matrimony.[22]

Observably, most of the decorative elements found in ketubbahs from Muslim lands, including Iran, to some extent echo various ornamental features of the Genizah ketubbahs. In most cases, however, these elements are also characteristic motifs of popular art in the Muslim cultural sphere in modern times—both among Jews and their Muslim compatriots. As such, there is no clear evidence for continuity in the use of these elements in the Middle Ages and their reappearance in Jewish communities in Iran. More decisive is the continuity in the choice of verses that decorate the ketubbahs in the Genizah. These verses form an integral part of the general ornamental scheme; and the order in which they are arranged, the way they are written, and mainly their content, change from place to place.[23] Consequently, we can treat these verses as central and characteristic elements in the ornamental pattern of a given ketubbah.

Among the decorative verses of the early ketubbah from Isfahan, for example, appears the beginning of a flowery, rhymed preamble, a kind of wedding song, which is also found more completely in ketubbahs from Afghanistan and Iran (with variants) in the course of the nineteenth century and the early twentieth century (the Hebrew verses carry a single rhyme throughout):

Light and merriment	*orah ve-tzahala*
And worth and greatness	*vi-yekar u-gedulah*
(For the blessing of the mighty)[24]	*(le-virkat eitanim)*
And a mantle of praise	*u-ma'ateh tehillah*
With happiness and with joy	*be-hedvah u-ve-gilah*
To sing doubly	*le-ranen kefulah*
For the noble groom	*la-hatan ha-na'aleh*
And the virgin bride[25]	*ve-la-kalah ha-betulah*

Anonymous popular wedding songs like this appear in the early ketubbahs from the Genizah. The notable feature of these flowery preambles is short lines of two or three words only, rhyming with the syllable '*la*'. The most famous rhymed preamble from the Egyptian Genizah follows this pattern:

At a noble hour	*be-sha'ah me'ulah*
And a praiseworthy season	*ve-onah mehullala*
And celebration and rejoicing	*ve-simha ve-tzahalah*
And happiness and joy	*ve-hedvah ve-gilah*
And fame and praise	*ve-yad va-shem u-tehillah*
And the fulfillment of every wish…	*u-milu'i kol mish'alah…*

These rhymed wedding greetings have been preserved almost in their entirety in modern times in ketubbahs from Yemen (and following the practice in Yemen, in India as well),[26] and their *similarity* to Iranian ketubbahs is not a mere coincidence. Moreover, other notable expressions from benedictory verses in the ketubbahs of the Genizah appear in ketubbahs from the Iranian sphere, such as the special Aramaic blessing "*banyin u-matzlihin*" taken from Ezra 6:14: "So the elders of the Jews *progressed in the building.*"[27] This blessing appears often and in the same context in nineteenth- and early twentieth-century ketubbahs from Afghanistan, Iran, and Bukhara (*Figures 5.5 and 5.6*). However, it is extremely rare in modern ketubbahs from anywhere else despite its regular occurrence in ketubbahs from the Genizah.[28]

An additional matter of principle that connects the decorative verses from the Genizah ketubbahs and the Iranian ones is the exceptional blessing for the Diaspora community and its leadership. In ketubbahs from the cities of Iran and Afghanistan the preferred expressions are "a chosen [treasured] community" [*adat segulah*], "sages of the Diaspora" [*hakhmei ha-golah*], "Diaspora of Ariel" [*golat ariel*]. In some of the ketubbahs from Herat, however, and nearly all of those from Bukhara, from the earliest surviving examples until today, a longer phrase is used: "To the chosen community and our master the head of the yeshiva of the Diaspora" (*Figures 5.5 and 5.6*).[29] The special

Figure 5.5 Ketubbah, Bukhara, 1861. Jerusalem, National Library, no. 901/33.

Afghani-Bukharan blessing for the head of the community,[30] which to the best of my knowledge does not occur in modern times in ketubbahs from any place outside the greater Iranian region,[31] appears to be clearly archaic. The phrase "the head of the yeshiva of the Diaspora" is, of course, reminiscent of the heads of the ancient academies in Babylonia, and indeed such blessings do occur in ketubbahs from the Genizah, in

Figure 5.6 Ketubbah, Bukhara, 1816. Shlomo Moussaieff Collection, Herzlia.

the decorative verses at the top of the document. For example, in the
ketubbah from Fustat 1128, which is nearly complete (Ms. Oxford Heb.
a. 3, fol. 40r), there is a seven-line lyrical inscription in beautiful
calligraphy, decorated by the scribe with tiny flowers between every
phrase (*Figure 5.7*):

> At a noble hour / And a praiseworthy season / And celebrating
> and rejoicing / And happiness and joy / And fame and praise /
> And the fulfillment of every wish / For our master Mazliah Ha-
> Cohen / Head of the Yeshiva / *Goren Agulah* [A round threshing
> floor] / *Ga'on Ya'akov* [The pride of Jacob] / Whom he loved *sela*
> / May He who abides above bless him / Son of our master
> Solomon Ha-Cohen / Head of the Yeshiva *Ga'on Ya'akov* / May
> his soul in Paradise / be included / And for the groom and the
> bride / And for all the community / May they rejoice and
> celebrate / May they sprout and flourish / May they shine and
> glow / May they build and succeed [II Chronicles 14:6] / as they
> build and succeed.

This text refers to a known individual and not to an anonymous head
of the yeshiva. Mazliah Ha-Cohen and his father Solomon, mentioned
in the decorative inscription, were both famous and admired spiritual
leaders in Eretz Israel and in Egypt in the eleventh and twelfth
centuries.[32] Solomon (d. 1083) headed the great yeshiva in
Jerusalem. In 1127—i.e. one year before this ketubbah was
written—his son Mazliah founded the yeshiva in Fustat as an
extension of the one in Jerusalem, and headed it until his death in
1139. Mazliah called himself "Head of the yeshiva of the pride of
Jacob," and the great respect that his community had for him as their
leader brought them to mention his name at the top of the
ketubbah,[33] which had evidently been the practice in ketubbahs from
Babylonia.

A remnant of this practice may be found in ketubbahs from the
greater Iranian region, where the phrase "the head of the yeshiva of
the Diaspora" is mentioned. The continued use of this phrase and its
systematic inscription at the top of the ketubbah—both features that

Figure 5.7   Ketubbah, Bukhara, 1809. Moldovan Family Collection, New York.

were common practice in the Middle Ages—testify to a long-standing decorative tradition that was preserved in greater Iran. Though the lacuna in historical samples makes it impossible to know how the ketubbah was decorated in this cultural region between the Middle Ages and the seventeenth century, it is reasonable to presume that geometric designs and floral motifs were used.[34] At any rate, we may conclude that the earliest extant decorated ketubbahs from Iran are evidently a direct continuation of a centuries-old tradition of which only a few pre-nineteenth-century examples have survived.

The Beginnings of Decorated Ketubbahs in Herat and Mashhad

Whether or not we attribute the design characteristics of nineteenth-century ketubbahs to earlier traditions, it is clear that ketubbah decoration flourished in an exceptional way at that time among the Jewish communities of the greater Iranian region. Even though the prevailing socioeconomic atmosphere made this a generally difficult period for the Jews of that region who routinely suffered persecution and forced conversion to Islam, many works of art and splendid ritual objects from this period have survived. Hundreds of exquisite ketubbahs, decorated in a characteristic style, were created in all of the central Jewish communities of Iran in the course of the nineteenth century. A few examples exist from smaller towns as well. One factor that may have contributed to the increased popularity of decorated ketubbahs during this period may be the parallel custom among Iran's dominant Shi'ite population to decorate the Muslim wedding contract [ghabāla], a custom that flourished particularly in the nineteenth century.[35] As scholars have suggested, there is unquestionably a correlation and evidence of mutual influence regarding the motifs, the general composition and layout of the page, and the relation between text and decoration between Jewish ketubbahs and Muslim wedding contracts.[36]

Nineteenth-century ketubbahs from Herat (Afghanistan) are an integral part of this cultural phenomenon. First of all these contracts are connected in many ways, socially and artistically, to the

Figure 5.8 Ketubbah, Herat, 1882. Gross Family Collection, Tel Aviv.

ketubbahs of other Jewish centers (and particularly to those of the community of forced converts to Islam in Mashhad) and to local folk art. On the other hand, they represent a unique and characteristic style of ornamentation, which is easy to recognize and identify (*Figure 5.8*). In this compositional scheme, the text is inscribed in the middle of the lower part of a rectangular sheet of paper. The ruling lines were delineated first, sometimes in watercolors, and the text was written in square letters—unlike the practice in most other Jewish communities in Muslim countries of writing the ketubbahs in rabbinic cursive script. Above this panel, we find an arcade of five arches with alternating flower vases and blessings. Narrow frames of flowers, more verses, and an alphabetical list of "good signs" surround the two central panels. This was also the basic plan of the early ketubbah from Isfahan (without the arcade, cf. *Figure 5.1*). The scribes in Herat used lighter and brighter colors, however, which immediately attract the viewer's eye.

This basic pattern can already be seen in the earliest extant ketubbah from Herat, dated 1812 (*Figure 5.9*).[37] Despite its similarity to later ketubbahs, however, the 1812 ketubbah displays a number of significant differences—both in the decorative text and in the pictorial motifs—which may contribute to our understanding of the source of the preferred pattern of ketubbahs from Herat. First, only three openings or windows appear at the top of the 1812 ketubbah, as opposed to the five that we find in ketubbahs from Herat in the second half of the nineteenth century. These windows frame previously quoted passages from the wedding poem *"Orah ve-zahalah."* This triple opening was common in the ketubbahs of other Jewish communities in the Muslim world, mainly in Iraq (Baghdad, Basra) and Kurdistan (Zakho, Irbil, and also Sanandaj in Iran; *Figure 5.10*).[38] The selection of the number three may indicate the influence of Muslim aesthetics, which displays a marked preference for odd numbers in various art forms in general, and architecture in particular, where we commonly find three openings in many structures. This tripartite division can also be observed in synagogues throughout Iran—e.g., the three niches in the sixteenth-century tiled synagogue wall from Isfahan in the collection of The Jewish Museum in New York or in the entrance of synagogues in Herat (*Figure 5.11*).[39] Additionally, ketubbahs from Herat are crowned by a multi-arched arcade, decorated with delicate flowers against a bluish background; a motif that directly echoes the decoration on the blue-glazed ceramic tiles of the *mihrab* [prayer niche] and dome of mosques and *madrasas* from the greater Iranian region.[40]

The most interesting text in the decoration of the Herat ketubbah of 1812 is in the central "window" of the tripartite opening: "May Reuben live and not die, by virtue of the Rock, who rides the clouds"

Figure 5.9   Ketubbah, Herat, 1812. Jerusalem, National Library, no. 901/424.

(*Figure 5.9*). This rhymed and metered greeting is obviously addressed to the groom Reuben bar Hananya. The first part of the expression is taken from the blessing of Moses to the tribe of Reuben before his death (Deuteronomy 33:6), and the second part applies the

Figure 5.10   Ketubbah, Sanandaj, 1903. Gross Family Collection, Tel Aviv.

Figure 5.11 Tripartite design of a synagogue wall, Mully-ye Garji Synagogue, Herat (photo after *Brides and Betrothals*, p. 29).

blessing to the groom by virtue of the Lord, who is a "Rock who rides the clouds" (see Psalm 68:5). Italian ketubbahs offer many examples of blessings for the groom with references to Jewish historical heroes with the same name. Such blessings also appear sometimes in ketubbahs from European Sephardic communities.[41] Such references, however, are extremely rare in ketubbahs from Eastern communities. In fact, no other known ketubbah from Afghanistan contains such a reference,[42] which suggests that its use here was evidently an innovation either of Samuel b. Abraham—the scribe (and decorator?) of the ketubbah[43]—or of the family of the groom who commissioned this magnificent document.

With respect to the text in the body of the ketubbah, the opening words were written in an exceptional manner, using large and ornate red display letters. Ample use of the color red was also made in the benedictory verses in the panel above the text, mainly for the words of the poem "*Orah ve-zahalah*" in the adjacent windows. In the list of signs for good fortune in the external frame, the words are written in red and black alternately, with the word *siman* [sign] appearing in red and the attribute itself in black. The more prevalent custom is to write the entire list in black. This uncharacteristic feature in the 1812 ketubbah from Herat[44] may indeed be reminiscent of the opening inscriptions in ketubbahs from the Genizah. Arguably, however, it reveals a more immediate connection to ketubbahs from Mashhad, in which we find a similar practice (*Figure 5.12*).[45]

Observably, however, the similarities between the 1812 ketubbah from Herat and ketubbahs from Mashhad are not limited to this pattern of alternating red and black ink. A closer analysis of other examples of ketubbahs from Mashhad reveals that the incorporation of benedictory verses in the 1812 Herat example as well as its entire ornamental scheme mirrors distinct characteristics of Mashhadi Jewish marriage contracts. It is important to note here that these remarkable similarities unquestionably predate the mass migration of many Mashhadi Jews to Herat after the community's forced conversion to Islam in 1839. Consider, for instance, the two examples of *Figures 5.12 and 5.13*.[46] While Iris Fishof maintains that "it would be wrong to associate the Herat ketubbahs exclusively with Mashhad,"[47] based on the features of the 1812 ketubbah from Herat it is my opinion that the development of ornamental characteristics of Jewish marriage contracts from Herat was a product of multifarious ties between the respective Jewish communities of the cities.[48] In support of Fishof's position, it is true that at first glance there is no evidence that the 1812 ketubbah was influenced by the Mashhad tradition, since its elements are identical to those produced in Mashhad later—i.e., after 1812, but before 1839. Existing documents, however, compel us to reevaluate this position. The 1812 ketubbah has a precedent from Mashhad: a ketubbah from Mashhad written in 1784, that is, one generation before the one from Herat (*Figure 5.14*).[49] As in the ketubbah from Herat, the upper panel is divided into three openings, not five, as was customary in the nineteenth century; and in the exterior border we find "signs" in alphabetical order, surrounded by a narrow frame with floral decoration. The color palette was evidently similar as well, but unfortunately this ketubbah exists only in an old black and white photograph.

The above provides a very strong argument for the fact that ketubbahs from Herat and Mashhad are closely related; a connection

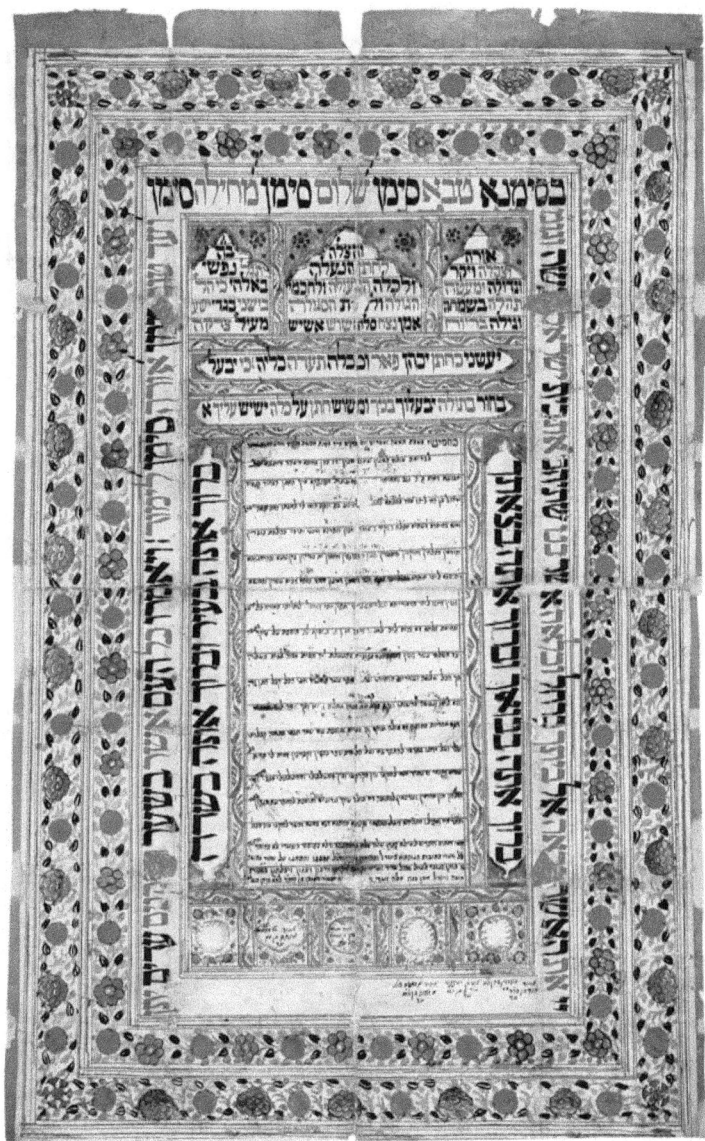

Figure 5.12   Ketubbah, Mashhad, 1831. Jerusalem, National Library, no. 901/503.

Figure 5.13   Ketubbah, Mashhad, 1834. Jerusalem, National Library, no. 901/426.

Figure 5.14 Ketubbah, Mashhad, 1784. Present whereabouts unknown (after Patai, "Marriage Among the Marannoes of Meshhed," facing p. 180).

that is supported by historical evidence. The early date of the eighteenth-century Mashhadi ketubbah indicates that the respective wedding was conducted only one generation after the Jews settled in the holy city.[50] The financial success of the Jews of Mashhad attracted Jewish migrants from other cities in Iran, such as Yazd and Kashan,[51] who brought their own sociocultural traditions with them. And as we have seen, the Mashhad ketubbah had many elements that connect it to other communities in Iran and to earlier traditions from the Middle Ages. As opposed to the flourishing community of Mashhad at the end of the eighteenth and the beginning of the nineteenth century, the community of Herat was small and dwindling, comprising no more than 20 to 40 families.[52] The Jews of Mashhad who migrated to Herat not only increased the Jewish population there, but also enriched it culturally and materially. Thus we may conclude that the compositional scheme under discussion reached Herat from Mashhad before the forced conversion thanks to the ties between the smaller community and its dominant sister community.[53] Evidently the Jews of Herat continued to use the Mashhad model until the mid-nineteenth century (*Figure 5.15*).[54] In the second half of the century a more sophisticated version of this model was adopted, which decorated the ketubbahs of many Jewish couples who were married in Herat.

Conclusion

The decorated ketubbah originated in Jewish society in the Muslim world in the early Middle Ages out of a social need to elevate the wedding celebration and to make it more elaborate in every way possible. In fact, ketubbahs from the Genizah were decorated in a relatively simple manner, but in the next generations the phenomenon gained strength throughout many parts of the Jewish Diaspora and reached Europe as well. While we have examples of decorated ketubbahs from Europe from a relatively early period, the overwhelming majority of the examples from Jewish communities in Muslim countries date from the nineteenth century and the first half of the twentieth. Among these, ketubbahs from Iran help to bridge the great gap between the Genizah period and modern times. The evidence from various cities in Iran, Afghanistan (mainly Herat), and Bukhara testify to the close connection between those ketubbahs that were written and decorated in modern times and their counterparts within the medieval tradition. In addition to drawing from past tradition, the large communities

Figure 5.15   Ketubbah, Herat, 1851. Jerusalem, National Library, no. 901/425.

in the greater Iranian region developed local patterns of ornamentation, featuring new motifs and bold uses of color, which in turn testify to a strong connection between neighboring communities, on the one hand, and between each Jewish community and its respective local art, on the other. This link is best illustrated in the case of ketubbahs from Afghanistan: the design characteristics first developed among the Jewish community of Mashhad eventually reached Herat, ultimately to become a famous and cherished symbol of the Jewish wedding; a symbol that combined both beloved tradition and creative continuity.

Notes

1 For a general introduction to the art of the ketubbah in Jewish communities, East and West, see David Davidovitch, *The Ketuba: Jewish Marriage Contracts through the Ages* (Bat Yam, 1978), pp. 114–95 [English section]; Shalom Sabar, *Ketubbah: Jewish Marriage Contracts of the Hebrew Union College Skirball Museum and Klau Library* (Philadelphia, 1990), pp. 6–32; for examples from Islamic lands, see ibid., pp. 301–64. It is important to note that in the early history of Jewish art in general and the art of the ketubbah in particular, ketubbahs from Muslim lands are generally not mentioned and all the examples cited by the various authors are European (save the occasional mention of a single example from the Cairo Genizah). See, for example, Moses Gaster, *The Ketubah: A Chapter from the History of the Jewish People* (Berlin, 1923); Karl Schwarz, "Ketubba," in *Jüdisches Lexikon*, vol. 3 (Berlin, 1927–30), cols. 668–78; Rachel Wischnitzer, "Schmuck der Ketubba," in *Encyclopaedia Judaica*, vol. 9 (Berlin, 1928–34), cols. 1186–91. Perhaps not totally unrelated is another noteworthy phenomenon: the practice of the handwritten and individually illuminated ketubbah in those Muslim lands where it was still popular in the first half of the twentieth century (e.g., Morocco, India, Iran) came to an abrupt end with the immigration of these communities to Israel, dominated in those years by Western-European culture.

2 For the Islamic approach, see for example Oleg Grabar, *The Formation of Islamic Art* (New Haven and London, 1977), pp. 75–103. For a classic, general introduction to the Jewish approach to painting and the visual arts in the lands of Islam, see: Leo A. Mayer, *L'Art juif en terre de l'Islam* (Geneva, 1959); (English translation: "Jewish Art in the Moslem World," in Cecil Roth (ed.), *Jewish Art: An Illustrated History* (New York, 1961), cols. 351–76).

3 For a large selection of examples from the various communities, see the reproductions in Davidovitch, *The Ketuba*; Sabar, *Marriage Contracts of HUC*; Liliana Grassi (ed.), *Ketubbot italiane: Antichi contratti nuziali ebraici miniati* (Milano, 1984); Shalom Sabar, *Ketubbah: The Art of the Jewish Marriage Contract* (Jerusalem and New York, 2000).

4 In rare cases, other techniques were employed—for example, readymade printed decorations that were cut out and affixed onto the ketubbah surface in Baghdad and Damascus, or decorative block prints that surrounded the text in Hamadan, Iran (see below).

5 For brief introductions on Persian ketubbahs and discussions of selected examples, see Davidovitch, *The Ketuba*, pp. 102–100; Sabar, *Marriage Contracts of HUC*, pp. 327–44 (examples from the collection of HUC Skirball Museum,

Los Angeles, arranged by the towns of their origin); Iris Fishof, "The 'Ketubbah'," in No'am Bar'am-Ben Yossef (ed.), *Brides and Betrothals: Jewish Wedding Rituals in Afghanistan* (Jerusalem, 1998), pp. 85–93; Yehuda L. Bialer and Estelle Fink, *Jewish Life in Art and Tradition from the Collection of the Sir Isaac and Lady Edith Wolfson Museum* (Jerusalem, 1980), pp. 24, 29–31; Claudia J. Nahson, *Ketubbot: Marriage Contracts from the Jewish Museum* (San Francisco and New York, 1998), pls. 2, 16, 17, 21, 23, 25–7, 31, 32; Houman Sarshar (ed.), *Esther's Children: A Portrait of Iranian Jews* (Beverly Hills, 2002), pp. 126–9, 328–9; Reuben Kashani, *Illustrated Jewish Marriage Contracts from Iran, Bukhara and Afghanistan* (Jerusalem, 2003); David Yeroushalmi (ed.), *Light and Shadows: The Story of Iranian Jews* (Tel Aviv & Los Angeles, 2012), pp. 75, 126, 130, 142–3, 148–9, 159–61. Selected Jewish examples are found also in Layla S. Diba (ed.), *Iranian Wedding Contracts of the Nineteenth and Twentieth Centuries* (Tehran, 1976), pp. 85–7 (in Persian and English). Many additional examples are reproduced in auction catalogs of Judaica, in particular by Sotheby's and Christie's. The largest selection of ketubbahs from Iran, Afghanistan, and Bukhara, arranged by location and date, appears in the Internet site of the National Library of Israel, Jerusalem (henceforth NL): http://web.nli.org.il/sites/NLI/English/collections/jewish-collection/ketubbot/Pages/default.aspx (some of those preserved in the NL, are described by Yisscahar Joel, "From the Collection of Marriage Contracts in the Library," in *Kirjath Sepher*, 22 (1944–5), pp. 302–3, 306–7 (in Hebrew)). For the text of an early Persian ketubbah found in a manuscript of the Persian *siddur*, see Shlomo Tal, "A Persian Ketubah," *Diné Israel*, 4 (1973), pp. 229–31 (in Hebrew).

6 Davidovitch, *The Ketuba*, p. 100; Reuven Kashani, *Illustrated Ketubot of Afghanistan* (Jerusalem, 1978) (in Hebrew); Sabar, *Marriage Contracts of HUC*, pp. 303–5; idem, "The Wedding: *Ketubbah* Decoration in Herat," in B. Yaniv and Z. Hanegbi (eds), *Afghanistan: The Synagogue and the Jewish Home* (Jerusalem, 1991), pp. 36–9; Fishof, "The 'Ketubbah'."

7 The early Isfahan contract was donated to the Jewish Museum by Dr. Harry G. Friedman (no. F 3901); see Nahson, *Ketubbot*, p. 19. The Maragheh contract is preserved in the Library of the Jewish Theological Seminary, New York (henceforth JTS), Ket. 145. It is not discussed in this essay, as its formulation and ornamentation in simple black ink represent the Kurdish tradition, which is different from the one analyzed here. This contract and other Kurdish ketubbahs from Iran (and other countries) are discussed by this writer in a comprehensive volume on the ketubbahs preserved at JTS (in press).

8 The high quality of the paper led to the supposition that the material is parchment and it is described as such in Nahson, *Ketubbot*, p. 19. However, a laboratory examination revealed it to be paper, not parchment. I am grateful to Claudia Nahson for this examination and update. Though parchment was not the normal writing material for ketubbahs in Muslim lands during the last centuries, in the Middle Ages the situation was apparently different. Most of the Cairo Genizah ketubbahs of Eretz Israel and Egypt are written on parchment (cf.

Mordechai A. Friedman, *Jewish Marriage in Palestine: A Cairo Geniza Study*, vol. 1 (Tel Aviv, 1980/81), p. 9). Parchment was still common in Egypt in the sixteenth century (e.g., a parchment ketubbah from Cairo, 1551, preserved at Temple Museum of Religious Art, Cleveland). It is not known when exactly paper became the dominant material and whether parchment was common also in the Iran of the Middle Ages. In modern times, only among Bukharan Jews were parchment or leather used at times for writing ketubbahs (along with paper).

9   See for example, Hamadan 1874 (JL Ket. 360; Davidovitch, *The Ketuba*, pl. IX). Note that the block print here has been hand colored. In another example from Hamadan (d. 1909; Skirball Museum Los Angeles—Sabar, *Marriage Contracts of HUC*, pp. 330–1) the impression has not been embellished with additional designs.

10   The last two Hebrew words of Prov. 31:11, "lacks nothing of value" (as in "Her husband has full confidence in her and lacks nothing of value") were not transcribed. Perhaps this omission is not a mistake but rather intentional— avoiding negative connotation in order to protect the bridal couple. Protective inscriptions and designs are common on many ketubbahs, especially in Muslim lands (see Shalom Sabar, "Words, Images, and Magic: The Protection of the Bride and Bridegroom in Jewish Marriage Contracts," in R. S. Boustan, M. Rustow, O. Kosansky (eds), *Jewish Studies at the Crossroads of Anthropology and History: Authority, Diaspora, Tradition* (Philadelphia, 2011), pp. 102–32, 361–5).

11   See Ezra Spicehandler, "The Persecution of the Jews of Isfahan under Shah Abbas II (1642–1666)," in *Hebrew Union College Annual*, 46 (1975), pp. 331–56; Vera Basch Moreen, *Iranian Jewry's Hour of Peril and Heroism: A Study of Babai ibn Lutf's Chronicle, 1617–1662* (Jerusalem, 1987).

12   Several studies of these miniatures have been published. For a comprehensive catalog of the extant manuscripts and their miniatures (including a list of the earlier literature), see Vera Basch Moreen, *Miniature Paintings in Judaeo-Persian Manuscripts* (Cincinnati, 1985). For the context of these manuscripts in the general (Shi'ite) book arts of Isfahan at the time, see Alice Taylor, *Book Arts of Isfahan: Diversity and Identity in Seventeenth-Century Persia* (Malibu, 1995), esp. pp. 31–46.

13   Cf. ibid., pp. 31–2.

14   In her historical background to the period, Taylor (ibid., pp. 1–8) remarks, in addition, that Shah Abbas II encouraged and supported the visual arts of his time. While it is implausible that his support included the Jews, the Jewish elite of the capital apparently did its utmost efforts to join the contemporary trends and commission manuscripts illuminated in the style and aesthetics of the time.

15   The 1781 ketubbah is preserved in the Skirball Museum, Los Angeles. See Sabar, *Marriage Contracts of HUC*, pp. 332–3.

16   Most of the decorated Genizah ketubbah fragments have not been published or analyzed yet. For some preliminary discussions, see: Shlomo D. Goitein, *A Mediterranean Society: The Jewish communities of the Arab World as Portrayed in the Documents of the Cairo Geniza*, 6 vols (Berkeley, 1967–93), vol. 3, pp. 110–13;

Friedman, *Jewish Marriage in Palestine*, vol. 1, pp. 96–7; Davidovitch, *The Ketuba*, pp. 110; Sabar, *Marriage Contracts of HUC*, pp. 6–8; Shalom Sabar, "Two Millennia of Ketubbot in Eretz Israel," in Nitza Behroozi Bar-Oz (ed.), *A Local Wedding: Ketubbot from Eretz Israel, 1800–1960* (Tel Aviv, 2005), pp. 8–10.

17 On the difficulties involved in the preparation of the dowries in the Genizah period, see Friedman, *Jewish Marriage in Palestine*, vol. 1, pp. 288–309. On the various items that comprise the dowry in the contracts, see Yedida K. Stillman, *Female Attire of Medieval Egypt According to Trousseau Lists and Cognate Material from the Cairo Geniza*, unpublished Ph.D. Dissertation, University of Pennsylvania, 1972; idem, "The Importance of the Cairo Geniza Manuscripts for the History of Medieval Female Attire," *International Journal of Middle East Studies*, 7 (1976), pp. 579–89; Shlomo D. Goitein, "Three Trousseaux of Jewish Brides from the Fatimid Period," *AJS Review*, 2 (1977), pp. 77–110. For a detailed transcription of one such list, taken from an early eleventh-century ketubbah from Tinnis, see: Friedman, *Jewish Marriage in Palestine*, vol. 2, pp. 1–34.

18 Cf. ibid., vol. 1, p. 296.

19 Ibid., vol. 1, pp. 96, 296, 467.

20 The importance given to the ketubbah as a physical object is demonstrated in yet another custom. Once the ketubbah was recited and shown to the public, it was folded (or rolled) and then the bridegroom would hand it to the bride, saying to her "Take the ketubbah in your hand and accept your kiddushin from me as final... according to the Law of Moses and Israel" (see Friedman, *Jewish Marriage in Palestine*, vol. 1, pp. 213–14). This medieval tradition was continued later in very few communities, significantly including Italy and Iran. For the Persian custom, see Shlomo Tal (ed.), *The Persian Prayer Book: A Facsimile Edition of MS Adler ENA 23 in the Jewish Theological Seminary Library* (Jerusalem, 1981), p. 31; Sabar, *Marriage Contracts of HUC*, pp. 328–9.

21 Micrography characterizes the decoration not only of ketubbahs but also of Bibles and other Hebrew manuscripts from the Genizah. For the beginnings of this phenomenon in Eretz Israel and Egypt and its continuation in other communities, see Leila Avrin, *Hebrew Micrography: One Thousand Years of Art in Script* (Jerusalem, 1981).

22 See the chapter "Praise Her in the Gates," in Sabar, *Ketubbah: Art of the Jewish Marriage Contract*, pp. 17–41.

23 For a partial list of the verses and blessings that commonly appear in ketubbahs of various communities, see Bracha Yaniv et al. (eds), *Hebrew Inscriptions and their Translations* (Jerusalem, 1988), pp. 16–31.

24 This verse appears only in the early ketubbah from Isfahan and not in the nineteenth-century ketubbahs from Iran and Afghanistan.

25 Alternatively, the last two lines are at times abbreviated to "for the groom and bride"—as in the Isfahan ketubbah of 1647. Two additional variations of this blessing are referred to in note 28, below. Selected sections appear also in the ketubbahs of Baghdad and Zakho (Kurdish Iraq)—see below.

26 See Shalom Sabar, "The Illuminated Ketubbah [of the Cochin Jews, Baghdadi Jews and Bene Israel]," in Orpa Slapak (ed.), *The Jews of India – A Story of Three Communities* (Jerusalem, 1995), pp. 166–202, esp. pp. 170–1.

27 For this Aramaic blessing see Friedman, *Jewish Marriage in Palestine*, vol. 1, pp. 93–4. In Indian and Yemenite ketubbahs preference was given to the parallel Hebrew expression, "May they build and succeed" (II Chronicles 14:6), which is likewise known from the Genizah ketubbahs (see below). See also Sabar, *Jews of India*, p. 170.

28 Slight variations of this blessing appear in nineteenth-century ketubbahs from Iran and Afghanistan. See, for example, a ketubbah from Yazd, 1857 (Skirball Museum Los Angeles—Sabar, *Marriage Contracts of HUC*, pp. 342–3); Herat, 1867, (formerly in the collection of David Sassoon—see David Solomon Sassoon, *Ohel Dawid: Descriptive Catalogue of the Hebrew and Samaritan Manuscripts in the Sassoon Library*, vol. 1 (London, 1932), p. 382 (no. 709). Note, however, that in Bukhara this blessing is part of the fixed decorative opening formula, appearing in practically every preserved ketubbah of the nineteenth and early twentieth century.

29 The earliest known ketubbah from Uzbekistan, dated 1791 is preserved at NL (ketubbah no. 1043; see the image in the aforementioned NL site [note 5]). Curiously, however, this final section is missing in the earliest decorated extant example (Bukhara, 1809—*Figure 5.7*; collection of the Moldovan Family, New York)—apparently for lack of space in the framed area of the superscription. It is worthy to note that the early decorated Bukharan ketubbahs from the collections of Moldovan and Moussaieff (*Figures 5.6 and 5.7*) are both signed by the noted religious and spiritual leader of the community, Rabbi Yosef Maman Ma'aravi (r. 1741–1822). Rabbi Maman was born in Morocco, immigrated to the Holy Land, and from his Yeshiva in Safed was sent as an rabbinical emissary (SHaDaR) to Jewish communities in the Persian sphere to raise funds; following several months with the Mashhad community, he went in 1793 to Bukhara, where he settled for good, introducing significant changes in the religious practices of the community. See on him Alanna Esther Cooper, "Reconsidering the Tale of Rabbi Yosef Maman and the Bukharan Jewish Diaspora," *Jewish Social Studies*, 10:2 (2004), pp. 80–115 (and there the earlier Hebrew literature on Maman). Of his respected position, one may learn from the fact that in both ketubbot his signature appears "first"—that is at bottom right, reading: *ha-tza'ir Yosef Ma'aravi, s{ofeh} t{av}* ("the humble [lit. the young man] Yosef Ma'aravi. May his end be good"). The other signatories are well-known rabbinical authorities of Bukhara at the time as well.

30 A similar blessing for the "Head of the Diaspora" was included in the special version of the Kaddish, which Bukharan Jews used to recite on the annual memorial day (*Yahrtzeit*): "In your lifetime and during your days, and within the life of the head of the Diaspora" (see Itzhak Ben-Zvi, *The Exiled and the Redeemed* (Philadelphia, 1957), p. 67; the full quote, however, appears only in the updated Hebrew edition of the book (Jerusalem, 1969), p. 158). Ben-Zvi hypothesizes

that this expression proves the early association of the community with the Diaspora centers of Iraq in the Gaonic period. The full blessing resurfaces along the decorative borders of Herat ketubbahs printed in Jerusalem at the printing shops of Luncz and Levy. The printed formulary was provided to these presses by Rabbi Ya'akov Garji, of Herat, who may have been influenced by the Bukharan examples. In one of the earlier manuscript ketubbahs of Herat the blessing is to the "presidents of the Diaspora" (Herat, 1879—Hechal Shlomo, Jerusalem; see Bialer, Fink, *Art and Tradition*, p. 30).

31 To a certain extent, the popular engraved border of Sephardi ketubbahs from Amsterdam and elsewhere provide a partial exception to this rule. After the venerated Hakham of the community Isaac Aboab de Fonseca passed away in 1693, an inscription in Latin letters was added to the ketubbahs indicating the date of his death: *H. Y. Aboab F. Adar Seni A°5453*. However, this inscription was used only during a brief period and not among the decorative opening verses, but rather at the bottom of the page.

32 See: Goitein, *A Mediterranean Society*, vol. 6, *s.v.* Index.

33 Another important ketubbah fragment in which the opening blessing mentions "The Head of the yeshiva of the pride of Jacob" is preserved in the Cambridge University Library (TS 12.453) (see Bezalel Narkiss, *Hebrew Illuminated Manuscripts* (Jerusalem, 2014) [Hebrew edition only], p. 28 and figure on p. 19). Narkiss's assumption that Ghaliya, the bride in the ketubbah, is the daughter of the "head of the yeshiva" is implausible, as the blessing to him was a standard feature in the ketubbahs of the community. In addition, the date he suggests is incorrect. In the reproduction of this image in *Encyclopaedia Judaica*, vol. 10 (Jerusalem, 1972), col. 926, the suggested date is 1125—which is still prior to the actual arrival of Solomon in Fustat. Based on the Oxford contract, the full date should read 1438 to the Deeds, which parallels 1126/7. This date fits the historical data and is thus reliable. Another contract, dated 1164, mentions an additional historical figure: the Gaon Netanel ha-Levi, who was then the head of the yeshiva in Cairo (see David Kaufmann, "Zur Geschichte der Khethubba," *Monatsschrift fur Geschichte und Wissenschaft des Judentums*, 41 (1897), p. 214).

34 Examples of Jewish art in Muslim lands during this period are very scarce. However, the few items that have survived, such as the 1551 Cairo ketubbah mentioned in note 8 or the decorative synagogue wall from Isfahan (see note 39, below), prove that during the period in question the basic motifs did not change considerably.

35 An important exhibition of decorated Shi'ite wedding contracts was held in Tehran in 1976; see Diba, *Iranian Wedding Contracts*. Another lavish catalog on the same topic: Amir H. Zekrgoo, *The Sacred Art of Marriage: Persian Marriage Certificates of the Qajar Dynasty* (Kuala Lumpur, 2000).

36 Cf. Sabar, *Marriage Contracts of HUC*, pp. 24–5; idem, "A Decorated Marriage Contract of the Crypto-Jews of Meshed from 1877," *Kresge Art Museum Bulletin*, 5 (1990), pp. 23–31 (esp. 26–9); Fishof, "The 'Ketubbah'," pp. 91–2.

37 NL, ketubbah no. 424. See Davidovitch, *The Ketuba*, pl. 12 (the date should be corrected); Kashani, *Illustrated Jewish Marriage Contracts*, p. 6; Fishof, "The 'Ketubbah'," p. 88.

38 This tripartite design appears in the earliest known decorated ketubbah from Baghdad, 1764 (see Sabar, "The Illuminated Ketubbah" [*Jews of India*], p. 173, fig. 3). It continued to appear in the printed Baghdadi ketubbahs of the late nineteenth and early twentieth centuries (Sabar, *Marriage Contracts of HUC*, pp. 346–8). For Kurdish examples, see: Ora Shwartz-Be'eri, *The Jews of Kurdistan: Daily Life, Customs, Arts and Crafts* (Jerusalem, 2000), pp. 225 (Zakho, 1925), 220, 222–3 (Sanandaj, 1900, 1913, 1929). This type flourished also among the Jews of Georgia, apparently under southern-Iranian influence (see: Rachel Arbel, Lily Magal (Magalashvili), (eds), *In the Land of the Golden Fleece: The Jews of Georgia – History and Culture* (Tel Aviv, 1992), pp. 130, 132; Rachel Arbel, "Georgian Ketubbot," *Rimonim*, 6–7 (1999), pp. 37–44 (in Hebrew)).

39 For the Isfahan wall, see Norman L. Kleeblatt, Vivian B. Mann (eds), *Treasures of the Jewish Museum* (New York, 1986), pp. 38–9; for the Herat synagogue, see *Brides and Betrothals*, pp. 26–30.

40 For examples from Isfahan, Bukhara, Samarkand, Herat, Balkh, and other towns, see: Alexandre Papadopoulo, *Islam and Muslim Art* (New York, 1979), pp. 354 ff.

41 Sabar, *Ketubbah: Art of the Jewish Marriage Contract*, p. 82.

42 Another early Herat ketubbah, dated 1851 (NL, Ket. 425—Figure 5.15, below), contains an unusual verse, which possibly implies the name of the bridegroom. In the left arch appear the words of Laban and Bethuel to Eliezer: "This is from the Lord; we can say nothing to you one way or the other. Here is Rebecca, take her and go, and let her become the wife of your master's son, as the Lord has directed" (Genesis 24:50–1). While these verses could fit the ketubbah of any couple and are common in Italian ketubbahs, for example, they are extremely rare in ketubbahs from Jewish communities in Muslim lands. Thus, their selection may allude in this case to the bridegroom Jacob and his father Isaac. As we will see below, there are additional features that link this document to the 1812 example.

43 His name appears in the closing line of the text, using several self-effacing adjectives—e.g., *ze'ira de-ze'irin* [the smallest among the small]. The signature of the scribe appears in a considerable number of other ketubbahs from Herat. It can also be found in ketubbahs from other towns in the greater Iranian region, Isfahan in particular. However, it is an extremely rare phenomenon among other communities, including European ones (with a few exceptions from Italy).

44 Perhaps it is not incidental that another Herat ketubbah in which this feature of alternating black and red words appears is that of 1851 (*Figure 5.15*).

45 The Mashhad ketubbah from 1831 (NL Ket. 503) is also reproduced in Fishof, "The 'Ketubbah'," p. 86, fig. 5 (and cf. p. 89).

46 Aside from these two contracts, a third example from Mashhad 1826 with a similar compositional scheme is preserved in the Zucker family collection, New York (unpublished); a fourth one is discussed below.

47 Fishof, "The 'Ketubbah'," p. 89.

48 Cf. also Sabar, "*Ketubbah* Decoration in Herat," p. 36.

49 The present whereabouts of this important ketubbah is unknown to this writer. It was formerly in the private collection of Farajullah Aminoff, who immigrated to pre-state Israel from Mashhad, and settled in Jerusalem. Around 1947 the contract was documented by Raphael Patai, who reproduced it for the first time in his pioneering essay "Marriage Among the Marannoes of Meshhed," *Edoth: A Quarterly for Folklore and Ethnology*, 2 (1947), pp. 165–92 (in Hebrew), esp. pl. 4 facing p. 180 (reprinted in Patai, *On Jewish Folklore* (Detroit, 1983), p. 220; Patai, *Jadid al-Islam: The Jewish "New Muslims" of Meshhed* (Detroit, 1997), p. 248). The old black and white photo was copied in many other publications, especially on the Jews of Mashhad, without mentioning the source.

50 Several dates in the eighteenth century ranging from 1735 to 1760 have been proposed for the first settlement of Jews in Mashhad. See Azaria Levy, "Evidence and Documents on the History of the Jews of Mashhad," *Pe'amin: Studies in the Cultural Heritage of Oriental Jewry*, 6 (1980), pp. 57–73, (esp. 57–62) in Hebrew); Houman M. Sarshar, "The Jewish Community of Mashhad," in Houman M. Sarshar (ed.), *Jewish Communities of Iran: Entries on Judeo-Persian Communities Published in the Encyclopaedia Iranica* (New York, 2011), pp. 157–69, esp. p. 157.

51 Cf. Azaria Levy, "Evidence and Documents," pp. 59–60.

52 Azaria Levy, "The Expulsion from Herat, 1856–1859," *Pe'amin: Studies in the Cultural Heritage of Oriental Jewry*, 14 (1982), pp. 77–91 (esp. p. 80; in Hebrew); Benzion D. Yehoshua Raz, *From the Lost Tribes in Afghanistan to the Mashhad Jewish Converts of Iran* (Jerusalem, 1992), p. 155 (in Hebrew).

53 Aside from commercial connections between the two communities, the Jews of Mashhad assisted their brethren in Herat in times of trouble and distress (see Levy, "Jews of Mashhad," p. 60).

54 For this ketubbah see also Fishof, "The 'Ketubbah'," p. 89, fig. 6. This contract is the latest known from Herat that is decorated in the early Mashhadi compositional scheme. Nonetheless, a ketubbah with this scheme, dated three years later (1854), survived from Mashhad itself (Zucker Family Collection, New York—unpublished). A related contract that preserves this composition is from Kabul in Afghanistan (Kabul 1854—preserved at the Israel Museum, Jerusalem—179/18; reproduced in Kashani, *Illustrated Ketubot of Afghanistan*, p. 11). As very few ketubbahs are known from the small community of Kabul, it is difficult to ascertain the characteristics of ketubbah decoration in this town and their sources of inspiration. In the case of this contract, however, it is safe to assume it was created under the influence of the Herat contracts.

CHAPTER 6

THE MATERIAL CULTURE AND RITUAL OBJECTS OF THE JEWS OF IRAN

Orit Carmeli

Introduction

The Jews of Iran who lived in that country for over 2,700 years created a rich and versatile culture in many areas such as literature, philosophy, science, medicine, music, and art. The study of the artistic history and the material culture of the Jewish communities of Iran—from their manufactured day-to-day and ritual objects to architecture—has hardly begun. Only a few studies have been published as yet on these subjects; and there is a great need for further analysis, as there are many lacunae in our knowledge.[1] Museums and private art collections worldwide house noteworthy ensembles of Iranian Jewish artifacts in metalwork, wood, paper, ceramics, and textile. Some of the significant public collections of Iranian Judaica are found in Israel: The Israel Museum, Jerusalem; Hechal Shlomo—The Wolfson Museum of Jewish Art, Jerusalem; Eretz-Isreal Museum, Tel Aviv. Other important collections are found in the United States: The Jewish Museum, New York; Judah L. Magnes Museum, Berkeley; Spertus Museum, Chicago.[2] Despite the long history of the Jews across

Iran, however, the majority of the artifacts that have survived are from the nineteenth and twentieth centuries. At the current state of research, these artifacts can be grouped according to stylistic affinities, information gleaned from dedicatory inscriptions, or contextual information. A comprehensive analysis of these works of art in the context of their artistic or workshop connections, their historical and social matrices, and their relationship to the larger field of Islamic art history is yet to be conducted. Given the scarcity of extensive published material, the aim of this present article is to portray a broad-spectrum overview of the material and artistic history of the Jews across Iran. Other than the actual artifacts that have lasted in private and public collections, additional sources of information that can assist in portraying the narrative of the material culture of the Jews of Iran are informants: the people who in fact used this array of objects and utensils and those who were involved in manufacturing them.[3]

In the field of art history, "material culture" refers to the technology and material artifacts of a human group within their environmental and cultural context. It creates the visual and tangible aspects of everyday life.[4] The position of the Jews living in Muslim lands was never secure. Changes in the political or social climate would often lead to persecution and violence. Overall, however, Jews under Islam were able to live in relative peace and flourish culturally and economically.[5] The material culture of the Jews of Iran indicates that they had a continuing interchange with the larger Muslim community and various degrees of symbiosis with it. Jews adopted many elements of local daily life and often bought items designed for general use to modify them for use in a Jewish context. As in many Muslim societies, the Jews of Iran also took part in the production of the local material culture, working as craftsmen or artisans. Other than demonstrating the artistic level achieved by these craftsmen, these beautiful and unique artifacts also reveal the assimilation of Muslim and Iranian cultural and aesthetic norms into the material culture and life of the Jews of Iran.

Works on Paper

Thus far, the earliest evidence known in research for the material culture of the Jews of Iran are works on paper: illuminated manuscripts and decorated marriage contracts.

Miniature Paintings

In the rich and versatile Judeo-Persian literary corpus, only 14 manuscripts illuminated with miniatures have been discovered to date.[6] Based on stylistic evaluation of the miniatures, these cycles of illustrations appear to be provincial products of the late Safavid (1501–1736) and Qajar (1786–1925) periods. However, the beginning of this form of art among the Jews of Iran is still obscure. Iconographically, many of the scenes depicted in these manuscripts are unique and have no parallel in Islamic art. Though the artists copied familiar models from the Persian painting repertoire, they adapted them to scenes dealing with Jewish iconography. Naturally, the copyists or scribes of the texts were Jewish. There is no clue or knowledge, however, about the identity of the artists who painted these miniature cycles.

One unique example is that depicting "Joshua and the Israelites circumcising the children" from the manuscript *Fath-nāmeh* (The Book of Conquest or Victory) by the Jewish poet Emrani (b. 1454), composed *c.*1474. This composition in verse recounts the main events from the books of Joshua, Judges, Ruth, and Samuel I–II. In it, Emrani follows the Biblical text and scarcely departs from the sequence of the narrative.[7] The manuscript (Ms. 4602), which is part of a large collection of Judeo-Persian manuscripts at the Ben-Zvi Institute in Jerusalem,[8] is an incomplete copy of Emrani's composition. It contains 291 folios and 23 miniatures, and dates to the second half of the seventeenth century.[9]

According to Emrani's text and the biblical source (Joshua 5: 2–5), the Israelites traveling in the desert did not perform the commandment of circumcision. Therefore, upon entering the Land of Israel, they were told to fulfill this act after a break of 40 years.

In the miniature,[10] comprising two parts, Joshua is shown in the upper part of the composition kneeling with a golden flame halo rising from his shoulders. In his right hand he is holding a circumcision knife and his left hand holds the leg of a boy he is about to circumcise. The same boy is being held by another man kneeling down. The lower part of the composition depicts a similar theme.

Although circumcision is a religious mandate in Islam, there are no realistic visual expressions of this ritual in Persian or Islamic art. There are very few miniatures relating to this subject, none depicting the act itself, but only the festivities attending the ceremony.[11] Pictorial portrayals of the act of circumcision can be found in Christian art portraying the circumcision of Christ, and in Jewish art from Christian lands, such as circumciser diaries, *Mohel* notebooks, Passover haggadahs, and prayer books. "The circumcision of Isaac" from the Regensburg *Humash* and "Moses's wife, Zippora circumcising their son" from the second Nuremberg haggadah are but two examples.[12] Interestingly, the episode of Zippora, Moses's wife, circumcising their son appears in another illuminated Judeo-Persian manuscript, Shāhin's *Musā-nāmeh*, in a totally different manner.[13]

Decorated Marriage Contracts

The Jewish marriage contract, ketubbah, is a significant part of the Jewish wedding ceremony. The contract spells out the obligations of the husband to his wife as a precondition to their marriage. Decorated ketubbahs were very common among Jews living in Muslim lands, as they were among European Jews, mostly in Italy. It is unknown, however, when this custom started among the Jews of Iran.[14] One of the notable examples is a ketubbah made in 1647 in Isfahan.[15] This contract is made out of paper and is decorated with ink, gouache and gold paint. This rare and unique document is one of the earliest known examples of an Iranian decorated ketubbah. Another early example belongs to GFC collection and dates from 1763 Isfahan. A continuous floral design in yellow and brown frames the paper document. In the center of the composition three large flowers stem out from a vase with two birds situated above it.[16]

Each town often developed its own tradition of decorating ketubbahs, reflecting local artistic styles while still preserving older iconographic traits. Contemporary local architectural forms, carpets and textiles, illuminated manuscripts, and bookbinding are just a few of the visual sources of influence in the design of Iranian ketubbahs. A case in point is a group of nineteenth-century ketubbahs from Isfahan kept in various collections worldwide.[17] The documents are made of large sheets of paper and decorated with watercolors and ink. Several depict two birds flanking a tree of life—a symbol of paradise or a gate to heaven—while others portray an ancient and prominent motif in Iranian art and culture—the lion and sun motif [*shir-o-khorshid*]—which the Jews of Isfahan adopted into their marriage contracts. Interestingly, this group of ketubbahs (*Figure 6.1*) is signed by the "scribe and painter Moshe ben Yeshu'a." Artifacts of Islamic Judaica that are both dated and signed by a Jewish maker or artist are extremely rare. In this case, Moshe son of Yeshu'a, the scribe and painter, came from a well known Isfahani family of artists. He and his brother, Eliyahu son of Yeshu'a, were prominent ketubbah painters with a very distinctive style, which many of their followers tried to copy.

Many Iranian marriage contracts are significant not only for their artistic value, but as historical cultural documents that shed light on Jewish life under Muslim rule. An 1870 ketubbah from the city of Damavand provides fascinating insights into external influences on Jewish life as well as domestic arrangements in nineteenth-century Iran.[18] The Jewish population of Damavand was devastated by famine in 1871/2[19]—one year after the couple was married. According to Hebrew and Judeo-Persian textual additions to the ketubbah, in 1885 the wife received a settlement from her husband, who had left her in Damavand for 15 years while he worked in Tehran where he had acquired a second wife.

Although the Jews of Mashhad were forced to convert to Islam in 1839 in what is known as the Allahdad incident, they continued to observe all aspects of Judaism in secret. After the forced conversion,

Figure 6.1 Ketubbah, Isfahan, 1887. Paper: watercolor and ink. Gross Family Collection, Tel Aviv 035.011.001.

they began living a double life as *Anusim* [crypto-Jews]: outside the home they acted as Muslims as their clothes, names, and way of life resembled those of their neighbors; at home, in contrast, they secretly observed their Jewish rituals and life.[20] Accordingly, two marriage contracts would be prepared, an Islamic document [*ghabāleh*] for public use and a Jewish one for the home. The ghabāleh containing Arabic verses from the Koran would be dated

according to the Hijri calendar and included the couple's Muslim
names. Interestingly, at times the ghabāleh of Mashhadi Jews was
signed in Hebrew by a few of the witnesses, as most of the Anusim
were only literate in Hebrew.[21] Thus, the Mashhadi ketubbahs serve
as a remarkable demonstration of how the Jews secretly adhered to
their traditions and their religion in a time of persecutions and forced
conversions.

Metalwork

The Jews of Iran participated in the production of the local material
culture, working alongside non-Jewish workers as craftsmen or
artisans. At times, they also took part in shaping segments of the
local material culture, as they were the main practitioners of some
crafts, which was the case with the decorative art of metalwork. One
of the almost exclusively Jewish professions throughout the Muslim
world was silversmithry and jewelry making.[22] There may be a
variety of reasons as to why Jews and other non-Muslims practiced
this art form. The traditional explanation is the Koranic prohibition
against working with precious metals because the recompense for
such work is viewed as usury, which is forbidden in Islam.[23]

Most of the Jewish Persian metal artifacts kept in private and
public art collections were manufactured in the late nineteenth to
mid-twentieth century in two major production centers: Shiraz and
Isfahan. Each center has its own unique style and design, drawn from
local artistic traditions. Decorative work on metal objects (mainly of
gold, silver, and brass, but sometimes of copper and white nickel
alloys) is executed in several techniques and is referred to by the
general term *ghalam-zani* [chisel work]. In Isfahan this work is
referred to as *ghalam-e 'aksi* [pictorial chiseling]. Both centers are
characterized by a combination of embossed and engraved
techniques. The Shiraz school, however, often incorporates motifs
from nearby Persepolis.[24] Jewish artisans were a major presence in
both centers. Consequently, many of the works created there
incorporate Jewish themes. Yet a good number of this type of artifact
were made primarily for the tourist market.[25]

Decorative and Household Objects

Decorative and household objects such as trays and platters, bowls, dishes, ewers, jugs and mortars, lamps and candlesticks, incense burners, mirrors, and many other utensils represent an important chapter in the material culture of the Jews of Iran. Some of these artifacts served a variety of decorative functions, while others were practical utensils for holidays and special occasions. In addition to Jewish themes and motifs, these objects are also decorated with a range of ornamental motifs and designs borrowed from or inspired by their respective local Iranian artistic repertoire. Said Jewish themes and motifs often include Biblical figures (e.g. Moses and Aaron; Jonah and the fish), Biblical scenes (e.g. stories of Joseph in Egypt), embalms of the 12 Tribes of Israel, Kabalistic inscriptions, and scenes from the Jewish holidays (predominantly Passover and Purim).

Among this group of decorative objects there is a group of metal plates, all made in the beginning of the twentieth century by an Isfahani artist named Taghi Pashutan. Like most Iranian metalwork of the time, the plates display the technique of pictorial chiseling. In this case, however, the artist used Western pictorial models rather than adhere to Islamic artistic traditions, perhaps indicating the market for which they were intended. Some examples of his work can be found at TJM collection. Among them is an oval copper plate (*Figure 6.2*) with a nearly flat bottom rising to a concave rim and a thick rounded edge. Occupying a large portion of the composition is a figural depiction of Aaron the priest holding a censor and wearing a breastplate with 12 compartments (the *hoshen*). The artist's signature is engraved below the image in Persian: "*ghalam-e Taghi Pashutan Isfahan.*" A passage from Psalms 19:1–3 is also engraved in Hebrew characters along the border of the plate.

At times the metalware was purchased abroad, mostly in Russia, and was decorated in Iran by local artisans. Often the artifacts were older than the engraved decoration. A case in point is a silver tray decorated with a scene from Moses's life (*Figure 6.3*). This is a silver rectangular tray with a curved outline and cast rim and handles. At the center of the tray is a scene depicting Moses striking a rock and

Figure 6.2   Plate, Taqi Pashutan, Isfahan, early twentieth century. Tinned copper: repoussé, engraved, traced, punched, and hammered. 1 3/16 × 15 1/8 × 10 3/16 in (3 × 38.4 × 25.8 cm). The Jewish Museum, New York. Gift of Dr. Harry G. Friedman, F 3386. Photo by Frank Darmstaedter.

water flowing out. To the left of Moses stands Aaron, hands raised to the sky, with onlookers in the background. Surrounding the figural scene are decorative bands with floral scrolls, and below it is a band of Hebrew inscription taken from Numbers 20:11. On the reverse side of the tray two marks are stamped: "St. Petersburg 1867" and "84." Unlike European gold and silver objects that are marked with the artist's symbol and often the city or country of production, in Islamic Judaica rarely do we have pieces with silver marks or country of

Figure 6.3 Tray, Russia (tray), Iran (decoration), 1867 to early twentieth century. Silver: engraved, traced, and cast handles. 7/8 × 13 5/8 × 21 1/2 in (2.3 × 34.6 × 54.6 cm). The Jewish Museum, New York. Gift of Dr. Harry G. Friedman, F 3222.

production on them.[26] The marks on the tray indicate the quality of the silver and the place and date of its production (in this case, Russia, 1867). However the engraved decoration was made in Iran in the beginning of the twentieth century, typical of the late Qajar style of the time, which strongly follows European models.

Overall, the pictorial element in the ornamentation of these decorative utensils is predominant. The motifs are Jewish and are executed in a distinctively Persian style. The total composition, however, strongly suggests an awareness of a new type of market— one aimed primarily at the foreign tourist trade. Unlike utensils formerly crafted solely for the Iranian market, the decorative value of these metal objects had become much more important than the functional.

Amulets

A widespread phenomenon among the Jews of Iran has been the frequent and prominent usage of amulets and amuletic jewelry. These artifacts were produced for various life-cycle occasions and rites of passage such as childbirth, circumcision, and weddings.[27] Usually made of silver, these metal pieces vary in shape (e.g., round, rectangular, case, cartouche) and in type (e.g., pendants, armlets, belt buckles). Almost all are decorated with Hebrew kabalistic inscriptions formed into varied elaborate designs and cryptograms. These kabalistic abbreviations also indicate the amulet's purpose: general protection; wishes for good health and remedies; pregnancy; assistance in difficult times; hopes for finding a life partner; means of livelihood; etc.[28] In the case of newborns, metal amulets were typically pinned to the sleeve of a shirt or dress near the shoulder and for boys were worn until the age of four or five years. Girls, in contrast, wore amulets until they were teenagers, and later during pregnancy from before childbirth until the baby was weaned from breast feeding. During labor the amulet was traditionally placed on the mother's stomach.[29]

Among amulets from Iran there is a subcategory known as *shiviti* amulets, characterized by the citation of Psalm 16:8 "I have set the Lord before me always" and Psalm 67:1–8. Psalm 67 consists of eight verses, the first of which is usually engraved horizontally on the amulet, with the remaining seven verses forming the design of a seven-branch menorah.[30] These amulets are frequently designed as pendant plaques in rectangular shape with a scalloped arch, and one or two suspension rings soldered to the top.[31] Although Psalm 67 is usually associated with a woman in childbirth, there are some rare examples of *shiviti* amulets with a man's name engraved on the back. On one example (*Figure 6.4*), kept in the GFC collection, the name "Abba ben Hajji" is engraved on the back side in addition to the names of some angels. On another silver *shiviti* amulet, part of TJM collection, the name "Mirza Khan ben Solayman" is engraved on its back.[32]

Other than kabalistic abbreviations, some of the Jewish Iranian amulets are decorated with human figures, especially the image of Lilith. According to folk tradition, Lilith, the mother of all demons who was the first Eve, had been created to harm newborn babies. She was convinced by three angels (Sanuai, Sansanuai, and Semanglof) that she would be unable to enter a house or harm a baby or its mother wherever she saw their images illustrated or their names written on an amulet.[33] On this type of amulet (*Figure 6.5*) the image of Lilith is portrayed as a frightening demon and engraved on the

Figure 6.4 Shiviti amulet, front and back, Iran, twentieth century. Silver: cut and engraved. 10.8 × 6 cm. Gross Family Collection, Tel Aviv 027.001.395.

front of the piece. The names of the three angels are usually inscribed on her belly or next to her.[34]

Ceremonial Art

Other than detailed instructions as to the writing of the Torah scroll, there are no specific directions or regulations concerning its adornments or the design and production of ceremonial objects. Consequently, Judaica artifacts evolved through different traditions and customs. In some cases Jews made the ceremonial objects. In other cases they were made by gentiles according to instructions or based on different models given to them. As in non-ceremonial secular articles, wide artistic diversity also exists in the design of Iranian Jewish religious ceremonial objects.

Figure 6.5 Amulet, Iran, first half of the twentieth century. Silver: cut and engraved. 9.7 × 6 cm. Gross Family Collection, Tel Aviv 027.001.407.

The Synagogue

The heart and center of the religious, communal, and educational lives of the Jews of Iran throughout the ages has always been the synagogue, called *kenisā* in Persian. Daily prayers during the week and congregational services on the Sabbath and holidays were held in the synagogue, which provided a sanctified space. The synagogue also served as the community's main gathering place, where an array of personal and communal interactions took place.[35] Thus far, no systematic art history research and documentation has been conducted on these monuments. We do not have sufficient information concerning the exact number and the specific artistic features of Iranian synagogues over the course of the centuries in which the Jews lived in Iran. The evidence we do possess at this stage is fragmentary and disjointed, and generally limited to descriptions by eyewitnesses from the eighteenth and nineteenth centuries in addition to visual material such as photographs from the late nineteenth through the twentieth century.[36] In recent years, however, private individuals have taken the initiative of documenting and photographing existing synagogues and other Jewish public spaces across Iran, posting all visual material online, where it is accessible.[37]

These partial sources of information point to the generally poor and shabby condition of many of the synagogues in Iran throughout the eighteenth and nineteenth centuries, during which time Jews suffered severe material hardship and almost constant emotional and physical persecution. Under Shi'ite restrictions, Jews were not permitted to build new synagogues, but were only allowed to maintain and repair old ones. As such, they faced considerable difficulties both in maintaining existing synagogues and building new ones. Following the restrictions of the pact of Umar, Muslim law and Shi'ite restriction controlled the synagogues' location, size, height, and the material used for their construction.[38] In part due to these restrictions, existing synagogues consequently became the focal point of areas that would eventually come to be known as Jewish quarters, or *mahalleh*s, in various cities throughout Iran. Typically, the structure of the synagogue would be low, not to exceed in height any Muslim monument as mandated by Shi'ite laws. The buildings are typically simple and modest on the outside as well as in the interior. Prior to the mid-twentieth century, there were neither galleries nor seats of any type in the synagogue, and the entire congregation would sit on the carpet-covered floor, having removed their shoes before entering the main sanctuary. The only article of furniture in the synagogue would be the *tevah* or *bimah* [the reader's desk], which was also covered with carpets or decorative textiles; a practice that is continued to date. The *heykhal* or ark is located in the wall oriented toward Jerusalem. Unlike those of Western synagogues, the ark consists of an arched niche or hollow in the wall with wooden doors or a curtain before it, or both.

An interesting and exceptional example of an architectural fragment of an Iranian synagogue is a portion of a mosaic wall currently in TJM's permanent collection.[39] The monumental wall, which possibly dates to sixteenth-century Isfahan, comprises three arched niches covered by monochromatic sections of faïence tiles that were cut after firing [*kāshi-kār*], forming an elaborate design of arabesques, flowers, and leaves. On the upper part of the wall we find two Hebrew inscriptions taken from Psalms 118:20 and 5:8, indicating that the wall was produced for a place of worship. On a different architectural fragment we find a passage from Genesis 28:17, which designates that this is the house of God. The arched fragment dates to the eighteenth or nineteenth century, and is also said to have come from a synagogue in Isfahan.[40] A small glazed tile form Kashan dating to the twelfth–thirteenth century with the Hebrew inscription "*sakhih khod*" is the earliest known evidence of a synagogue or Jewish communal building in Iran.[41] However, since none of the fragments here mentioned were found *in situ*, it is impossible to determine whether or not they were actually installed in any particular synagogue.

Torah Ornaments

Torah Cases
Traditionally, the Torah scroll is housed in a wooden or metal case known as *tiq*, which contributes both to the beautification and

adornment of the ritual and to the protection of the penned parchment. Regional variations in the shape and decoration of the Torah case can be noted among the various Jewish communities. However, there is no sufficient literary evidence or material findings that enable us to portray accurately the development of the Torah case in Iran prior to the nineteenth century. Nevertheless, research conducted thus far points to two main prototypes of a Torah case, each with its own subcategories and variations (*Figure 6.6*).[42] The first type emerged in Baghdad according to the Babylonian tradition and continued to appear and develop in western Iran. It consists of cylindrical or faceted cases, with either an onion- or bulbous-shaped dome. Two rods for Torah finials are set in the onion-shaped crown. At times four or six rods stick out diagonally from the bulbous-shaped crown case. Usually, the case is made of wood, often covered with richly decorated plaques of silver repoussé and chased work. Alternatively, such cases are sometimes covered in leather or a kind of rich fabric with metal decorations attached. The inner halves of the crown are decorated with dedication inscriptions.[43] The second type, distinctive to eastern and central Iran, consists of polyhedrons or cylindrical wood cases with a flat top and rods for two or three pairs of Torah finials. One pair of rods act as the upper ends of the Torah staves [*atzei haim*], and they stick out through round openings in the center of the case top. The reaming pairs are smaller rods placed in front and behind the Torah staves. At times, the case is richly covered with luxurious fabric, such as velvet, that is bound to the wood with silver nails, often in a decorative design. Customarily, a dedicatory silver plaque adorns the case.[44] Both types of cases were customarily decorated with women's silk scarves or other fine textiles donated for this purpose.

Torah Finials

Customarily, Torah finials are placed upon the Torah staves in order to beautify and glorify the Torah scroll. Among the Jewish communities across Iran two main types of Torah finials have evolved, each with its own subgroups (*Figure 6.7*).[45] The first type is a pair of globular finials referred to by the Hebrew word

Figure 6.6 Torah case, Persia, 1861/2 (date of inscription). Wood: painted. Silver, brass: cut, chased, punched. 103.3 × 31 cm. Gross Family Collection, Tel Aviv 048.010.001.

Figure 6.7 Torah finials, Persia, 1862 (date of inscription). Silver: chased. Each 12 × 4 in (30.5 × 10.2 cm). The Jewish Museum, New York. Gift of Dr. Harry G. Friedman, F 3342a–b. Photo by John Parnell.

rimonim [pomegranates]. Rimonim are usually made out of chased and/or repoussé silver decorated in floral and/or geometric patterns. A dedicatory inscription may also be engraved on a horizontal band around the body of the rimonim, which in most cases commemorates the name of the donor.[46] The second type, most common among the Jewish communities of eastern Iran, consists of a pair of flat finials called *ketarim* [crowns]. Dedicatory inscriptions of passages from the Torah and Kabalistic texts generally adorn both sides of these finials.[47] Both types of finials are additionally adorned with sets of bells that hang either around the narrow shaft, the globular body, or the top disk. Other than the aesthetic purpose of embellishing the Torah scroll, the Torah finials of the Jews of Iran also demonstrate the use of a common artistic vocabulary. A case in point is the *boteh* [paisley] shaped finials. The boteh (a droplet-shaped vegetable motif of Persian and Indian origin) has been widespread in Iranian art and material culture since the Sassanid period. Its unique shape consists of a stylized floral spray and a cypress tree, which symbolized eternal life in Zoroastrian tradition.[48]

Torah Pointers

The Torah pointer is an object used by the person reading from the Torah scroll in the synagogue to indicate the exact place of reading. Interestingly, the pointer is not considered a ritual object since its use is purely functional and intended only to assist the reader. However, it is considered holy when used as a decorative element of the Torah, either when hanging from one of its staves or attached to the shield. Middle Eastern Jewish communities call the pointer *ghalam* [pen]; and Iranian Jews in particular call it *ghalam-turā* [Torah-pen]. The typical shape of the pointers used by the Jews of Iran is of a straight bar with a pointing end shaped like an open hand.[49]

Elijah's Chair and Staff

Typically, two chairs are used in the Jewish circumcision [*brit milah*] ceremony: one for the prophet Elijah and the other for the godfather, the *sandak*. According to the Midrash (Pirke De-Rabbi Eliezer, 28), Elijah complained that Israel had forsaken the covenant of the Lord, whereupon God ordained that no circumcision should take place without Elijah being present. As "The Angel of Covenant," Elijah is thus thought to be the guardian of the child at the circumcision ritual.[50] Called *takht-e milla* [circumcision seat] or *sandali-ye elyāhu hannāvi* [prophet Elijah's chair], among the Jews of Iran the chair was the property of the community and was thus kept in the synagogue. When needed, the chair was brought to the family's home for use at the ceremony. Lavishly embroidered textiles were draped over the back of the chair and a decorated cane known as Elijah's staff was placed next to it. The staff was further placed on or near the baby boy's bed for a few weeks for protection against the evil eye.[51] According to an Afghani Jewish folktale, Elijah the prophet, somewhat exhausted from participating in so many circumcision ceremonies, pauses to rest in his chair or lean upon his staff.[52]

As furniture and chairs in particular were introduced into Iranian homes during the Qajar period under European influence, no Iranian

Elijah chairs have been discovered hitherto predating the nineteenth century. A unique example from a private collection, made of carved wood and gesso and decorated with lacquer work and silver plaques, is said to have been rescued from a synagogue in Shiraz in the early twentieth century.[53] A lavishly engraved silver Elijah's staff, presently part of TJM collection, had been in the possession of a Jewish Iranian family for some generations and was in use in the family's circumcision ceremonies until the mid-twentieth century.[54] Interestingly, this ritual of Elijah's staff lingers nowadays, as demonstrated by a contemporary wooden staff belonging to a private collection.[55]

Spice Containers

The Jewish religious ceremony *havdalah* [separation] marks the symbolic end of Shabbat and holidays and ushers in the new week. Part of the ceremony requires sniffing a sweet-smelling spice or plant. Among Jewish communities living in Muslim lands, including the Jews of Iran, branches of aromatic plants such as myrtle or mint are used for this purpose. Among European Jews, in contrast, the use of a specially designed spice box or container is most common. The common type of this ceremonial vessel in synagogues across Iran was a glazed ceramic vase, in which fresh plants were placed. One pair example of this vessel is kept in TJM collection.[56] It is dedicated to two brothers: "Reuven and Shim'on sons of Shemuel" and dates to 1923. The passage (taken from Song of Songs 2:6) and the blessing over the spices ("Blessed art thou, God, our Lord, King of the universe, creator of spices") that adorn the two pieces clearly indicate their function. In the twentieth century, rosewater sprinklers and incense burners were adopted from the native Muslim culture, and their function was altered occasionally, when they would serve as spice containers. In the Muslim world, rosewater sprinklers are common for everyday use as well as special occasions as a sign of hospitality when welcoming visitors. During the *brit milah* ceremony, for example, a rosewater bottle was available for the fragrance to be sprinkled in the room and for the guests to sprinkle a few drops on their fingers.[57]

Textiles

Decorated textiles are one of the distinctive features of affluent domestic interiors. They provide household furnishing and clothing, function as symbols of power and social status, and play a vital economic role in industry and trade.[58] Generally, textiles and costumes convey messages regarding the economic and social class of the wearer, as well as the individual's occupation, ethnoreligious affiliation, and marital status.[59] Textiles in different shapes and sizes, decorated with various techniques, fulfilled many ceremonial and non-ceremonial functions in the life of the Jews of Iran. They were used at home, especially in life-cycle festivities and on holidays, as well as in public spaces such as synagogues and bath houses. As in many traditional societies, decorated textiles of various kinds played a central role in the formation of the dowry and contributed to defining one's status within the community.

Needlecraft/Embroidery

Needlecraft or embroidery [*sokmeh-duzi, nakh-duzi, golabetun*] is generally not an industry or a formed craft, but work done by women (and sometimes men) in the house. Little is known in research about its development or expansion, and it would be somewhat challenging to portray an overview of this domestic skill. Over the centuries, embroidery techniques—e.g., "stiches"—have developed across Iran. The satin-stitch, known in Iran as *tiraz*, developed under Chinese influence and was common during the thirteen and fourteen centuries. In the sixteenth–seventeenth centuries a regional technique of cross-stitch characterized northwest Iran; however, the style of gold embroidery called *malileh-duzi* flourished all over Iran until the present. The term *malileh* applies to fine gold and silver threads used for textile work and also for jewelry making, in what is called filigree work [*malileh-kari*] in the West.[60] In this type of embroidery the metal thread is initially twisted into a spring-like coil before being applied to the fabric. This particular technique also allowed for pearls to be added occasionally to the embroidery.[61]

Malileh-duzi was frequently used in decorating household items such as cushion covers, and in outfits and clothes such as jackets, gowns, and skirts. Velvet women's jackets kept at the EIM collection are but two such examples.[62] In addition to velvet, gold and silver embroidery was also employed on silks and brocades. Examples from the same collection include a blue silk and taffeta woman's urban costume form nineteenth-century Mashhad, and a twentieth-century pink brocade silk head kerchief.[63]

A special embroidery technique most common among the Jews of Iran is the *naghdeh-duzi*, or tinsel. In this case the flattened metal thread is directly embroidered onto a tulle fabric.[64] Among the Jews of Iran the dowry items were usually listed in a document known as *shtar* (a Talmudic term for an agreement, similar to a contract). The items listed in this document usually included clothing, household furnishings, money, silver objects, and sets of velvet or tulle bed and pillow covers that were embroidered with metallic gold or silver thread.[65] The traditional bridal dress of the Jewish Iranian women was made of white tulle decorated with the naghdeh-duzi technique of embroidery. In an interesting nineteenth-century example from TJM collection, the skirt and sleeves are embroidered with sprigs of flowers alternating with sequins.[66] The wide collar is decorated with larger flowers in gold tinsel and is bordered by an undulating line from which sprigs emerge. The waistband bears a Hebrew inscription, which makes the piece unusual. In addition to the dress, a tulle scarf [*chahār-ghad*] or veil [*chādor*] was used to cover the bride's hair during the ceremony. On the first Shabbat after her wedding and during other ceremonial occasions, the tulle scarf was used by the bride to cover her hair at the synagogue.[67] The embroidered veils were customarily handed down from generation to generation in many families. Nowadays, some tend to frame pieces from the *naghdeh* to be hung on the wall as artwork.

Ghalamkār: Woodblock Printing

Ghalamkār is the craft of woodblock printing, which typically combines block-printing, dyeing, and hand-painting in four colors

Figure 6.8 Wall hanging, Persia, *c*.1850. Cotton: block-printed and painted. 96 × 54 in (243.8 × 137.2 cm). The Jewish Museum, New York, U 7025. Photo by Richard Goodbody, Inc.

(black, red, yellow, blue) on cotton fabrics. These textiles have customarily been used for a variety of purposes, including wall hangings, tablecloths, bed covers and clothing.[68] Prior to the nineteenth century, Indian imports had dominated this branch of the textile industry in Iran. Since the mid-nineteenth century, domestic ghalamkar production has suffered a decline due to the importation of cheaper and better quality fabric from Europe. The craft of ghalamkar was revived again after World War II due to demand from the international market. This type of craft was a specialty of Isfahan, where a number of workshops and guild masters operated. In the 1970s another slowdown of the ghalamkar industry occurred as a result of anti-pollution laws and import limitation after the 1979 revolution.[69] Long rectangular or square sheets of ghalamkar work were generally used for hanging in front of niches, as decorative wall hangings, or as floor covering. Identifiable Jewish examples served both in Jewish homes and in synagogues and are usually stamped with Hebrew inscriptions (*Figure 6.8*). At times, the fabrics have been used for ceremonial purposes on Shabbat or festive occasions (e.g., Passover, Purim)[70] and others used in decorating the Sukkoth.[71] Often, they were used as *parokhet* [Torah ark curtain] in synagogues and for covering the Torah cases. An array of symbolic and religious motifs are depicted on these colorful and lively textiles according to traditional Persian and Jewish artistic conventions.

Carpets

Due to the absence of both fitted and movable furnishing up until the nineteenth century, the most important textile in Iranian domestic culture was floor coverings, more specifically carpets.[72] Heavy textiles, commonly made of wool and cotton and sometimes silk, used to cover floors, walls, and other large surfaces, comprise an essential part of Iranian art and culture. Although carpet weaving has a long history in Iran, the earliest surviving Persian carpets are from the sixteenth–seventeenth centuries when royal Safavid carpet workshops were established in Isfahan, Kashan, and Kerman. There is much variety in Persian carpets, which were frequently designed by illuminators of manuscripts.[73] Common motifs include scrolling vine networks, arabesques, palmettes, medallions, and overlapping geometric compartments, rather than animals and human figures.[74] The preferred choice for floral patterns was mainly to harmonize with the lavish interior decoration of the house and revealed a strong affinity to tilework and to carved and painted plaster work (stucco). During the nineteenth century, a taste for large-scale pictorial carpets began to develop with the influence of Qajar art.[75] Jewish Persian carpets often featured Jewish figural motifs. Biblical imagery, scenes of the Holy Land, and sites of Jewish religious significance, as well as Hebrew inscription were included in the design of these beautifully woven carpets.[76]

Summary

The material culture of the Jews of Iran encompasses a wide range of mediums such as textiles, metalwork, woodwork, ceramics, painting, and more. While most of these objects served either a decorative or practical function, some were also part of various social rituals and customs, as well as part of religious life. On some occasions Jews themselves made the ceremonial objects, while in others the objects were made by non-Jews according to specific instructions or by copying familiar models. At times, Jews borrowed some of these objects from the surrounding Iranian culture, adapting them to Jewish ritual function either through modification of the object or the addition of Hebrew inscriptions. Overall, these material culture and ritual objects are a living testimony to the assimilation of Muslim and Persian cultural and aesthetic values into the daily life of the Jews of Iran.

Acknowledgements

I wish to thank Shalom Sabar and Houman Sarshar for reading the draft of this article and for their helpful remarks. List of abbreviations used here: GFC—Gross Family Collection, Tel Aviv; EIM—Eretz-Israel Museum, Tel Aviv; IMJ—Israel Museum Jerusalem; JLMM—Judah L. Magnes Museum Berkeley; JNUL—Jewish National University Library Jerusalem; TJM—The Jewish Museum New York; YBZ – Yad Ben Zvi Jerusalem.

Notes

1 Most of the studies published up to now focus mainly on the ceremonial and ritual objects of the Jews of Iran. Two of the subjects in which most research was conducted are the decorated ketubbah and the Torah ornaments. For examples see: Shalom Sabar, *Ketubbah: Jewish Marriage Contracts of the Hebrew Union College Skirball Museum and Klau Library* (Philadelphia, 1990); Shalom Sabar, "Ha-Hatkhalot shel ha-ktubah ha-me'uteret be-kehilot Paras ve-Afganistan," *Pe'amim*, 79 (1999), pp. 129–58; Bracha Yaniv, *Ma'aseh khoshev: Ha-tiq lesefer Torah ve-toldotav* (Jerusalem & Ramat-Gan, 1998); Bracha Yaniv, "Tokhen ve-tzurah be-rimone keter mi-mizrakh Paras ve-Afganistan," *Pe'amim*, 79 (1999), pp. 96–128. In 2010 the first ever art exhibit about Iranian Jewry was held in Tel Aviv. For the catalogue see: *Light and Shadows: The Story of Iran and the Jews* (Tel Aviv, 2010).

2 As of the time of this publication, not all art collections listed above have been fully catalogued, documented, and published in research. As regards the collection of The Jewish Museum New York, in the years 2008–10, the author conducted a comprehensive research project, funded by the Leon Levy Foundation, cataloguing and documenting the museum's collection of Islamic Judaica. A large number of examples discussed in this article are taken, therefore, from this collection.

3 The author is relying on oral testimonies given to her by members of the Jewish Iranian community in Israel, New York, Los Angeles, and Milan.

4 Esther Juhasz, "Material Culture," in Reeva Spector Simon, Michael Menachem Laskier, and Sara Reguer (eds), *The Jews of the Middle East and North Africa in Modern Times* (New York, 2003), pp. 205–23.

5 For more about the political and social position of the Jews in Iran, see: Sorour Soroudi, "Jews in Islamic Iran," *The Jerusalem Quarterly*, 21 (1981), pp. 99–114; Daniel Tsadik, *Between Foreigners and Shi'is: Nineteenth-Century Iran and its Jewish Minority* (Stanford, 2007); David Yeroushalmi, *The Jews of Iran in the Nineteenth Century: Aspects of History, Community, and Culture* (Leiden, 2009).

6 For a detailed index of 12 of the illustrated Judeo-Persian manuscripts and the subjects of the paintings, see: Vera B. Moreen, *Miniature Paintings to Judeo Persian Manuscripts* (Cincinnati, 1985). As opposed to the comprehensive study of the Judeo Persian language and literature, only a handful of studies have been published about the illustrated Judeo Persian manuscripts. For examples see: Joseph Gutmann, "Judeo Persian Miniature," *Studies in Bibliography and Booklore*, 8 (1968), pp. 54–76; Alice Taylor, *Book Arts of Isfahan: Diversity and Identity in 17th Century Persia* (Malibu, 1995); Orit Carmeli, "Persian Jewish Art in a Time of Religious Persecutions," *Iran, Bukhara, Afghanistan*, 2 (2008), pp. 156–68.

7 For more about the poet and his literary works see: David Yeroushalmi, *The Judeo Persian Poet Emrani and his Book of Treasure* (Leiden, 1995).

8 For a survey of the Ben-Zvi Institute's collection of Judeo-Persian manuscripts see: Amnon Netzer, *Otzar kitve ha-yad shel yehude Paras be-makhon Ben-Zvi* (Jerusalem, 1986).

9 Another illustrated copy of Emrani's text is kept in the British Library in London, Ms. Or. 13704. For comparison between the two manuscripts, see: Orit Carmeli, "Ha-Eurim me-toch ktav ha-yad Fath-namah le-Emrani, Yerushalaim, Yad Itzhak ben Zvi, Mispar 4602" (unpublished M.A. Thesis, The Hebrew University, Jerusalem, 2004).

10 For image see: Hayim Sa'adoun (ed.), *Jewish Communities in the East in the Nineteenth and Twentieth Centuries: Iran* (Jerusalem, 2005), p.192.

11 For visual examples from the Ottoman Empire see: D. Terzioglu, "The Imperial Circumcision Festival of 1582: An Interpretation," *Muqarnas*, 12 (1995), pp. 84–100. For an example from Moghul India, see "Humayun at the Celebrations of Akbar's Circumcision," in Abu'l Fazl ibn Mubarak, *Akbar-Nameh* (India, 1603–4). London, The British Library, Or. 12988, fol. 114.

12 Natalia Berger, "Kley milah: bien tashmishe mitzvah le-bien kelim refueeim," *Rimonim*, 5 (1997), pp. 29–42, figs 2–3.

13 IMJ 180/54, fol. 38a.

14 The subject of the Iranian decorated ketubbah has been researched extensively. For examples see: David Davidovitch, *The Ketuba: Jewish Marriage Contracts through the Ages* (Tel Aviv, 1985); Sabar, 1990; Sabar, 1999.

15 Vivian B. Mann & Norman L. Kleeblatt, *Masterworks of The Jewish Museum* (New Haven & London, 2004), pp. 106–7.

16 Sabar, 1999, fig. b.

17 For examples see: TJM – F4224, F 4225; YBZ – 251, 252; JUNL – 436, 413.

18 Claudia J. Nahson, *Ketubbot: Marriage Contracts from The Jewish Museum* (New York, 1998), plate 25.

19 For more about the great famine of 1871/2 in Iran see: Yeroushalmi, 2009, pp. 321–45.

20 Raphael Patai, *Jadīd al-Islām: The Jewish New Muslims of Meshhed* (Michigan, 1997); Jaleh Pirnazar, "The Anusim of Mashhad," in Houman Sarshar (ed.), *Esther's Children: A Portrait of Iranian Jews* (Philadelphia, 2002), pp. 115–36.

21 Nahson, 1998, plate 31. IMJ – 179/196.

22 For more about Islamic metalwork see: A. S. Melikian-Chirvnani, *Islamic Metalwork from the Iranian World 8th–18th Centuries* (London, 1982). For more about Jewish silversmithry and jewelry making in Iran and Kurdistan see: Amnon Netzer, "Hatzurfot ve-hakhkshuri bekerev yehudei Iran," *Pe'amim*, 11 (1982), pp. 56–62; Ora Shwartz-Be'eri, "Tzurfot kesef shel yehudim be-Kurdistan," *Pe'amim*, 25 (1985), pp. 102–22.

23 Myriam Rosen-Ayalon, "Tachshitim ve-tzurfot be-olam ha-islam," *Pe'amim*, 11 (1982), pp. 7–16.

24 Jay & Sumi Gluck (eds), *A Survey of Persian Handicraft: A Pictorial Introduction to the Contemporary Folk Arts and Art Crafts of Modern Iran* (Tehran, 1977), pp. 18, 127–30, 143; H. E. Wulff, *The Traditional Crafts of Persia: Their Development, Technology, and Influence on Eastern and Western Civilizations* (Cambridge, 1966), pp. 8, 35–7.

25 Laurence D. Loeb, "Creating Antiques for Fun and Profit: Encounters Between Iranian Jewish Merchants and Touring Coreligionists," in Valene L. Smith (ed.), *Hosts and Guests: The Anthropology of Tourism* (Philadelphia, 1977), pp. 236–45.

26 Nevertheless, silver marks and workshop names can be found on Yemenite jewelry. For examples see: Naomi Feuchtwanger, "Tsamid neillo teymani ve-yikhodo," *Pe'amim*, 11 (1982), pp. 94–101; Esther Muchawsky-Schnapper, *The Yemenites: Two Thousand Years of Jewish Culture* (Jerusalem, 2000).

27 Shalom Sabar, "Hakmei'ot shel yehudei Iran," in Hayim Sa'adoun (ed.), *Kehilot Yisrael ba-mizrakh ha-me'ot ha-tesha 'esreh ve-ha-'esrim: Iran* (Jerusalem, 2005), pp. 220–1.

28 T. Schrire, *Hebrew Magic Amulets: Their Decipherment and Interpretation* (New York, 1982).

29 Leah Baer, "Life's Events: Birth, Bar Mitzva, Wedding and Burial Customs," in Houman Sarshar (ed.), 2002, pp. 311–36.

30 For more about the symbolism of the shiviti see: Esther Juhasz, *Ha-Shiviti— Menorah: Bein mufshat le-khomri, 'eyunim be-yitzug ha-kodesh*, unpublished Ph.D. dissertation, The Hebrew University Jerusalem, 2004.

31 For examples see: Isaiah Shachar, *Jewish Tradition in Art: The Feuchtwanger Collection of Judaica* (Jerusalem, 1971), nos. 875–7.

32 TJM – F 2920.

33 Shalom Sabar, "Childbirth and Magic: Jewish Folklore and Material Culture" in D. Biale (ed.), *Cultures of the Jews: A New History* (New York, 2002), pp. 671–722.

34 IMJ – 103/545, 103/513.

35 Yeroushalmi, 2009, pp. 121–4.

36 For example: Laurence D. Loeb, "Travels Through Iran: A Photo Journal," in Houman Sarshar (ed.), 2002, pp. 337–72.

37 The website 7dorim.com has recently started a photo archive of many of the synagogues in Iran. Although not all Iranian cities with a Jewish population are yet represented in the archive, the majority of the synagogues in Tehran were already covered at the time of this publication. The webmasters plan to include all the synagogues in Iran in their archive [editor's note].

38 Yeroushalmi, 2009, pp. 121–30; Elkan Nathan Adler, *Jews in Many Lands*, (Philadelphia, 1905), pp. 173–95; Azaria Levy, "Batei Kenest be-Iran," Et-Mol, 12:6 (1987), pp. 18–19.

39 Mann & Kleeblatt, 2004, pp. 100–1.

40 Sarshar (ed.), 2002, p. 71, figure 1342.

41 Rachel Hasson, "Ktovet 'ivrit 'al haftzim muslemyiem me-yemei ha-beynaim be-Paras," in Shalom Sabar (ed.), *Bein yahadot le-islam be-rei ha-omanot: divre hakenes ha-'esrim ve-shiv'ah shel ha-agodah le-omanot yehudit* (Jerusalem, 1995), pp. 42–3.

42 Yaniv, 1998, pp. 61–73; Ruth Jacoby, "Al tisha'h tikim le-sefer Torah me-Paras," *Iran, Bukhara, Afghanistan*, 4 (2011), pp. 96–112.

43 IMJ – 145/034; *Light and Shadows*, 2010, p.143.

44 For examples see: Zohar Hanegbi and Bracha Yaniv, *Afghanistan: The Synagogue and the Jewish Home* (Jerusalem, 1991), figures 19, 20, 21, 25; *Light and Shadows*, 2010, p. 139.

45 Much has been written about the Persian Torah finials. For examples see: Bracha Yaniv, "The Mystery of the Flat Torah Finials from East Persia," in Amnon Netzer (ed.), *Pādyāvand*, vol. 1 (Costa Mesa, 1996–7), pp. 63–74; Yaniv, 1999.

46 For examples see: Rafi Grafman & Vivian B. Mann, *Crowning Glory: Silver Torah Ornaments of The Jewish Museum New York* (Boston, 1996), cat. 436–9.

47 For images see: Yaniv, 1999, figures 2, 9, 10.

48 IMJ – 145/034. *Light and Shadows*, 2010, pp. 136, 239.

49 For image see: Sa'adoun, 2005, p. 107; Ruth Jacoby, *Etzba and Kulmos: The Torah Pointer in the Persian World*, unpublished Ph.D. dissertation, The Hebrew University Jerusalem, 2005.

50 For more about the Midrash and the ritual see: Shalom Sabar, *Jewish Communities in the East in the Nineteenth and Twentieth Centuries: The Life Cycle* (Jerusalem, 2006), pp 61–6.

51 Baer, 2002, p. 313.

52 Hanegbi & Yaniv, 1991, pp. 34–5. It has been suggested in research that the use of Elijah's staff and chair was practiced by the Jews of Bukhara and Afghanistan and was not an Iranian Jewish tradition. Oral testimonies of members of the

community, however, indicate that these ceremonial objects were in use among the Jews of Iran in the late nineteenth century through the twentieth century.

53 Sarshar, 2002, figure 1030, p. 312. For example from mid-twentieth century see: *Light and Shadows*, 2010, p. 136

54 TJM – 1993–233.

55 Sarshar, 2002, p. 314.

56 TJM – F 1111a,b.

57 For examples see: Sa'adoun, 2005, p. 204; Sarshar, 2002, figure 1101, pp. 323, 313.

58 Jenifer Scarce, *Domestic Culture in the Middle East: An Exploration of the Household Interior* (Edinburgh, 1996), p. 5.

59 Juhasz, 2003, p. 208.

60 Wulff, 1966, pp. 33, 217–19.

61 Sarshar, 2002, p. 322, figure 1108.

62 Nitza Behroozi-Baroz (ed.), *Shimmering Gold: The Splendor of Gold Embroidered Textiles* (Tel Aviv, 2007), cat. 31–2.

63 Behroozi-Baroz, 2007, cat. 30, 33.

64 Sarshar, 2002, p. 322, Figure 1108. The *naghdeh* technique is often cited by members of the Persian Jewish community; however it is not discussed anywhere in research other than the aforementioned source.

65 Baer, 2002, p. 319.

66 TJM – 1983–300.

67 TJM – 1980–51, 1993–231; Sarshar, 2002, p. 132, figure 319; p. 322, figure 1104.

68 Wulff 1966, pp. 224–6; Aliza Baginski, "A Group of Qalamkār Fabrics in the Israel Museum," *Iranian Studies*, 25 (1992), pp. 91–101.

69 Gluck, 1977, pp. 192–3.

70 TJM – U 7025, U 7026; JLMM – 2009.19.8; Isaiah Shachar, *Jewish Tradition in Art: The Feuchtwanger Collection Judaica* (Jerusalem, 1971), no. 474.

71 Sa'adoun, 2005, p. 207.

72 Scarce, 1996, p. 68.

73 B. Bier, (ed.), *Woven from the Soul, Spun from the Heart: Textile Arts of Safavid and Qajar Iran* (Washington, 1987).

74 Still, some examples show figures engaged either in the hunt or feasting scenes.

75 Scarce, 1996, pp. 69–70.

76 Anton Felton, "Jewish Persian Carpets," in Houman Sarshar (ed.), 2002, pp. 295–310; Anton Felton, *Jewish Carpets: A History and Guide* (Woodbridge, 1997).

CHAPTER 7

THE THINGS THEY LEFT BEHIND[1]

Judith L. Goldstein

In the past, a big house, a luxury car, a fat bank account, a sea
coast resort, being associated with the treacherous regime and
possibly with foreigners or with America itself, even having a
bigger desk in the office, was the mark of values [. . .]. Today the
revolution has completely reversed this [. . .]. These have
become anti-values. Those who have a bit of luxurious life are
embarrassed. Those who are above average keep a low profile, do
not brag about it. No longer can people be deceived by these
fancy appearances [. . .].[2]

A teacup, cufflinks, a copper tray: these everyday things, when
recalled in speech and writing, sometimes become witness-objects
through which the emotional and physical cost of change can be
measured. Delineating the remembered object—the thing left
behind—as a narrative strategy refocuses our readings of diasporic
women's literature. Contemporary Jewish Iranian women's writing
records a picture of life in Iran before and after leaving Iran (following
the 1979 Islamic Revolution),[3] and provides examples of how history
works through objects. Material objects structure both the memories
of the novels' characters and the novels and memoirs themselves.

Ordinary objects, rendered extraordinary in their absence, act as vehicles that transport the narrator to other times and places, and enable the reader access to those experiences.

By focusing on the material world, I displace the self onto the surrounding world of objects and environments (home, place of business, prison, street). Considering the role of material possessions in Iran, life-writing offers an entry into the themes that concern me in what follows: witnessing, ownership, identity and value. What happens to the idea of a common culture when inclusiveness is redefined? In the time of dramatic change recounted in Iranian diasporic life-writing, new regimes of value confront older ones. The resulting contestations are articulated not only through persons, but through the medium of objects as well.

The Fates of Persons and Things

I start with one book, Dalia Sofer's *The Septembers of Shiraz*, to initiate a more general discussion of remembered objects and their role in what I call "genealogies of diminishment."

The chapters of Dalia Sofer's novel *The Septembers of Shiraz* alternate among the lives of the members of a Jewish Iranian family: the father Isaac Amin who is in prison in Tehran, Isaac's wife Farnaz and daughter Shirin who remain in their home in Tehran, and their son Parviz who is living in New York City. Looked at from a slightly different point of view, however, we can say that the book alternates between two dominant intersecting narratives. One concerns the fate of Isaac and his fellow prisoners, and the other traces the status of his possessions (appropriately, the original hardback version of the novel featured a tilted copper tea pot instead of the images of women on the covers of other memoirs and novels). Both these narratives—the first through the medium of persons, the second through the medium of things—are genealogies of diminishment.

Isaac Amin is arrested by the Revolutionary Guard in the office of his gem factory in the very first pages of *The Septembers of Shiraz*. "Isaac shuts the inventory notebook before him. He looks down at his desk, at the indifferent items witnessing this event—the scattered files, a metal paperweight, a box of Dunhill cigarettes, a crystal ashtray, and a cup of tea, freshly brewed, two mint leaves floating inside" (Sofer, p. 1). What does it mean that these items were "witnessing this event"? As witnesses, they vouched for the life that Isaac was forced to leave. Some of the witness-objects, like the metal paperweight or crystal ashtray, could potentially outlive Isaac, while the more ephemeral ones—a fresh cup of tea, a cigarette— stood for the simple freedoms that Isaac would lose. They would be the sole "indifferent" or neutral observers in what would be the battle of wills and ideologies that constitutes much of the novel.

Isaac, on his release months later, his life entirely overturned, visits his office and finds these objects still there, still "indifferent" to the revolution in his life:

> His desk is the only object in the office left untouched. His files are scattered everywhere, the calendar still open to the date of his arrest, the scribbled appointments now infused with the knowledge that they would never be met. Even the glass of tea is where he left it, filled now with greenish layers of fungus. Everything else, including the furniture, the stonecutting equipment, and the jewels, is gone. (Sofer, p. 281)

The most ephemeral object—the cup of tea he never got to drink on the day of his arrest—is still there, no longer drinkable. Isaac's physical condition has also changed. He is thin, hesitant, anxious; his feet, swollen from lashings, won't fit into his shoes. The novel tells the story of what happened to the "furniture, the stonecutting equipment, and the jewels" that are now gone, and what happened to Isaac that changed him physically and emotionally.

In *The Septembers of Shiraz* objects are witnesses, as noted above. They are also carriers of their owners' identities. For the most part, these identities are unstable; the owners (only) imagine that their longed-for identities are carried and communicated by the objects with which they surround themselves. For these people, the objects and the identities they are meant to create are "aspirational"—they indicate a status desired but not quite achieved. As such, the objects are believed to be important as a means of moving Jews from the provincial lower classes they occupied, to the urban middle and upper middle classes of Tehran. Ironically, perhaps, the more possessions matter to their owners, the more threatened their status appears.

Even before the revolution, the exaggerated importance of the objects signified insecurity as much or more than it signified the materialism of which their owners are accused in the course of the book. After the revolution the imagined identities are even more unstable, because they index social relations that the revolution has unsettled and because the interpretations of what the objects signify are no longer shared. The novel provides the narrative for the ideological turn Ali Akbar Hashemi Rafsanjani is proposing (as much or more than describing) when he said that luxuries have become "anti-values."

The two intersecting narratives in *The Septembers of Shiraz* document the destabilization of identity. In the prison narrative, Isaac undergoes the physical hardship of prison life and a series of interrogations in which he progressively loses agency as he tries, with increasing desperation, to find a common ground, an agreed upon point of reality, with his interrogator Mohsen. He struggles not so much to clarify what is in his own mind as to figure out what will satisfy his interrogator, thus displacing his identity onto his interrogator rather than external objects or social roles.

In this place of no possessions, Isaac uses memorized texts to help himself endure and to connect with others. Isaac does this with his fellow prisoners when he diffuses a difficult situation by citing the poetry of Hafez. The poetry—his possession, as well as theirs—is exchanged with his fellow prisoners with whom he does not, or has not, shared an ideology. Isaac makes a kind of offering to his cellmates of these texts, a *ta'arof* of the invisible but collectively owned.

Reza, Isaac's fellow prisoner (a leftist whose father worked for the shah) says to him: "You know what your problem is? [...] You have no beliefs. As long as you can buy your Italian shoes and your fancy watches and your villas by the sea, you're happy. 'Who cares what kind of regime it is, as long as I make money!' Right? [...] Isn't that what you're all about?" (Sofer, p. 100). Isaac thinks to himself that he is indeed not willing to die for his beliefs the way Reza is.

> 'So what?' [Isaac] says finally. 'So what if I wanted a good life [...] and waking up with my wife and children by the sea? [...] You know what is my belief [...]? My belief is that life is to be enjoyed [...]'. In the silence that follows he remembers some Hafez verses [and] recites them, without further thought. 'Give thanks for nights in good company' [...]. The other men smile; some begin to recite whatever they can remember, throwing in words here and there. (Sofer, pp. 100–1)

A memorized text is treated like a possession enjoyed in common through exchange.

In the contrasting narrative that takes place in Isaac's house, with which the prison scenes alternate, it is Isaac's possessions that come under attack. Farnaz, Isaac's wife, watches as

> they pull out their knives and split open the pillows and sofa cushions, sliding their hands through the slits in the hope of finding more evidence sewn inside. From the tops of shelves and drawers they take down her trinkets—the porcelain creamer, the copper plate, the antique silverware—and park them in a corner of the room as if preparing them for an auction. (Sofer, p. 137)

These objects, in turn, become texts that Farnaz and the searchers do not interpret in the same terms. Here there is no common ground for the exchange of goods, either material or immaterial, only destruction or appropriation.

The searcher "runs his hands through the tangled silk" of Isaac's ties.

> 'Tell me, did your husband always wear ties?' he says. 'Most of the time, yes,' Farnaz says [...]. 'So he took himself for a *farangui*—a westerner, didn't he?' 'No. He was a businessman.

He wore business attire.' 'Couldn't he conduct his business in ordinary clothes?' [...] 'I'm not sure what is considered "ordinary," Brother. A suit and tie used to be quite ordinary.' 'You're wrong. This was "ordinary" for westernized dandies, not anyone else.' (Sofer, p. 131)

Both before and after the revolution, clothing, in context, was read for social messages; but in the search of Isaac's house the meanings of dress are reframed, thus making past behavior a predictor of current status and ideology.[4]

The term "westernized dandies" is a potentially threatening ascription, as the most famous recent "westernized dandy" was the shah's prime minister from 1965–77, Amir Abbas Hoveyda, whose photographs always showed him with the orchid he wore in his button-hole, leaning on his cane, a tie or bow-tie around his neck. His dress marked him as effeminate, and he was rumored to be homosexual and Baha'i. Thus Hoveyda was caricatured as problematic for his implied sexual and religious deviance. The threat is there because Hoveyda was executed in 1979 after secret trials conducted by the "Hanging Judge" Sadeq Khalkhali. According to Afsaneh Najmabadi, the "over-Europeanized male dandy" became a "figure of cultural alterity" for twentieth-century Islamists who sought to "protect a public heterosexual space," but were deflected in their search for an Islamic modern because modernity had become identified "with either the Pahlavi state or with the nationalist, socialist, and communist Left."[5] An open collar has become a public sign of allegiance to the Islamic Republic for men, and thus, in his absence, Isaac's ties, in themselves, witnessed against him.

While excavating the house, the searchers find a silver teapot that Farnaz had thought lost. "When she sees her silver teapot, which had been missing for some time, she thanks them for finding it. 'Look how happy a piece of silver makes you,' the scruffy one says, shaking his head. 'There is no cure for your kind.' 'I bought this with my husband in Isfahan, right after our wedding,' she starts, but stops" (Sofer, p. 137). We learn that Farnaz is indeed attached to her objects, but she thinks of this attachment differently. "'So many things,

Sister,' the man says. 'Why so many?'" (Sofer, p. 138). For Farnaz, the
things measure memories, not material success.

"On long, silent afternoons, when Isaac would be at work and the
children at school, she would sit in her sun-filled living room and look
at each one [. . .]. Living among these objects assured her that hers was
a populated world" (Sofer, p. 138). Her objects return her through her
memories to another time and place. To lose an object such as the silver
teapot is to lose the possibility to be suddenly transported, at the sight
of it, to the past and to a happier time. The objects enchant her daily
life through their ability to transport her elsewhere. Beyond that,
however, after Isaac's imprisonment, those objects that mark important
stages in their relationship—such as their marriage—become
identified for her with Isaac. Losing such objects makes her fear for
his life, makes her fear she will lose him. "Look how happy a silver
teapot makes you" is right for all the wrong reasons.

Isaac, until his imprisonment, did not share Farnaz's attachment to
objects. He grew up very poor. When Farnaz married him, Isaac's
"only belongings were one old suit, a few poetry volumes, and a
photograph of his mother" (Sofer, p. 135). Once in prison, however,
he also free-associates in the presence of objects that transport him to
other places and times through the memories they invoke.

In Isaac's case, it can be the most common of objects that call forth
memories.

A slight man, masked also, [enters] holding a tarnished copper
tray on which a small glass of tea and a pyramid of sugar cubes
rest. [. . .] The spicy aroma reaches Isaac's nose from across the
table; he stares at the steaming orange liquid through the glass.
It has been freshly brewed, he can tell, and the glass, just like
the ones he has at home, just like the ones everyone has at home,
is the kind they call *kamar-barik*—'slim waisted,' because it
curves in the middle like a woman's body. (*Figure 7.1*)

Then come the personal associations that accompany the standard
object: "He bought the set with Farnaz on their first trip to Isfahan
some twenty-five years earlier, shortly after their wedding." Then the

Figure 7.1   Tea glass. Photo by Judith L. Goldstein.

association, which links the fates of objects, especially fragile objects, and people:

> The night the first one chipped, Farnaz stood still by the sink, water running over her hands. He was there, had witnessed it from his seat at the kitchen table. 'Oh, no,' he had heard her say. 'Oh, no.' And when he casually told her not to worry, they would get another set, he thought he heard a sniffle. (Sofer, pp. 13–14)

In this incident, it is one of the most ordinary and shared objects—a tea glass—that stands in for the future of a person. In prison the single tea glass—it is for the interrogator, not Isaac—also indexes a lost common culture; the culture of hospitality, and the culture in which the environment of the house and its objects—tea glasses and teapots—was familiar and shared across classes and religions.

Who now has a share in the common culture, and what is the common culture to be? This is a different—and, I think, a more central—formulation than the more familiar ones that pair opposites like religious and secular, or reformist and hardline (or Muslim and non-Muslim, Persian and ethnic). The lack of *ta'arof* on the part of Isaac's interrogator questions their common humanity as well as their respective social statuses. That no glass is offered to Isaac separates him from any social context for the senses, physical and emotional, that he experiences: "The spicy aroma reaches Isaac's nose from across the table; he stares at the steaming orange liquid through the glass. It has been freshly brewed, he can tell." The taste and comfort of tea— like the glasses, a standard part of everyday life, and one that would ordinarily give shape to each day—is denied him. His mind and body are prepared for an event that does not take place. On what grounds can claims to a common culture be made? And another question is linked to this one: on what grounds can claims to a common nation be made? Or from a slightly different point of view, what would the nation have to look like to include Isaac?

Collecting the Past: Material Culture/Common Culture

Markets for goods that are nonstandard (or nonsubstitutable in terms of quality and quantity) operate differently than markets for goods that are standardized [. . .]. Buyers and sellers of these heterogeneous goods [hand-woven carpets, used goods, antiques] face profound impediments in acquiring and trusting information about the goods traded and, by implication, trading partners.[6]

Iranian Jews have played a culturally particular, and historically deep, role in the definition and preservation of Iranian material culture. They have done this by occupying a variety of economic niches in which they have created and sustained markets for used and antique goods (and, in another register, music and traditional performance genres). Jews in the decades before the revolution moved from their traditional role as itinerant peddlers and sellers of second-hand goods to owning or managing antiques stores. During my fieldwork in Iran in the mid-1970s, I could see that these antiques stores functioned as unofficial museums and as ethnographic displays, the range of their offerings emblematic of the cultural diversity of Iran. The objects amassed in Jewish-owned antiques stores carried messages about a shared culture and a shared national identity. These messages, too, are subject to reinterpretation.

For example, it has been suggested that the indifference after the Iranian Revolution to some aspects of popular tradition has now been followed by a restored interest on the part of at least some Iranians, an artistic and intellectual elite.

> During the Shah's time it seemed that no one but foreigners collected Iranian antiques, and no one stopped them from carrying bags full of them out of the country. Nor did anyone protest when traditional old houses, with their mirrored arches and over-grown gardens and tiled courtyards, were demolished to make way for new apartment buildings. Now, though there seems to be a new regard for the old Iran. Airport officials check suitcases to stop antiques from leaving the country. The government has begun to put money into restoring old houses before they crumble away. There has been a recent proliferation of coffeehouses, restaurants, and plays, and often they have a line out the door. When I mention that I want to buy some old embroidered tapestries [...] Kambiz laughs. 'Good luck,' he says. 'Everyone wants those now. Everyone from Shahrak has already gone down to Kerman on vacation and raided the bazaars.'[7]

Bahrampour understands this change as follows: "The banning of Western influences, for all its extreme consequences, forced many middle-class, Westernized Iranians to turn to Iranian influences, and often they discovered that they liked them."[8] However, the exodus of many Jews from Iran, and the appropriation or sale of formerly Jewish-owned antiques and music stores, means an aspect of Jewish cultural activity is lost.

Isaac, with his transition from a poverty-stricken youth in Shiraz to economic success in Tehran, shows this attachment to the antique in the décor he chooses for his home. On the walls of his study Isaac had hung "newspaper clippings with yellow edges, family photographs, greeting cards, and antique swords and daggers hanging like half-moons one beneath the other, from as far back as the time of Cyrus and as recently as the 1920s" (Sofer, p. 44). As with Farnaz's mementoes, the accumulation is meaningful, not just material.

A similarly heterogeneous collection is displayed in a Jewish-owned antiques shop in Tehran. Farnaz, Isaac's wife,

surveys the shop—the pregnant belly of a sitar leaning against the round metallic face of a medieval shield, carpets and kilims hung along the walls, the footprints of their previous owners, now dead and buried, imprinted in their memory. There are French china sets, and Indian silk pillows. Silver tables engraved with figures of Cyrus or Darius stand in one corner, while in the other, in a glass-enclosed shelf, are Achaemenian jewels—a gold pendant shaped like a lion, an armlet with griffins—prized relics of an age long gone but to which people cling like proud but destitute heirs to a dead tycoon. (Sofer, pp. 214–15)

"I am a slave to my relics," the owner tells her, not without pride. As a "slave to his relics" he also serves a particular idea of an inclusive past, one that both merges with past orientalist tropes and also preserves oppositional political force; one whose valence, therefore, is not easily defined. The owner spends night and day guarding his shop, but in the end he is arrested and his store expropriated.

Through these displays, the novel's characters, and many Iranian Jews more generally, attached themselves to Iran and its past. This identity, too, has aspects of the "aspirational," especially since the revolution. The references to Cyrus in both of the descriptions cited above make this clear; the longed-for identity is one in which the pre-Islamic balances the Islamic, and Jews could live in the atmosphere of tolerance for which the reign of Cyrus (and the images that represented it) were always a shorthand signifier. Those symbols of a longed-for common culture—Cyrus and Ferdowsi's epic about pre-Islamic Iran, the *Shahnameh* (written about 1000 CE)—became explicit "anti-values" (to borrow Rafsanjani's term used in a different but related context) for some after the revolution.

Was Cyrus a tolerant ruler or the forefather of future tyrannical monarchies? "Shortly after Iran's 1979 revolution, Ayatollah Khalkhali, the infamous 'Hanging Judge,' published a book branding Cyrus a tyrant, a liar, and a homosexual. He called for the destruction of the Cyrus tomb and [...] Persepolis."[9] Some local revolutionary councils forbade the naming of newborns Cyrus (or Darius), and today "very few Iranian teenagers claim the name Kurosh or Darius (Dariush in Persian)."[10] The trajectory of Cyrus's reputation is instructive.

Both Pahlavi shahs—Reza Shah (r. 1925–41) and Mohammad Reza Shah (r. 1941–79)—used Cyrus and Persepolis as symbols of the nation in implicit and explicit opposition to the clergy (and Reza Shah built a monument to Ferdowsi in 1935).[11] Journalist Afshin Molavi cites Davoud, his friend and guide to Cyrus's tomb, on the issue (2002):

> The legacy of Cyrus the Great has been mixed up in twentieth-century Iranian politics. [...] The political discourse of this time created two prevailing views on Cyrus, both extremes. The first view is the part-royalist, part-nationalist caricature of the king as the unequaled founder of the Persian Empire, a king we should worship for achieving Iranian greatness, though this view rarely focuses on Cyrus's progressive views on religious tolerance. On the other side, the side of the Cyrus-bashers—mainly leftist intellectuals and the group of Islamic clerics who supported the revolution— Cyrus is condemned as the first in the long line of absolute monarchs strangling Iran for twenty-five hundred years. He is not a king to be loved and emulated, but just another tyrannical Shah.[12]

Figure 7.2 Persepolis figures on silver fruit bowl, courtesy of Pourustamian family. Photo by Judith L. Goldstein.

Cyrus's status (as well as Ferdowsi's) began to be renegotiated with the presidencies of Ali Akbar Hashemi Rafsanjani (1989–97) and Mohammad Khatami (1997–2005).

The evaluation of Cyrus on the part of the Jewish community (perhaps particularly of the Tehran-based middle class) was bound up with their desire to belong to a common culture and to a certain kind of inclusive nation, and the manifestations of that desire in the material culture with which they surrounded themselves. Jewish institutions were commonly named after Cyrus before the revolution, and the symbols of pre-Islamic culture were saved as "heritage" in the form of the decorative items—silver and tinned copper and carpets with figures of Persepolis (*Figure 7.2*), manuscript pages with illustrations of the *Shahnameh*—found in their homes and in their stores to be sold to tourists. When Farnaz asks the antiques dealer to lend her something of value to cover the money she has given to Isaac's brother so he can escape, he gives her a page from a sixteenth-century *Shahnameh*, with the comment, "Now schools don't teach the Shahnameh anymore. But we should all continue to read it, so we can understand how great our nation once was" (Sofer, p. 216).

It is hard, however, as we have seen, to stabilize the identities of persons and things. This is poignantly addressed in *The Septembers of Shiraz* in an exchange between Isaac's sister Shahla and her husband Keyvan during which Farnaz is present. Keyvan's great grandfather was an artist, and a portrait of the Qajar king Naser al-Din Shah (r. 1848–96) that he painted in 1892 hangs in their house. Keyvan's family's claim to identity is one that links a Jewish family to the nation and to a dynasty (thus extending the link between Jews and the Pahlavi dynasty to an earlier one under which, by most accounts, the historic reality of their relation to the throne was quite different: the Qajar dynasty (1796–1925)).

Today, in consonance with the post-revolutionary political culture, some Jewish spokespersons emphasize the inclusive possibilities of a shared monotheism.

> In 2009, at the official gathering to mark the thirtieth anniversary of the revolution, Siamak Moreh-Zedek (the Jewish representative in Parliament) said that the Islamic Revolution strengthened the possibility of brotherhood between the believers of different monotheistic religions. The 1979 revolution had been neither political nor economic in nature but a cultural and religious uprising, he said, and one of its more important achievements was the transformation of a secular society into a religious one.[13]

The turn to religion and to religious institutions as social centers is becoming a substitute or reformulation of the inclusiveness that many Jews sought under the Pahlavi regime.

Keyvan, especially since Isaac's arrest, is worried about their future in Iran and wants to leave. "'This painting alone is reason enough to stay,' Shahla responds. 'How can you leave all this family history behind?' [. . .] 'But what if they arrest me: How will this painting—and all the pages I've written about it in all those useless art magazines—help me in jail? Or this tea set, or that chandelier, or this stupid eighteenth-century chair—what will they do for me?'" (Sofer, p. 55). Shahla answers: "If we leave this country without taking care of our belongings, who...will understand who we once were?" (Sofer, p. 56). We began with "indifferent objects witnessing the event" of Isaac's arrest. We end with a more complex and more personal object, also a witness, in this case to a family's role in Iranian history and its attachment to their country. Without this proof, they will lose status, fears Shahla (who, as we have already learned in the course of the novel, is very attached to hers). The painting is a witness, but responds Keyvan, how can it be an actor: "How will this painting [...] help me in jail?"

Redress

In its description of objects, *The Septembers of Shiraz* tells the story of what was taken away and what was left behind. By tracking the combined narratives of people and objects through the novel, we see that the text is also a kind of re-appropriation in that it describes, and displays, the objects left behind, because expropriated or exchanged, for money. "Since every commodity disappears when it becomes money it is impossible to tell from the money itself how it got into the hands of its possessor, or what article has been changed into it. *Non olet* [It does not smell]."[14] The novel gives the "smell" back to the objects by placing them in their former environments, and by connecting them to their former owners by recounting the memories they evoked.

In the years 1978–9, I spent many hours in an apartment complex in Jerusalem where new immigrants found temporary housing (a *maon olim*).[15] The many Iranian women who lived there turned the building entrance hall into a kind of shared living room. I was struck then by the amount of time they gave in their conversations to the recounting of the homes and the objects they had left behind. Some spoke of simply shutting the door on full apartments. Others gave keys to neighbors, expecting to return. Almost all of the women listed the number of carpets, of futons, of dishes, pots and pans they once had. I recall finding this recounting often tedious; it seemed to go nowhere, the remembered objects floating free of any framework or analysis.[16] With hindsight, I can see more clearly that the women were fighting their losses through their remembered objects. "Lokht am" [I am naked], one woman told me. The women were collectively inventing a way to counter the diminishment—personal, social and material—of exile. In their recounting, they re-clothed themselves. "Who will understand who we once were?" Fighting diminishment through the process of expansion, in fiction and in life, begins by giving an account of what was left behind.

Notes

1 Versions of this paper were presented at the Association for Jewish Studies Annual Meeting, Los Angeles, December 2009, and the Frankel Institute for Advanced Judaic Studies, University of Michigan, February 2010. I thank the audience and my colleagues who were at these events.

2 Ali Akbar Hashemi Rafsanjani, in the 1986 speech on the seventh anniversary of the Islamic Revolution in Iran, as cited in Afsaneh Najmabadi, "Iran's Turn to Islam: From Modernism to a Moral Order," *Middle East Journal*, 41:2 (Spring 1987), pp. 202–17; see page 216.

3 There is already an extensive literature by and about Iranian American women writers and Iranian American Jewish women writers. On the Jewish writers, see: Marla Harris, "Consuming Words: Memoirs by Iranian Jewish Women," *Nashim*, 15 (2008), pp. 138–64; the special issue of *Nashim* on the subject of Iranian Jewish women (*Nashim* 18, 2009); and essays by the writers themselves. This essay on remembered objects forms a pair with my piece "The Tear Jar," *Nashim*, 18 (2009), pp. 71–86, on the materiality of the books themselves. For the use of domestic objects in Iranian Jewish folklore, also see my article, "Iranian Jewish Women's Magical Narratives," in P. Chock and J. Wyman (eds), *Discourse and the Social Life of Meaning* (Washington, 1986), pp. 147–68.

One important and particular aspect of the work of the Jewish diasporic writers that has not been discussed elsewhere is the relation between that writing and (Iranian) Jewish Studies. The early nineties saw not only the development of an Iranian Jewish diasporic literature, but the formation of a number of community organizations that were established to collect and to archive Jewish Iranian history. Both initiatives proceeded from similar feelings about the lack of, and the need for, a community history.

An interviewer suggested to Gina Nahai: "In depicting the experience of Iran's Jews—their long history of persecution, departure from the ghettos in the 1930s, and exile to the West—your novels occupy a unique place in the literature of the Iranian diaspora" (Darznik and Nahai, "Dreaming in Persian: An Interview with Novelist Gina Barkhordar Nahai," *MELUS*, 33:2 (Summer 2008), pp. 159–67; see pp. 161–2). Nahai responded: "When I first started writing *Cry of the Peacock*, I went to the library a lot, looking for sources, but I found nothing. This was in the late eighties, before the Iranian Jewish community in the West and Israel started documenting our history. There were references to Iran's Jewish communities in travelogues written by Europeans, and there was a three-volume book by Dr. Habib Levy, written in Farsi, and out of print at that time. That was all" (ibid., p. 163). So, she said in the interview, she proceeded to collect oral histories.

The current interest in histories of Iranian Jews on the part of the generation that grew up in the United States has also been a motivating factor (Habib Levy's history is back in print in an abridged version in English). As a recent statement from the New York chapter of 30 Years After (founded by a "sandwich generation" of "young Iranian Jewish professionals" in 2008) put it, "As first-generation Iranian American Jews, we are not only divided between our dual identities, but more importantly, we stand at a critical position where we face the inevitable reality of being the ones to take responsibility for preserving 2700 years of ancestry and heritage" (Sharon Udasin, "Young Iranian Jews Now Pushing Beyond Old Boundaries," in *The Jewish Week* (January 28, 2010), accessed online.

Gina Nahai's *Cry of the Peacock* came out in 1991, and in 1995 the Center for Iranian Jewish Oral History (CIJOH) was founded in Los Angeles; in 2002, CIJOH, along with the Jewish Publication Society, published the heavily illustrated volume *Esther's Children: A Portrait of Iranian Jews* edited by Houman Sarshar with contributions from many Iranian American Jewish scholars. The novels and memoirs ("blurred genres" as they are) therefore occupy a wider discursive field that privileges both oral history and the active participation of the Jewish Iranian community in recording and archiving that history.

4   On interpretations of the dandy in a Middle Eastern context, see; H. E. Chehabi, "The Imam as Dandy: The Case of Musa Sadr," *The Harvard Middle Eastern and Islamic Review*, 3:1–2 (1996), pp. 20–42. I have analyzed the domain of clothing and Jews in Iran in a series of papers, the most recent of which is, "The Mission of Dress: The Alliance Israelite Universelle and the Politics of Appearance in Iran" (Conference on "Israel and Iran: From Cyrus the Great to the Islamic Republic," Center for Jewish History, October 2010).

5   Afsaneh Najmabadi, "Gender and Secularism of Modernity: How Can a Muslim Woman be French?" *Feminist Studies*, 32:2 (Summer 2006), pp. 239–55; see p. 250. See also Mohamad Tavakoli-Targhi, *Refashioning Iran: Orientalism, Occidentalism, and Historiography* (Palgrave, 2001).

6   Arang Keshavarzian, *Bazaar and State in Iran* (Cambridge, 2007), p. 189.

7   Tara Bahrampour, *To See and See Again* (New York, 1999), pp. 292–3; see also footnote 5.

8 Bahrampour, p. 293. For an aspect of selling antiques to tourists during the 1970s, see Laurence Loeb, "Creating Antiques for Fun and Profit: Encounters Between Iranian Jewish Merchants and Touring Coreligionists," in Valene Smith, (ed.), *Hosts and Guests: The Anthropology of Tourism* (Pennsylvania, 1977).

9 Afshin Molavi, *Persian Pilgrimages* (New York, 2002), p. 13.

10 Ibid.

11 Ibid., p. 70.

12 Ibid., p. 13.

13 Miriam Nissimov, "The Jews of Iran between Antisemitism and Anti-Zionism," Stephen Roth Institute for the Study of Contemporary Antisemitism and Racism, Tel Aviv University, Topical Brief No 3, 2009, p. 2.

14 Karl Marx, cited in Christopher Flint, "Speaking Objects: The Circulation of Stories in Eighteenth-Century Prose Fiction," *PMLA*, 113:2 (March 1998), pp. 212–26; see p. 223.

15 Judith L. Goldstein, Fieldnotes, Israel, 1978–9.

16 The narrator of Gina Nahai's novel *Moonlight on the Avenue of Faith* provides a related picture of Iranian immigrants in Los Angeles: "They always walked in groups, the men wearing business suits even in the August sun, as if to prove to themselves and to others, that they were not exiles [...] that their jobs and offices were still waiting for them [...]. Behind them, the women walked [...] looking tired and pale, talking about the homes they had left behind: 'just furnished,' 'just bought,' just built from the ground up'" (Gina Nahai, *Moonlight on the Avenue of Faith* (New York, 1999), pp. 261–2).

CHAPTER 8

VOICES OF MARGINALITY: DIVERSITY IN JEWISH IRANIAN WOMEN'S MEMOIRS AND BEYOND

Jaleh Pirnazar

In this review I examine two memoirs written by Jewish Iranian women, Farideh Goldin and Roya Hakakian. In addition to discussing the distinct voices of the memoirists, I will examine the voices of other women in their communities to hear a polyphony of narratives emerging from marginal lives in Iran. The tapestry of stories presented by these Jewish Iranian women, we will discover, displays as many common threads and as much texture as diversity in the lives it weaves.

The first memoir to be discussed is Farideh Goldin's *Wedding Song: Memoirs of An Iranian Jewish Woman* (Hanover and London, 2003). The setting for Goldin's memoir is her childhood neighborhood, the mahalleh or Jewish quarter in Shiraz. On the cultural landscape of Iran, the mahalleh has always represented an incommensurable sphere of existence of the "other," untouched by mainstream society (other than at times of pogroms), and unfamiliar even to the integrated Iranian Jews of the 1960s. Goldin takes us to the heart of that segregated impoverished corner of Shiraz of that decade.

The author vividly paints for us the unfolding lives of these mahalleh dwellers as they have lived for centuries within a majority Muslim country. She describes how members of this closed community lived with a dual consciousness of themselves as Jews and also as Iranians. They spoke their own language, *Judi* (Judeo-Persian), which was not always shared with other residents of Jewish quarters in other Iranian cities (such as Hamadan, for example). As observant Jews, they performed religious prayers and other rituals, sang songs in Hebrew, spoke Judeo-Persian among themselves, and communicated in Persian outside the mahalleh. Goldin captures the diversity and nuances in languages and dialects used daily by people in her neighborhood. Further, by recording the silence and absence of speech, she gives voice to the quiet voiceless females in her segregated world. One such person is her own mother, to whom we will turn shortly. In fact, Goldin's memoir can be read as a study on the lives of four generations of Iranian Jewish women as they are introduced to us. We hear them in their own distinct voices. Let us begin with her voiceless mother.

As a young girl of eight or nine, Goldin is acutely aware of her mother's unhappiness in her life, and the little girl observes how her mother carries her sorrow in silence. Farideh's mother, she tells us, had been married off to Farideh's father who had come from Shiraz to the Jewish neighborhoods in Hamadan looking for a bride to take home. The young bride of 13 is thus uprooted against her will and taken to her new home in the mahalleh of Shiraz. Feeling abandoned by her own family, and losing all support, she never finds roots or happiness here. She was brought here, Farideh tells us, to clean, raise kids, and take care of the never-ending needs of her manipulative mother-in-law, her two unmarried sisters-in-law, one married brother-in-law, as well as her increasingly unapproving and unsupporting husband. Her upbringing in the Jewish community of Hamadan is viewed as "inferior" to the lifestyle of her new family in the mahalleh of Shiraz, where the matriarch of the household—her mother-in-law—boasts of being the widow of a *dayan*, a judge. Never accepted as an equal among other women in Shiraz's mahalleh, Farideh's mother is quietly resigned to her fate, accepting it without a fight. She is the silent Jew who learns to keep a low profile and hide when facing hostile surroundings. Her fears and uncertainties render her paralyzed.

Farideh's mother is thus marginalized within a marginalized community that lives within the limits of the mahalleh, as she draws deeper and deeper into her silent isolation. Her desire for approval and her fear of being ill-treated and rejected are all overshadowed by her longing to belong. She is the reed cut off from her reed bed, lamenting separation. Denied visitation or reunion with her own family for many decades, she eventually leaves Iran to reside in Israel, where she hopes to belong and find acceptance. Growing up, Farideh resents her mother's sadness and her voiceless position in their household: "I hated my Mom for creating such sad emotions in me" (p. 54).

Rejecting her mother as "weak," Farideh forges emotional bonds with a strong woman in her family, her grandmother. Grandmother is the matriarch heading her large household, enjoying respect and obedience from her sons and many others within the mahalleh. As the widow of a community leader, she exerts a degree of leadership herself. In contrast to Farideh's uprooted mother, she is resourceful and firmly grounded in her communal life of traditional values, and she carries a rooted self-awareness about her, with which she exercises authority over her sons and other women in the mahalleh. Knowledgeable in folk medicine, she is consulted on cases of malady and child diseases, and in her own manipulative ways she arranges marriages, consoles others, punishes her offenders, demands and receives attention and respect. Grandmother is strongly protective of her commune and its ways; fearful of losing the only identity she knows, she adheres to the traditions and rituals of Jewish life as she sees them, persuading other household members to follow them.

Despite these character traits, we see that Grandmother is aware of her twice-subordinate position, both as a Jew and a woman, within the larger community of Shiraz. Once after a rare excursion outside the mahalleh into the Shiraz Bazaar, with young Farideh hanging tightly to her grandmother's *chador*, Khanom Bozorg (Farideh's grandmother) walks by the tea house where several Muslim men sat idly outside smoking water pipes. The men make passes at Khanom Bozorg, cracking offensive jokes at her as they eye her young granddaughter. They laugh out loud, insulting her. Having been humiliated earlier that day in the bazaar (p. 60), Grandmother is impatient and angered in the face of so much disrespect and discriminatory insult: "I wondered if they would dare ask a woman of their own faith to go to the mountains with them" (pp. 96–7). Farideh recalls that in her attempt to respond to the ridicule and to defuse the vulgarity, Grandmother addresses the men in Persian with a heavy Judeo-Persian accent. Farideh is scared by the encounter and infuriated by her grandmother's unnecessarily polite *ta'arof* (ceremonial niceties) and inadequate response. She runs away, out of breath, knowing that Khanom Bozorg does not seem to have much of a voice outside her sphere of influence within the mahalleh (pp. 96–7).

Goldin recalls the day out shopping with her grandmother as a rare occasion outside the mahalleh exploring the unknown. Toys, candy, a mule, the scents and colors of the bazaar are all fascinating. Amid childhood excitements, she is also frightened at the idea of getting lost in the huge market place. The scene described here is, in many ways, a mirror image of a scene narrated by Simin Daneshvar in her short story "*Bāzār-e Vakil*." Daneshvar, herself from Shiraz, writes about a little girl tightly holding on to her nanny's *chador*, following her in the narrow crowded alleys of the famous Vakil Bazaar in Shiraz. At one point, lost in the excitement of toys, the little girl lets go of the *chador* and soon finds herself hopelessly lost in that unfriendly crowd of passers-by with stern and gravely serious faces: "A tremendous fear developed in her little tummy. Through her tears she looked at the people around her with a peculiar suspicion."[1] Terrified and utterly helpless, she begins to cry when an elderly man notices her and walks to her offering help: "Don't be afraid. There is nothing to worry about. I'll take you home." The little girl looks him over and her horror grows. "She said to herself, 'Oh, that is he. This is the one my nanny was talking about. This is the Jew who snatches Muslim children, takes them to their quarter, kills them and makes bread with their blood'" (Daneshvar, p. 24).

In *Wedding Song*, Goldin presents a counter narrative to Daneshvar's dominant one cited above. This is how Goldin describes her fear

of "the other" when she, the young Farideh, is horrified at the idea
of getting lost:

The world outside our immediate neighborhood frightened
me. My parents, family members and children my own age
told me repeatedly that evil lurked outside the gates of the
mahalleh.[2] Genteel-looking grandfathers enticed young children
with drug-covered candy and kidnapped them to slavery. Nice
old ladies, covered modestly in chadors, asked for directions and
made the children disappear. Kidnappers [. . .] cornered children
[. . .] and took them by force for prostitution. (pp. 93–4)

In another scene, second-graders surround Farideh, no older than ten,
in their new neighborhood outside the mahalleh. These are Muslim
girls curious about the new kid on the block; curious enough to talk
to her from a distance to check her out, but not curious enough to
come close and perhaps make friends: "We talked a bit longer from a
distance. I assumed that they worried that my touch would defile
them. I was afraid to ask for a piece of bread or a glass of tea. What if
the food wasn't kosher? What if they poisoned it to kill me? Would
they allow me to touch their utensils anyway? They surely feared that
I would make them 'najes' (religiously/ritually impure)" (p. 119).
Here Goldin sees herself through the eyes of "the other."

Mistrust and fear of "the other" have reinforced lives of segregation
for many generations, to be sure. Yet despite discriminations and
daily violations of rights against Jews and Jewish communities in
Iran as reported in her memoir, Goldin is also quick to give credit
where credit is due. She recalls it was "a Muslim man who trusted my
father with a bag of gold, his first real assignment as a goldsmith"
(p. 14). Years later, her father still remembered that while he suffered
back stabbings from certain family members and from his fellow
Jews, it was the support of a trusting Muslim client that set him up
in his career. And Farideh's father never forgot (p. 122).

While Farideh's grandmother represents for her the rooted
Jewish Iranian woman who provides guidance and spiritual substance
for her Jewish family, and while her mother, in contrast, represents

the non-belonging passive Jew resigned to a spiritless life of daily maintenance and preservation of her segregated existence, the memoirist herself represents yet another generation of Iranian Jewish women—one that steps out of the confines in search of independence. Farideh is not content with the traditional life of early marriage, child raising and domesticity that her upbringing dictates. Hers is a new voice emerging from the mahalleh. She is literate in Persian and an avid reader, and she dreams of a life outside the mahalleh and its bondage. She manages to go to college and to educate herself. Gradually she prepares to travel to the US in pursuit of higher education. Farideh meets very harsh resistance by her family members who, in their attempt to control her, burn her books and go to extreme lengths to pressure her into submission. Yet Farideh knows she wants to leave Iran, because she is aware that she no longer belongs. In that suffocating atmosphere "I was becoming them [. . .]. I was being transformed into a person I didn't know and now didn't like [. . .]. I had to leave Iran soon in order to save myself" (p. 183).

As members of the fourth generation of Iranian Jewish women mentioned in this memoir, Goldin's Iranian American daughters living in the US know little about Iran and even less about their mother's life in that mahalleh of Shiraz. Goldin wrote her memoir "at my daughters' request who wanted to know about a country they might never be able to visit."[3] The Judeo-Persian language of the mahalleh is a forgotten language for them, and they wonder whether some day they will ever visit Iran. They are able to live their lives free of the social, religious and familial restrictions ever so present in Farideh's life in Iran.

In the span of this memoir, the journey of Iranian Jewish women is outlined through four interdependent and connected spheres of existence:

(a) the communal/social sphere occupied by the grandmother within the mahalleh, providing substance and definition to her Jewish life;

(b) the private inner sphere of the unfulfilled and withdrawn mother, preoccupied solely with the daily maintenance of her life in the mahalleh;

(c) the movement into the public sphere, stepping out into the larger
     Iranian non-Jewish community and beyond by Farideh; and
(d) the Diaspora Iranian Jewish woman part of the global sphere
     today, represented by Farideh's daughters who are given
     opportunities for education and social freedom.

A close look at another memoir written by another Jewish Iranian
woman reminds us of how diverse and non-monolithic Jewish lives in
Iran have been. In her *Journey from the Land of No: A Childhood Caught
in Revolutionary Iran* (New York, 2004), Roya Hakakian portrays a
dramatically dissimilar and yet common account of Jewish life in
Iran. Her family residence, in contrast to Goldin's conservative
Jewish quarters in the Shiraz mahalleh, is situated in western Tehran,
a cosmopolitan city in the 1970s where Jewish families were far more
economically integrated and socially accepted than they were in any
other part of Iran. Hakakian's parents are both college educated, and
her father is a schoolmaster, an educator and a poet. We recall that
Farideh's mother, by contrast, was married off at 13, at which time
her education came to an abrupt end. Farideh's father, too, had had to
earn a living at a young age, leaving him no opportunity for further
schooling. While numerous domestic responsibilities weighed on
Farideh's shoulders as the oldest daughter with younger siblings, and
while Farideh was presumably being prepared for an early marriage
and traditional female roles, Roya, the only daughter, was the
youngest child of the family and raised with no responsibilities.
Furthermore, both Farideh and Roya were loquacious young girls
growing up (*verrāj*). Goldin soon learns to swallow her words and
her fury, however, and to keep her silence in order to survive in
peace—a lesson she learns resentfully from her mother. Roya, in
contrast, becomes the spokesperson for her classmates as they rebel
against Mrs. Moghadam, the Muslim schoolmaster assigned to Roya's
all-girls' Jewish school after the revolution (pp. 168–9).

     As Roya begins to write, she describes herself as a secular Iranian
girl who has witnessed a revolution and now embarks on writing her
memoir. She gradually realizes, though, how much more there has
been to her story.[4] One afternoon, the 12-year-old Roya is dismissed

from school early and she begins to roam about Tehran, where she comes close to the gates of Tehran University. She chooses to walk bare feet: "I wanted hardness to seep through my skin while Tehran's tenderness enveloped me. Tehran had never failed me: the music of water in the canals, the cry of the peddlers, and the generosity of its vendors giving away a hearty sampling of cooked beets or fava beans to a lost girl" (p. 92).

This memorable excursion by the young Roya into the crowded streets of Tehran is indeed a far cry from the scene in *Wedding Song*, where Farideh Goldin is struck by horror at the idea of getting lost in the neighborhood bazaar among the Muslim crowd. Or, again, so dramatically apart from the account of the little Muslim girl traumatized by fear of being kidnapped and murdered by the Jews when she gets lost in the Vakil Bazaar. Roya seems to blend in effortlessly. Her presence alone on this diverse and colorful landscape of upper Tehran in that afternoon in 1978 was seamless and far from lonely and fearful. In fact it seemed so natural—yet it was deceivingly so. Tehran was fast heading toward major shakeups, the aftershocks of which were to uproot the Hakakians and thousands of others for good. Major hostilities toward Jews and other non-Muslim communities of Iran were soon unleashed, uprooting and dispersing large populations, thereby dealing heavy blows to Iran's vibrant multiculturalism and once thriving ethnic/ religious diversity.

Roya finally reaches home. "I had a view of the building across from our home. Next to 'Down with the Shah' on the wall, a new graffiti sign appeared, 'Johoods[5] get lost!'" (p. 134). Roya then proceeds to tell us that 40 years prior to this experience, over 70 years ago, in the small town of Khonsar, Roya's father, a young student then, had come face-to-face with anti-Semitism in his childhood days. Yet the bitter experience had at the same time taught him a memorable lesson in decency and humility.

On rainy days father was told to stay home lest a splash off his body sully a Muslim classmate. Once when the rain had not stopped for four days, his mother went to meet the district superintendent from the greater Khonsar and begged to let her son attend school. Moved by her appeal for her son's education, the superintendent stormed into my father's classroom, interrupted the lesson, and demanded that someone fetch him a glass of water. The class representative obliged. Then the superintendent handed the glass to Father and ordered him to take a sip. Eager to please, Father took a huge gulp. Then the superintendent grabbed the glass, drank the rest, slammed the empty glass on the bench and roared, 'If that water was good enough for me, it's good enough for all of you. From now on, Hakakian will be in class everyday, in all kinds of weather.' (pp. 134–5)

That message in humility and humanity delivered in a small classroom in Khonsar was now completely lost on Roya's neighborhood in upper Tehran where the inscription "Johood get lost" was punctuated by a sign "from the Nazi days," a swastika (p. 135).

In Goldin's memoir, when Farideh's father was finally able to move his family out of the mahalleh and into a more integrated part of the city, the Goldins had also faced an unwelcoming and frightening swastika sign painted on the neighbor's window across their alley—a rude awakening into the Goldins' ever-segregated status in the larger Muslim community of Shiraz (Goldin, p. 122). Some years later, after the Islamic Revolution had robbed him of all his hard-earned possessions, Mr. Goldin finally broke down, consumed with despair and utter helplessness in the face of rising tides of anti-Semitism. Farideh recalls how her father held his head tightly in his hands and sobbed. He sank into himself, humiliated, as "his wrinkles deeped" (p. 195). In comparison, when Roya's father sees the swastika on the wall, this reserved gentle educator, this logical and calm schoolmaster is at once struck with sudden madness. Unlike Mr. Goldin, Mr. Hakakian bursts out of the room and into the courtyard where he whirls and raves unabashedly, unbuttoning his shirt, baring his torso and taking off his pants as he spins with frightening madness in front of Roya's eyes (pp. 136–7). The reactions of both fathers to the rising anti-Semitic sentiments in their respective communities, and what they each felt as betrayals by their fellow Iranians, leave memorable and potent imprints on their daughters' psyche. Both episodes scorched unforgettable images in their memories.

Earlier in her narrative, Roya Hakakian, who was quite comfortable in the houses of her Muslim friends and had felt integrated with them, had reminded us of how she felt in the company of "the other." Being among Jews, she tells us, was effortless, like being comfortably in your pajamas. Being among Muslims, on the other hand, was "like being in my party dress... the fabric itched. The zipper pinched. I had to adjust myself to fitting into something less familiar. [...] It took effort being in it, but I liked the way it changed me. I liked how I looked in it" (p. 56). On that afternoon in 1978 Tehran, however, Roya's "party dress" became too tight and suffocating to tolerate. The squeeze became alarming. A strong determining blow hit her family, and something shattered deep inside Roya. That moment proved a turning point in the lives of the well-integrated Hakakians. The family soon prepared to leave Iran.

Before and during the revolution of 1979, many assimilated Jews had thought of themselves as Iranians first. This was the case, that is, before the revolution adopted the designation "Islamic" as its defining adjective and turned harshly and fatally against its critics. Thousands of socially integrated Iranian Jews found themselves forced to leave the country they knew as home. Homa Sarshar, an Jewish Iranian woman journalist, recorded those unsettling days of betrayals in her Persian memoirs *Dar Kucheh Pas-Kucheh–hāyeh Ghorbat* (*In the Back Alleys of Exile*, Los Angeles, 1993).[6] Unlike the younger memoirists Goldin and Hakakian, whose parents decide to move the family outside of Iran, in Sarshar's writing (the first published autobiographical account by a Jewish Iranian woman in the Diaspora) we hear a first-hand account of the experience of those who faced the very difficult decision to leave, taking their families with them.

Among a polyphony of voices of Jewish Iranian women of the revolutionary era, one voice unheard and one story untold, is that of a young Jewish Iranian woman political activist who stayed in Iran and whose promising young life was brutally cut short in the prisons of the Islamic Republic. Her voice was thus forever silenced and her memory almost faded. Edna Sabet, an engineering student turned political activist, was arrested in 1982 at the age of 26. Her repeated torturous interrogations and her eventual execution in the fall of 1983 were later reported by her loyal cellmate, and recorded by international organizations on human rights in Iran. Prison officials and government authorities claim no knowledge of this case, and they continue to cover up this crime. Edna's family abroad had also maintained a painful silence on her life and death as it grieved in private. Edna's story, and perhaps those of other Jewish political activists, thus remains untold and shrouded in silence.

While the few cases highlighted here demonstrate how diverse and nuanced the lives of Jewish Iranian women in Iran have been, they also show how commonly threatened and endangered the very fabric of Jewish life in that country became in the face of growing anti-Semitism in post-revolutionary Iran. What remains a common thread running through these stories and others is the fact that the Islamic Republic of Iran, by its exclusionist attitude toward Iran's religious minorities, has cut deep into the very fabric of Iran's society, robbing Iran itself of its legacy of cultural richness, ethnic and religious diversity, and multi-layered social life.

Notes

1 Simin Daneshvar, *Daneshvar's Playhouse: A Collection of Stories*, tr. Maryam Mafi (Washington, 2008), p. 12.

2 Farideh Goldin makes a factual mistake in her account here: the mahalleh in Shiraz has never had any gates. Though the limits of the Jewish quarter in Shiraz are clearly known to all, there never have been any external signs such as gates or walls delineating its perimeters [editor's note].

3 Marla Harris, "Consuming Words: Memoirs by Iranian Jewish Women," *Nashim: A Journal of Jewish Women's Studies and Gender Issues*, 15 (Spring 2008), pp. 138–64.

4 Ibid.

5 Kikes [editor's note].
6 See, for example, vol. 2, pp. 317–23. For an English translation of these pages, see: Homa Sarshar, "In Exile at Home," in L. Khazzoom, *The Flying Camel: Essays on Identity by Women of North Africa and Middle Eastern Jewish Heritage* (New York, 2003), pp. 123–30.

CHAPTER 9

FLIGHTS FROM HISTORY IN GINA BARKHORDAR NAHAI AND DALIA SOFER'S FICTION

Nasrin Rahimieh

The workings of memory have been central to the emergence of Iranian American writing, and the prevalence of the genre of memoir among Iranian American writers attests to this apparent dominance of memory in the Iranian American literary corpus. The penchant toward autobiographical writing has, however, sometimes led to conflations of these memoirs and of historical realities by both readers and reviewers, resulting in heated debates about the purported political objectives of the memoirists.[1] The discussions surrounding these memoirs and their manner of representation of a personal or collective past underline how they are read for their reliable depiction of given moments in time.[2] Such readings neglect the extent to which the act of writing is itself formative of the narrating subject, or to cite Michael Sprinker, "no autobiography can take place except within the boundaries of a writing where concepts of subject, self, and author collapse into the act of producing a text."[3] Gina Barkhordar Nahai, a Jewish Iranian American novelist, provides a different perspective on the fraught relationship between the author, her memories, and their integration into a narrative. Addressing a question about her own relationship to memory, she challenges the view that memory can serve as a reliable form of documentary evidence: "Memory, of course, is a selective device; it never retains the entirety of an experience. What we remember is not what was, but what we saw, and that recollection, in turn, is altered and amended over time by other subjective factors."[4] And yet, as Nahai points out in the same interview, her novels are means of bearing witness to the collective history of Jewish Iranians. Quoting from one of her novels, *Caspian Rain*, she states: "'Memory does not often serve the truth. I have learned this. I know I might have heard a vow my father never uttered, held on to the pipe dream of a promise he never made. But imperfect as it may be, memory is all I have to help me bear witness.'"[5] Nahai's declaration highlights an alternative intersection of memory and narrative that creates a space in which the real competes with the improbable and the unreal, shifting the focus away from a direct and exclusive correspondence between fictional representation and factual reality. In Dorrit Cohn's formulation, "fiction is subject to two closely interrelated distinguishing features: (1) its references to the world outside the text are not bound to accuracy; and (2) it does not refer exclusively to the real world outside the text."[6] One of the possibilities opened up as a result of the decoupling of the text and the "real world" is to heighten neglected aspects of history or to create alternative and imaginative realities in which the marginalized and the abject are foregrounded. Gina Barkhordar Nahai and Dalia Sofer, two writers who will be the focus of this analysis, draw on fictional representation to develop an oblique relationship to the history of Jewish Iranian experience, to mine and interrogate communal memory and tradition, and to lay bare the mechanisms of subjection and how they reproduce themselves within the Jewish community. Disentangled from the imperative to represent the past accurately, Nahai and Sofer's works realign the power relations between and across lines of traditional authority. Their fiction, in contrast to the memoirs drawn from a similar history, sheds the yoke of the past, carving out an imaginative site of potential for change and self-transformation.

The reworking of collective history into fiction is evident in Gina Barkhordar Nahai's works. Her first novel, *Cry of the Peacock*, published in 1991, is a historical novel that weaves together representations of Jewish Iranian life from the eighteenth century to the 1980s. In the acknowledgements that appear at the end of the novel, Nahai outlines the sources on which she drew:

> I began with my own memories, and then asked questions. I spoke to hundreds of Iranians, Jews and Muslims, old and young. Through years of interviews and volumes of books, I became familiar with a history—albeit recent—that had been buried by the last of the ghetto generation "as if to wipe away three thousand years of suffering."[7]

The plurality of voices that served Nahai lays the groundwork for a fictional narration that defies the strictures of historical time and the dictates of the real. For instance, in the opening chapter of the novel we are introduced to Peacock, a woman whose very appearance poses a challenge to the Islamic revolutionaries who have imprisoned her:

> She had been in jail for three weeks, and still no one had decided her fate. She had arrived one summer afternoon surrounded by Guards, sitting in the back of a military jeep with her face unveiled and her hair uncovered. She had sat in her clothes that shocked the eye and defied all Islamic codes, in layers of bright chiffon and fiery silk, yellow scarves and sequined shirts and a gold-embroidered belt above a crushed velvet skirt. [. . .] Still, it was not her clothes that so shocked the mullahs, it was her age. Peacock the Jew was so old, they said, she remembered God when he was a child.[8]

The post-revolutionary Islamic dress code imposed rules of modesty on women, forbidding them to show their hair and to wear bright colors. Peacock's mode of dress and the panoply of colors in which she has enveloped her body diminish the power her captors hold over her. Moreover, as she sits in her prison cell and listens to the daily execution of prisoners, she refuses to see herself as one of their potential victims. When a guard questions her about her in the past tense, "as if her life were over," she responds: "I am a hundred and sixteen years old. . . and still I intend to live."[9] Peacock's defiance is graphically illustrated in the closing chapter of the novel:

> And there was a moment of calm, an instant when Peacock's eyes locked into the Guard's and she found herself purged of fear, understood that she must act, speak out, if only once, before she died. She stepped into the execution yard—removed and rational—picked up the machine gun with an unwavering hand, and placed the barrel on the man's chest. She did not fire.[10]

That Peacock holds the machine gun but does not use it against her jailor/executioner places her in a power relationship that supersedes physical might. Opting to die in defiance rather than deference to revolutionary authority is the ultimate power she wields in this moment. As in this scene, throughout the novel, the reality of the revolution and the impossibility of escaping the executioners are offset by the extraordinary power exerted by women like Peacock, descendents of Esther the Soothsayer, their foremother, whose own story begins in 1796. While anchoring female characters in a historical frame, *Cry of the Peacock* highlights their exceptional abilities to transcend the confines of time, religious taboo and the power of patriarchy.

Esther the Soothsayer is endowed with the ability to "read people's eyes, walk into their dreams when they were asleep, and probe their minds,"[11] and yet she is trapped in a life of servitude: "She was a Jew, born of a mother who had worked and died in the service of the Sheikh's family, inherited by him and doomed to spend her youth and desire as a slave without a face, until she was too old to work and they sent her back to die in the ghetto [. . .]."[12] When she chooses to travel to places she has seen in her dreams, she finds herself rejected by the Jewish quarter or mahalleh on the assumption that "she must have been driven out [. . .]—punished by her own people and banned for a crime she had come here to hide. She must have been a thief, an adulteress, a whore."[13] Her supernatural powers remain her only means of transcending her fate as a Jewish woman. Her daring to leave, her ability to insert herself in others' dreams, and her seduction of the man whom she coerces into marrying her make her suspicious in the eyes of the new community she chooses to settle in. Driven from her new home, she becomes a wanderer with a unique power to oversee generations of her offspring.

Esther the Soothsayer's unabashed desire and her forthright manner of commanding make the men of the mahalleh very nervous. In her refusal to be contained and possessed, she embodies the libidinal economy Hélène Cixous describes:

> She doesn't hold still, she overflows. An outpouring that can be agonizing, since she may fear, make the other fear, endless aberration and madness is her release. Yet, vertiginous, it can also be intoxicating—as long as the personal, the permanence of identity is not fetishized—a "where-am-I," a "who-enjoys-there," a "who-I-where-delight": questions that drive reason, the principle of unity, mad, and that are not asked, that ask for no answer, that open up the space where woman is wandering, roaming (a rogue wave), flying (thieving).[14]

This unleashing, like Esther the Soothsayer's unauthorized roaming, questions the underlying assumption of women's inferiority, inscribed in myths, legends and cultural tradition. The "subordination of the feminine to the masculine order, which gives the appearance of being the condition for the machinery's functioning"[15] is repeatedly destabilized by female characters in the *Cry of the Peacock*.

The female character that best epitomizes the tension between the male domination and female resistance is Taraneh the Tulip. Daughter of a rabbi in Shiraz, she learns the price of disobeying her father when she tries to look at her likeness in a block of melting ice. Her father punishes her by shaving her head. To hide her shame, she locks herself away in the basement of their house where she discovers a *santur*,[16] musical instrument, which she takes up playing and continues to play secretly for ten years. When her secret is discovered, this time at the hands of her husband, Taraneh the Tulip leaves home

never to return. Her flight from home is a first step toward her
self-transformation into a musician and performer:

> She traveled across Persia, chased from one ghetto and into
> another, and in every place she learned the people's music and
> dances. When she arrived in Juyy Bar she was twenty-six years
> old and resolved to stay. The first time Raab Yahya attacked her
> at his Sabbath sermon, warning the people against "the stranger
> with the wicked instrument," Taraneh the Tulip realized she
> must fight. That night she appeared in the ghetto square,
> dressed in a scarlet gown, her hands and face painted crimson,
> her hair glowing red. She waited for an audience to gather, took
> a bow, and then began to dance—a slow, graceful performance
> that lasted twelve minutes, and in the course of which she
> managed to re-create a tulip's life from inception to end. No
> one ever called Taraneh "whore" again.[17]

Taraneh the Tulip's transformation empowers her not only vis-à-vis
the inhabitants of the mahalleh, it entitles her to act on her desires
and to disrupt the order of life both in the Jewish and the Muslim
communities. In 1869, when she is asked to perform at the wedding
of the governor's son to the daughter of Esfahan's Friday prayer leader,
she becomes the source of the wedding's disruption:

> It was an unprecedented event, the greatest wedding in a
> hundred years, and every person of rank and reputation was
> invited. The groom was twenty years old, educated in Baghdad,
> and so rich he had waived his right to a dowry. The bride's
> family were so eager to form the union, they had insisted on a
> wedding only two weeks after the courtship had begun. The
> night of the celebrations, they were outraged to find a Jew
> among the performers. Still, not wishing to spoil the festivities,
> they had allowed Taraneh to make her appearance. Halfway
> through her Tulip act, the governor's son annulled the
> wedding. He had fallen in love, he said, with the Jew in the
> scarlet gown.[18]

Her dreams are realized with her marriage to the governor's son and the move into a "house with rooms full of music."[19] Taking possession of her own desires, Taraneh the Tulip becomes a symbol of resistance to a history that condemns Jews and women, as the narrator of the novel indicates, to a life of abnegation:

> The Jews, as anywhere else in Persia, were considered impure and untouchable. They were not allowed to live and work outside their ghetto, to plant their own food or drink from public waters. The men wore red or yellow patches on their clothes, the women covered their faces with thicker veils than those reserved for Muslims. Anything a Jew touched became soiled forever. If accused of a crime, a Jew could not testify in his own defense. He could not even step out of the ghetto on a rainy day for fear that the rain may wash the impurity off his body and onto a Muslim's.[20]

Against such historical imperatives, the novel posits the seemingly unreal women capable of crossing barriers and taboos and altering their fate. The women's potential for transformation is even more pointedly inscribed in Nahai's 1999 novel, *Moonlight on the Avenue of Faith*.

If *Cry of the Peacock* moves across centuries, *Moonlight on the Avenue of Faith* is concerned primarily with Jewish life in twentieth-century Iran and the migration of Iranian Jews to the United States in the aftermath of the 1979 revolution. The double movement between confinement and self-actualization is equally pronounced in this novel, as is one of the central character's seemingly unreal attributes.

The novel begins with such an improbable predicament faced by the first-person narrator, Lili's mother, Roxanna the Angel:

> As I watch her now, three hundred and ninety pounds and gaining by the day, her frame so vast she has not been able to pull it upright in more than two months or to fit through any doorway without first having to take the door off its hinges, her breath so stormy it makes the dogs bark all the way up

and down the street where she now lives with her sister in
Los Angeles, and sets the piano in their neighbor's house playing
mad tunes at odd hours of the night, it is impossible to believe
that my mother, Roxanna the Angel, was once a young woman
with watercolor eyes and translucent skin, that she could stop the
world with her laughter and compel men, my father among
them, to follow her across an entire city without knowing why
they chased her or what they could do if ever she stopped and
answered their calls, that she had been so light and delicate, so
undisturbed by the rules of gravity and the drudgery of human
existence, she had grown wings, one night when the darkness
was the color of her dreams, and flown into the star-studded
night of Iran that claimed her.[21]

Roxanna the Angel's immobility signals a reverse transformation,
from a woman capable of taking flight to one shackled by enormous
weight. Roxanna's condition literalizes the metaphor of the weight of
sorrow she has accumulated in the process of fleeing her home and
leaving her five-year-old daughter behind. Her sister Miriam spells
this out for Lili, Roxanna the Angel's daughter, pointing the way to a
possible cure:

> She is dying of guilt, you see. Over what she did to you, and
> to your father before you. She is dying of Sorrow, over the
> life that she wasted, that she could have fixed but didn't. So
> much pain bottles up in you, so many tears, and after a while it
> has nowhere to go, and it begins to kill you. There is a word for
> it in Farsi: *Degh*, 'to die of Sorrow.' I figure Roxana never got the
> chance—gave herself the chance—to go back and ask for
> forgiveness. I figure if she did that—with you, at least, if not
> with Sohrab—she might release some if those tears and start to
> recuperate.[22]

Roxanna's inability to give voice to the sorrow she has buried deeply
within her is reflected in the inner monologue we witness as she
watches her daughter prepare the ritual cure of almond tears:

There is a sorrow within me so deep, I have not been able to give it a name, I want to tell Lili.

It is my mother's sorrow, and her mother's—the tears that they shed in the tear jar, that they drank alone, inconsolable.

I did not want my daughter to have this sorrow. I did not want to leave you those tears.

That is why I left: to take the sorrow out of your eyes.

It is not as if I sacrificed myself to save you. It was not your needs I was thinking of, but my own. More than anything else, more than the need to be with my child or the love I felt for Teymur, more than the instinct to simply live, I wanted to end the sorrow.

I came back and saw that I had lost.[23]

Roxanna's condition, as revealed in her own words, is caused not only by the weight of guilt: it also stems from self-betrayal. She runs away from home to suppress her desires, mimicking the edicts of tradition and male authority. Her exile thus becomes a self-banishment that renders her immobile and silent.

While Roxanna the Angel gives up her ability to fly, her daughter Lili turns exile into a potential for freeing herself from the weight of the past. Lili's recollection of her first encounters with the waves of Iranian exiles arriving in Los Angeles encapsulates her own sense of exile and the newcomers' malaise with their sense of being in limbo:

Often in those days, I saw Iranians who had come to Los Angeles to escape the riots that would turn into a revolution. They always walked in groups, the men wearing business suits even in the August sun, as if to prove to themselves and to others that they were not exiles, that they had had important work to do all their lives, that their jobs and offices were still waiting for them. They walked ahead of their wives, hands clasped behind their backs and heads lowered in conversation with their friends. They spoke of the latest news from Iran—the banks that had shut down, the companies that had burned to the ground, the exchange rate of the rial.[24]

The purposefulness with which the newly displaced Iranians comport themselves attests to their unwillingness to let go of the idea of an imminent return. By continuing to situate their gaze toward the home they have unwillingly left behind they maintain the ties Roxanna deliberately severs. Her daughter Lili's reaction is initially to envy her compatriots: "I watched them—travelers in a foreign land, exiles waiting to go home. As lost and homesick as they were, they clung together and managed to recreate, every day that they spent away from home, a sense of belonging, a community that I had never known. I was the real exile, I thought on those afternoons in the park—the traveler who would never find her destination."[25] But the sense of loss is quickly replaced by the recognition of a mobility she has acquired through painful ruptures and losses: "But on other occasions, watching my compatriots and how they had brought with them not only their sense of home and community but also their pasts loaded with failed hopes and lost expectations – on these occasions I would remember [...] that Sohrab might have done me a favor by sending me away."[26] What we see in Lili's grappling with her position vis-à-vis her past is a movement away from the hold the past has on her to a present of her own making. A similar movement has been foreclosed in her mother's self-imposed exile.

Other forms of immobility are captured in Nahai's latest novel, *Caspian Rain*. The novel is the story of Yaas, the single daughter of an unlikely couple. Her mother, Bahar, whose name means spring, is born into a poor family in Tehran's Jewish quarter. True to her name, Bahar is filled with exuberance, but mistakenly assumes that beyond the mahalleh lie mobility and freedom. She imagines that love and marriage will provide her with an entrée to a new life, and she believes that marrying a man from a higher class will allow her to pursue her dream of studying and becoming a teacher.

When she first meets her future husband, Omid, she overlooks all that separates her from Omid's affluent family. In Persian Omid means hope, and on him Bahar pins all her hopes. Class differences between Bahar and Omid's families prove insurmountable:

It is true that the Arbabs are Jews, but that's where the similarities end between them and Bahar's family. Mr. Arbab's wealth makes him a person who deserves to be admired and envied. His wife's life of comfort makes it inevitable that she would have nothing but disdain for Bahar's mother—look at this woman, she probably isn't so old, but she looks decades older than I, her skin is cracked like the desert floor and she obviously hasn't heard of hair dye or she would have done something about that gray; it's people like her who give Jews a bad name.

Not for them—no thanks—these trappings of ghetto life.[27]

Living with the Arbabs introduces Bahar to a whole new set of internalized taboos. For instance, while she can and must dress the part of the modern and fashionable woman, she cannot go to school.

Instead of gaining access to higher education and a professional life, Bahar enters a circle of women preoccupied with the latest fashions and interminable dinner parties. The city's elite, she discovers, flaunt their wealth, mimic Western norms but continue to view women as extensions of their husbands. The women appear to have internalized the society's image of themselves: "Every woman I know, even the ones who refer to themselves as 'thinking people,' which means they understand more than most women but not as much as men, believes that girls are like weeds; they grow anywhere, survive illness and misfortune, even if you don't want them to."[28]

There is little room for women to maneuver outside the bounds of marriage. In an attempt to gain control through her marriage, Bahar succumbs to the expected role of motherhood, but her daughter is born with a debilitating genetic disease, leading to yet another disappointment:

So she lived in a state of perpetual loss—the runner who gives her all to the race and always comes short. She couldn't give up the fight and couldn't quite win and so she was caught between the pride of battle and the shame of defeat. And in that state, in that place where rest was impossible and wanting led only to more sorrow, she bore me expecting that I, at least, would not fail.

What if you bet your whole life on a single wish, and lost?[29]

While Bahar is caught between these two contradictory impulses, Yaas observes and internalizes her parents' anguish. When her father broaches the possibility of divorce with his own father, he receives a lesson from his father in the social, cultural and religious taboos that he, like generations before him, have upheld:

> "Like it or not," he says, "there are things we allow ourselves, and boundaries we don't cross. No one is telling you to give up your mistress, but you have to realize you're a Jew and she's a Muslim, you have a name to honor and she's the child of an opium addict and a woman who whored herself for a new husband. I don't like your wife and I don't know what you're going to do with your kid but they're *your* burden to bear and I won't have the stigma of divorce haunting us in this town."[30]

The power structures close in on themselves, re-consolidating the very order Bahar had hoped to escape through her marriage.

The only moments of resistance and defiance we find in the novel are experienced by women who do not fit the expected norms and stand on the margins of society. For example, we find a character called the Tango Dancer: "Every afternoon at the hour of sleep, the woman in the yellow house opens all the windows and plays her wild, breathless music on a giant gramophone till she has awakened every soul on the Alley of the Champions and June Street. She plays the music at other times too, without regard for her neighbors or for the Islamic calendar that forbids music and dance and other displays of immorality during certain parts of the year,"[31] and the Kurdish servant Ruby who has the "presumptuous manners and earsplitting laugh of a rebel who has, by sheer resolve, made a life for herself in Tehran."[32] Omid's paramour, Niyaz, represents the possibility of escaping the margins. Niyaz, whose name means "need," defies the norms with no apparent harm to her standing: "So she lives with him in sin without bothering to hide herself, and yet, instead of being stoned or spat on or at least shunned for her immoral ways, she is the darling of Tehran's high society and the object of admiration by both men and women, and there is no telling how she pulls this off, no way to make sense of it except to say that God loves some people more than others."[33] Niaz's figurative authority is encapsulated in her name: needs whose dictates, when disregarded, stand in opposition to social conventions, mores and taboos. Omid, Bahar and Yaas all succumb to the laws that delimit social conduct between men and women, among members of different religions, and across class distinctions. But Niyaz imposes herself on the accepted and the normative, wreaking havoc in the social order.

Women like Niyaz, Esther the Soothsayer and Taraneh the Tulip embody the potential to disrupt the order of things. Like the revolution that looms over three of Nahai's novels, they represent the potential for turmoil, but they also tap into a mobility that is otherwise foreclosed within the limits of Jewish Iranian tradition and lore. Drawing on fiction as a means of writing about the past positions, Nahai's novels speak against a tradition of women's marginalization. In the new diaspora setting, Barkhordar Nahai takes charge of how to redraw the lines between a past marked by marginalization and victimization and a present in the making.

In Dalia Sofer's novel *The Septembers of Shiraz*, the revolution also occupies a central position. The novel begins with Isaac Amin's imprisonment and ends with the family's escape from Iran. Despite the novel's depiction of the ordeal of a Jewish Iranian family caught in the early days of the revolution, it too captures the potential to wrest mobility and change from turmoil and loss. The final passage of the novel, narrated from Isaac's perspective, encapsulates this potential: "But for now he looks at his wife, with whom he has shared an education in grief, and at his daughter, who is falling asleep standing up. Later in Istanbul they will sit by the Bosporus, squirting lemon on their grilled fish, remembering the Caspian and imagining all the waters that await them elsewhere."[34] This time of possibility and the "elsewhere" is inscribed throughout the novel so thoroughly that it engulfs the past and makes the memory of the past pregnant with a loss that is yet to come.

Shirin, Amin's daughter, anticipates their departure and imagines a "not being"[35] she projects onto her home:

> What happens to a house full of nonbeings? What if, like her father, she, her mother, and Habibeh would one day disappear also? The house, of course, would not know it. That would be the sad part. The house would continue to exist. Its walls would remain in the same place, the doors ready to be opened and closed. The plates and glasses too, would stay, even though there would be no one to eat or drink out of them. The chairs would stand still, their laps ready to serve. And the clocks' needles would continue moving forward, and at midnight starting all over again, as though the day that just ended have never been.[36]

By imagining that the movement of time and life would continue without the inhabitants of the house, Shirin removes herself and her family not only from the home that has become associated with her father's absence and the revolutionary guards' intrusions, but also a history of herself that had seemed irrevocably linked to this site. Seeing her family home devoid of the family members, she takes the first step toward moving to the "elsewhere" her father embraces at the end of the novel.

The psychological distantiation Shirin practices conditions her moment of departure. This moment, too, is filled with a conscious self-possession:

> Looking out the window, she realizes that they will never travel on this road again. Miles of asphalt disappear under their wheels, bringing them closer to the sea and to the end of their lives here. Yet it is not sadness she feels, but an emptiness, a certain guilt even, for not feeling sad enough. A departure like this, so definite, should devastate her. It doesn't. She tries to memorize her surroundings—the ridges on the rocks, the color

of the sun as it illuminates the road, the stretches of sea coming in and out of view according to the curves of the road—knowing that someday she will miss them. But there are too many details to remember, too much to record in a single viewing, and she wishes now that she had paid more attention back when she believed that, like the mountain, and the sun, and the sea, she would always be there.[37]

Interestingly, the overabundance of the details do not overwhelm her, and even the awareness that some day she might look back nostalgically is rationalized and put into a perspective she has already mastered.

The novel's thematization of a refusal to become caught up in the imperative of nostalgia and its alternating chapters between Iran and New York, where one of Amin's sons lives and studies, complicates the conflation of the narrative with historical specificity. This is not to say that *The Septembers of Shiraz* eradicates any links with the fate of Iranian Jews after the revolution, but rather that it makes the relationship to the past secondary to the creation of a new imaginative landscape that anticipates and carves out an "elsewhere." This is signaled in the tropes of movement and mobility in Sofer's novel, aligning it with Nahai's works.

Nahai and Sofer's respective works move further beyond the imperative of Iranian American memoirs and autobiographies, which in Gillian Whitlock's words are

narratives of trauma that remain preoccupied with an experience of estrangement, a "little death" of the self and a painful loss of the known world. The intensity of this death of a self and its habitus engenders resurrection through memoir as a Western metropolitan intellectual, and a Diasporic subject, with a troubled and ambivalent relation to a lost homeland and, it follows, to contemporary Iranian society and culture.[38]

If Nahai and Sofer's novels represent loss and estrangement, they situate this loss and estrangement not as a "little death," but rather as an integral factor in a movement and process of becoming. To counter the power of a past laden with painful memories, Nahai and Sofer make memory and history into material to be reworked through representations that locate the possibilities for alternative histories that signal the path to what is to come.

Notes

1 The most well-known example centers on Azar Nafisi's *Reading Lolita in Tehran*, which has been the subject of extensive discussion. For detailed discussions, see Gillian Whitlock, *Soft Weapons: Autobiography in Transit* (Chicago, 2007), particularly Chapter 7, "The Pangs of Exile: Memoir Ouy of Iran;" and Sharareh Frouzesh Bennett and Nasrin Rahimieh, "Representations: Memoirs, Autobiographies, Biographies: Writing in Another Language: Iranian Women Writing in English," in *Encyclopedia of Women and Islamic Cultures* [online] < http://sjoseph.ucdavis.edu/Images_Homepage/ewic/preview-of-ewic-online-supplement-i>, first published spring 2010, last accessed on July 2, 2014.

2 As Amy Malek reminds us in her 2006 article on memoir as Iranian exile cultural production, many issues are integral to the analysis of memoir writing: "The fact that [. . .] women have gained more commercial success for their memoirs than their poetic anthologies, novels, or academic articles, points, I would argue, to the implicit reason behind their writing in memoir genre: the command of the market economy and the commercial inaccessibility of non-memoir genres to Iranian women. It appears that, while Iranian women's voices may appeal to readers in this particular moment for a variety of reasons, they are still confined and pigeonholed within the memoir genre by an industry—unable or unwilling—to recognize them beyond their perceived status as 'formerly oppressed Third-World women,' and rather for their real intellectual, literary, or artistic talents. This only perpetuates several frustrations in Iranian exile culture within the larger Western culture: memoir and film have become the only two creative vehicles through which mainstream Western consumers can view Iran and Iranians outside of the one-dimensional view provided by commercial news outlets." Amy Malek, "Memoir as Iranian Exile Cultural Production: A Case Study of Marjane Satrapi's Persepolis Series," *Iranian Studies*, 39 (2006), pp. 353–80; see p. 364.

3 Michael Sprinker, "The End of Autobiography," in James Olney (ed.), *Autobiography: Essays Theoretical and Critical* (Princeton, 1980), pp. 321–42; see p. 342.

4 Jasmin Darznik, "Dreaming in Persian: An Interview with Novelist Gina Barkhordar Nahai," *MELUS*, 33:2 (2008), pp. 159–67. See p. 160.

5 Ibid.

6 Dorrit Cohn, *The Distinction of Fiction* (Baltimore, 1999), p. 15.

7 Gina Barkhordar Nahai, *Cry of the Peacock* (New York), 1991, p. 341.

8 Ibid., p. 5.

9 Ibid.

10 Ibid., p. 332.

11 Ibid., p. 10.

12 Ibid.

13 Ibid., p. 14.

14 Hélène Cixous and Catherine Clément, "Out and Out: Attacks/Ways Out/ Forays," in *The Newly Born Woman*, tr. Betsy Wing, Theory and History of Literature, 24 (Minneapolis, 1991), pp. 63–132; see p. 91.

15 Ibid., p. 65.

16 Hammer dulcimer.

17 *Cry of the Peacock*, p. 92.

18 Ibid.

19 Ibid.

20 Ibid., p. 13.

21 Gina Barkhordar Nahai, *Moonlight in the Avenue of Faith* (New York, 1999), p. 5.

22 Ibid., p. 356.

23 Ibid., p. 367.

24 Ibid., p. 261.

25 Ibid., p. 262.

26 Ibid.

27 Gina Barkhordar Nahai, *Caspian Rain* (San Francisco, 2007), p. 20.

28 Ibid., p. 111.

29 Ibid., p. 107.

30 Ibid., p. 148.

31 Ibid., p. 89.

32 Ibid., p. 128.

33 Ibid.

34 Dalia Sofer, *The Septembers of Shiraz* (New York, 2008), p. 338.

35 Ibid., p. 114.

36 Ibid.

37 Ibid., p. 306.

38 Gillian Whitlock, *Soft Weapons: Autobiography in Transit* (Chicago, 2007), p. 165.

CHAPTER 10

FANTASIES OF FLIGHT AND INCLUSION: GINA BARKHORDAR NAHAI'S RECLAIMING OF JEWISH IRANIAN IDENTITY IN THE AMERICAN DIASPORA

Mojgan Behmand

All the generations before me / donated me, bit by bit, so that I'd be / erected all at once / here in Jerusalem, [. . .] / It binds. My name's / my donors' name. / It binds. [. . .] / I have to change my life and death / daily to fulfill all the prophesies / prophesied for me. / So they're not lies. / It binds.[1]

Gina Barkhordar Nahai, born in 1961 in Iran, is the Jewish Iranian American author of four novels, *Cry of the Peacock*, *Moonlight on the Avenue of Faith*, *Sunday's Silence* and *Caspian Rain*. Her focal concern is the question of identity, an identity that for her characters is formed in varying degrees by religion, gender and ethnicity. Her forefronted representation of a religious minority, the Jewish community in Iran, serves to distinguish her novels from other Iranian American narratives, though recent publications such as *The Septembers of Shiraz* now tread on similar ground.

Notably, the poetic beauty of her work fuels the reader's imagination and elevates her novels, especially the first two—*Cry of the Peacock* and *Moonlight on the Avenue of Faith*—to a level beyond that of other literary depictions of Iran. In addition, Nahai uses her status as a writer of the Iranian diaspora to portray the life of another diaspora in Iran: her protagonists are mainly women defined by their Jewish heritage, circumvention of female repression, and an amalgam of assumed and shed nationalities. Three of her four novels focus on the constrained lives of Jewish characters in Iran, while the other muses on the restricted existence of Kurdish Jews living tenuous lives on ephemeral territory, Kurdistan.

The attractive cover art of Nahai's books is conspicuous in its lack of overt Middle East references—no veils, no bodiless women, no menacing dark men—and thus underlines that her work is distinct from sundry other publications in the genre: where most popular Iranian American works are memoirs depicting the aftermath of the Islamic Revolution with its inherent losses and indignities, Nahai's novels are works of fiction with a greater thematic and historical scope. They are narratives of transgression—transgressions against established authority, traditional gender roles, received history and everyday laws of nature. She paints with the broad brush of magic realism, creating accounts of Jewish life in Iran that establish a hitherto disdained presence within the story of Iran, the nation; and they do so for the expanse of centuries, even millennia. Firmly placing her characters within a sprawling Iranian history, her depictions predate the Islamic Republic of Iran and even the nation's name change from Persia to Iran outside the country. In this manner, Nahai undermines the popular imagining and imaging of the Jewish "other" and creates a new and modern collective Persian/Iranian narrative that integrates the Jewish Iranian people.

While doing so, Nahai's four novels exhibit a gradual development, an arc, with the various components of individual and communal identity evolving or devolving. First and foremost, the amalgam of ethnic and national identity is foregrounded. The author demonstrates an intense but eventually declining arc of focus on the intertwined Jewish and Iranian identities. Her first novel, *Cry of the Peacock*, published in 1991, rewrites Iran's collective memory. She weaves a narrative expanse of some 200 years into an intermittently recalled 2,500-year history of Jewish life in Iran, reaching all the way to the twentieth century and the ascent to power of the Iranian ayatollahs. In her second novel, *Moonlight on the Avenue of Faith* from 1999, the historical expanse decreases, placing center stage Iran's Jewish quarters. Here Nahai portrays the ultimate cost of being Jewish and female. Both components of identity receive equal treatment, as the limitations of lives led by such characters in Iran are emphasized. Female fantasies of escape and flight rivaling those of any Victorian novel dominate the narrative landscape, as women are doubly confined. Both early novels, *Cry of the Peacock* and *Moonlight on the Avenue of Faith*, make extensive use of the literary device of magic realism so deftly used by Gabriel García Márquez in his creation of a revisionist national history. Making unabashed use of the same device, Nahai circumvents physical and temporal boundaries: if her female characters are denied opportunity for self-assertion and fulfillment, literal and metaphorical flights follow until exile to the West, the new twentieth-century diaspora, frees them or their surrogates from the old patriarchal bonds.

The redemptive power of exile appears late in *Moonlight on the Avenue of Faith* but is center stage in Nahai's third novel, *Sunday's Silence* of 2001, and recurs in her fourth novel *Caspian Rain* of 2007. This is part of the shifting arc of focus on components of identity. The central characters in these novels are incidentally created Jewish, but purposefully painted female. *Sunday's Silence* is at first glance a seeming aberration of Nahai's recurrent theme of Iranian Jewish identity as it is set in the mountains and tents of the snake-handling, tongue-speaking Holy Rollers of Appalachia; yet the character who provides the focal narrative 150 pages into the novel is a Jewish Kurdish girl-bride fleeing an uncongenial home and identity. This figure, Blue, whose presence imprints on the reader's mind, lives in married exile in America, where the men in her life set out to destroy her old self by giving her a new name, a new religion and a new education.[2] By the end of the novel the kindness of (female) strangers affords her room for growth and the strength to destroy the man seeking her undoing. Ultimately, she is able to choose union with the man most suited to her: he also is an outsider and the forger of a new identity. Published six years later, *Caspian Rain*, Nahai's most pessimistic novel yet, marks the author's return to an Iranian setting. The intention and scope of Nahai's fiction have, however, greatly diminished since her former integration of Jewish Iranian history into the story of Iran. This fourth novel retreats from the communal to the individual: women suffer defeat, loss and disillusionment because they are women, not because they are Jewish. Even the potential of exile and its happy ending are not reserved for the female protagonists Bahar and Yaas, but rather for their philandering husband/father who, in possession of money and power, chooses to move to America and create a new family while abandoning his wife and child to their literally ghost-ridden life in Iran.

In examining Nahai's work, we see her craft imbue her characters and narratives with poignancy as she creates a world instilled with magic through the recurrent use of specific literary devices and modes of storytelling: her primary concern in her first novel is the centering of Jewish characters within the story of Iran to transform the traditionally marginalized or absent Iranian Jew into an acknowledged presence in literature, thus transplanting the figure into the cultural memory of Iran. In *Cry of the Peacock*, the use of magic realism permits Nahai a circumvention of temporal and physical restrictions that aid her in achieving this end: her characters easily cross boundaries and revise the Jewish Iranian story. Her secondary concern—a concern gaining a position of foremost prominence in her next three novels—is the female experience of life in the Iranian and Middle Eastern Jewish community. She depicts the havoc such a life wreaks, and ultimately evaluates the potential of exile and the American Dream for her protagonists.

The Fantasy of Inclusion:
Reclaiming Jewish Iranian Identity

Nahai's Western audience and reviewers have struggled to categorize her work. Even in the absence of the ever-familiar veiled woman gracing the cover of books concerned with women's lives in the East, her novels have been variously classified, as "riveting family drama and compelling historical fiction"[3] with overtones of "a fairy tale" (*Caspian Rain*, back cover), and "an account of Jewish history" (*Moonlight*, back cover). The historical component, the Iranian setting, and the fantastical elements have rendered classification difficult. Yet these fantastic elements, permitted and incorporated through the use of magic realism, constitute a fundamental feature of Nahai's novels and an overt indication of her novels' intent.

Magic realism is when magical or fantastical images or events occur in a realistic text and are treated as realistic; but this mode of storytelling "relies upon an 'absence of obvious judgments about the veracity of the events and the authenticity of the world view expressed by characters in the text.' "[4] Thus magic realism relies "upon the reader to follow the example of the narrator in accepting both realistic and magical perspectives of reality on the same level."[5] This suspension of disbelief is central to reading Nahai's first two novels, as the opening paragraphs set the magical realist framework. The prologue of *Cry of the Peacock* introduces the fantastical elements: "She had sat there in her clothes that shocked the eye and defied all Islamic codes, in layers of bright chiffon and fiery silk. [...] Her pockets were stuffed with gold and precious stones. In her shoes she had thousand-rial bills. Still, it was not her clothes that so shocked the mullahs, it was her age. Peacock the Jew was so old, they said, she remembered God when he was a child" (pp. 3–4). The first page of *Moonlight on the Avenue of Faith* urges the same suspension of disbelief: "[Roxana] had been so light and delicate, so undisturbed by the rules of gravity and the drudgery of human existence, she had grown wings, one night when the darkness was the color of her dreams, and flown into the star-studded night of Iran that claimed her. [...] Roxana the Angel had kept flying, never once bothered by the pull of the earth or the sound of her loved ones calling her" (p. 5).

In *Magic(al) Realism*, a historical and regional study of magic realism, the author Bowers asserts that the "predominant and increasingly frequent form of magical realism in the United States tends to be written by cross-cultural women with a political agenda relating to gender and the marginalization of cultures."[6] Subverting "the marginalization of culture" is precisely what Nahai does in *Cry of the Peacock* and *Moonlight on the Avenue of Faith*: she brings to the forefront stories of voiceless and unrepresented minorities by incorporating disregarded figures into a collective's story, undermining the versions authorized by monarchial or Islamic governments or the literary cannon. Gabriel García Márquez saw storytelling as "a way of expressing his own cultural context" and realized "that reality is also the myths of the common people, it is the beliefs, their legends; they are in their every day life and they affect their triumphs and failures."[7] Nahai, too, mirrors Márquez in using family lore as a source.[8] Growing up with the stories of the Jewish Iranian community and of the women in her family, she incorporates Márquez's confusion of time scales where characters, such as Esther the Soothsayer and the 116-year-old Peacock, live beyond usual life spans; she presents exaggerations and superstitions as reality, such as the changing of the order of night and day in the *mahalleh* in Tehran at the birth of Roxana, or the surrounding smell of sea and fish that causes a near-pogrom (*Moonlight*, p. 26). To adapt Márquez's phrase, Nahai expresses her own cultural context and allows beliefs and legends to be part of everyday life, affecting triumph and failure.

In achieving this suspension of disbelief in the reader, Nahai's liberation from temporal, physical and historical restrictions provides an unprecedented opportunity to address issues of Jewish Iranian history and identity. Identity, as we know, derives from one's own story and one's role within a collective's story. Stories are narratives that define individuals, communities and nations. As such, the self-understanding of US Americans is grounded on stories of Plymouth Rock, the Founding Fathers and the Civil War. Revisions are constantly made as the story expands to include the Native American tribes, the enslavement of Africans, and the Civil Rights movement. The self-understanding of Iranians is founded on 2,500 years of monarchy, Cyrus the Great and Persepolis, linguistic and nationalist revival through Ferdowsi's *Shahnameh*, the poetry of Hafez and Saadi and Rumi, the magnificence of Isfahan, and the nationalistic and democratic drives of the twentieth century. Like the story of any nation, it is a story of conflicts, but it is also a homage to the power of the word, of literature. Conspicuous in the mainstream version of the Iranian story is the absence of Iranian Jews. Through her fiction, Nahai incorporates this community into the national story, echoing Amichai's acknowledgement of the obligation to the past. After all, what is history but a recorded memory and is memory not malleable? For Nahai and her characters, it is an amalgam, "all the disparate, jagged pieces of that imperfect, forever-changing truth we call memory" (*Caspian Rain*, p. 16), and that flexible entity she sets out to knead and cast in new form.

In her first book, *Cry of the Peacock*, Nahai is completely bound to the history of the Jewish Iranian community and embarks on a recreation and revision of it in its entirety. She recounts the lives of five generations of men and women in and outside the *mahalleh*s of Isfahan and Tehran, while asserting Jewish Iranian presence over the course of 2,500 years. This effort is supported through a relentless incorporation of authentic locations and historical figures into the plot. Many of her characters are "so colorfully eccentric that they seem to inhabit a borderline territory between sanity and visionary madness,"[9] yet that does not stop Nahai's reviewers from reading her fiction as history. Perhaps this can be attributed to the fact that, despite the fantastical elements of her fiction, many of the details of Jewish life in Iran that Nahai includes in her novels are authentic. As David Yeroushelmi's painstaking study of nineteenth-century Jewish life in Iran reveals, 11 Shi'ite decrees were

implemented and enforced in most part of Iran roughly through the Constitutional Revolution of 1905–6. [...] 1. The ritual impurity of Jews. 2. The payment of poll-tax. 3. Subjection to commands issued by the Muslim state and its religious authorities. 4. The obligation to demonstrate due respect toward the Islamic religion and its sanctified traditions and symbols. 5. The obligation to comply with laws and regulations pertaining to the supremacy and security needs of the Islamic court. 7. The unequal and comparatively negligible entitlement of Jews to blood-money in cases involving murder or killing of Jews by Muslims. 8. Denial of inheritance rights from Jewish heirs. i.e. a Jewish heir who converts to Islam becomes entitled to the entire inheritance. 9. The prohibition against bearing arms. 10. The prohibition against riding horses. 11. The prohibition against marrying Muslim women.[10]

Thus it is not surprising that the New York *Newsday* finds "Nahai is the only writer who has given us an intimate account of Jewish history in Iran during the last two centuries" (*Cry of the Peacock*, front cover) and *The Washington Post* finds that "the Persia-Iran Gina Barkhordar Nahai depicts in *Cry of the Peacock* will seem as alien to most of its American readers as it does to Yasmine. That's one reason why this is an important novel. For it does shed light on an enigmatic part of the world with which Westerners must reckon."[11] Thus reviewers absurdly frame this fictional account of Jewish life in Iran as a textbook delivering insight into the threat of the Middle East. In *The Guardian*, Shrapnel's link between *Cry of the Peacock* and historical events seems more on point as he asserts:

Any lingering doubts about who won in the Gulf may perhaps be resolved by *Cry of the Peacock*, which leaves us with the central character 116 years old and still going strong. This is a highly coloured novel in the nature of things and there's no surprise in learning that "the world was filled with the sound of a deaf scream that only Peacock could hear". It's hard to overwrite about a corner of the world so blatantly overlived.[12]

Cry of the Peacock also showcases Nahai's most conspicuous use of authentic location and historical figures, as it provides a general history of ancient Iran through two characters who overcome the boundaries of space and time: Esther the Soothsayer and her granddaughter Peacock. The first central character, Esther the Soothsayer, wanders between the world of the living and the dead; the second central character, Peacock, has a life span of 116 and even then proudly declares: "and still, I intend to live" (p. 5). Some highlights from these two central characters' historical involvement are: Esther the Soothsayer imagines a new life in Isfahan's Jewish quarter, Juyy Bar (p. 13),[13] fails and is shamed. She wanders into Shah Square and the Palace of Forty Pillars (p. 24) only to run into Agha Mohammad Shah (p. 25) and prophesize his end: "Beware [...] of the avenging hands of slaves" (p. 31). She visits her son every night in his dreams and whispers a story of the time of creation and Ahura Mazda's twin sons Ohrmazd and Ahriman (p. 38), of Iran and King Cyrus who "conquered Babylon [...] freed the Jews [...] became founder of the Persian Empire" (p. 38), of Alexander marching on Iran, followed by the Turks and Muslims as "Islam brought an age of enlightenment [...] a tolerance of other religions. [...] But in the fourteenth century, Ismael I [...] made [Iran] Shiite [...] The mullahs declared the followers of all other religions [...] impure and untouchable" (p. 40). At Fath Ali Shah's court, she predicts: "You will die old [...] at peace in your throne," (p. 54) and as Esther's granddaughter, the second central character, is born, the Soothsayer says:

A man shall come, riding from the north, with blood on his hands and the anger of God in his eyes. He shall sit on the Throne of Sun, and with a sweep of his hand he shall reach across his empire to free our people. His son shall call himself the King of Kings, heir to the empire of Cyrus. He shall raise this child from the ashes and give her pride. But beware! For the King of Kings shall fall, and his throne shall crumble, and the men of God shall paint the skies of this nation with blood. (p. 89)

Aptly, the child receiving this forewarning of the Peacock Throne is called Peacock. During the 1871 famine, Peacock is asleep as her nine-year-old sister Hannah is dressed in bridal finery (pp. 102–5),

led through Isfahan's Chahar Bagh, Shah Square, and abandoned in
Ali Ghapoo to finally be taken into the Palace of Forty Pillars by
Nasser al-Din Shah's son, Zel al-Sultan as his child bride (pp. 104–
5). Peacock's husband, Solomon the Man, leaves Peacock for Tala,
granddaughter to Nasser al-Din Shah, the Qajar monarch of Iran, and
daughter of Hannah (p. 127). Peacock's journey to Tehran shows her
moving through such well-known locations as "Tekkyeh, Tehran's
central square" (p. 160) to Sar Cheshmeh and the Square of Cannons,
and makes possible meetings between Peacock and Reza Khan
(p. 180), the future Pahlavi king, who learns that he is to "never
underestimate the friendship of a Jew" (p. 181) and who, when
disheartened by lack of success in his studies, is consoled by Peacock:
"Doesn't matter what they say. [. . .] Doesn't matter that you were a
peasant. You're going to be King someday" (p. 182). Peacock's son
Arash is trained by Reza Khan (p. 197), is present at the assassination
of Nasser al-Din Shah (p. 198–202), and guards the young king,
Ahmad Shah (p. 221). In 1926, after the Pahlavis's ascension to
power, Peacock helps with the "building of a crown, the mending of
the Throne of the Sun" (p. 241) for Reza Khan's coronation. Reza
Shah's favor leads to a relaxation of the *mahalleh* perimeters[14] (p. 257)
and he consequently hires Peacock's son-in-law to purchase ladies'
ready-to-wear apparel from Europe before his famed *chādor bardāri* or
kashf-e hejāb, the forcible banning of the veil in 1936 (p. 260). And,
as in his support of Hitler, Reza Shah betrays the Jews of Iran
(p. 267), it is Peacock who can voice the tribe's disillusionment
and ask: "What of the Jews you saved?" (p. 269). Peacock's family
witnesses the rise and fall of Iran's nationalist prime minister
Mohammad Mossadeq (p. 295ff.) in the 1963 CIA-operated coup
Ajax, and the family saga comes to an end with the Islamic
Revolution as Peacock is nearly executed for speaking truth to
power, the bloodthirsty Revolutionary Guards (pp. 332, 336). The
sole survivors of this family are those who have made their way to
America (pp. 308, 320).

In Nahai's second novel, *Moonlight on the Avenue of Faith*, the
regional and historical scope is smaller, as if having placed Iranian
Jews within mainstream Iranian history and having acknowledged

the previous generations that bound her, Nahai is now free to move on to individualistic stories focusing on Jewish Iranian women who dream of flight and freedom. The sea and "everlasting waters" (*Moonlight*, p. 36) of the Caspian come to represent hope and freedom. Within the general history of Iran in *Cry of the Peacock*, Nahai had embedded landmarks of Jewish Iranian history, such as the massacres of Iranian Jews—in 1831 in Tabriz (p. 55), in 1853 in Isfahan's Juyy Bar (p. 73), and in 1906 in Kermanshah (p. 212)—and the recurrence of the blood libel (p. 55). The restriction to *mahalleh*s (p. 12ff.) and the wearing of identifying clothing (pp. 11, 99) had also been included in *Cry of the Peacock*. In *Moonlight on the Avenue of Faith*, the first chapter bears the title "The Ghetto: 1938"[15] and the scale shifts to foreground routine details of Jewish Iranian life. The narrative recounts the daily hardships: the lack of "access to fresh produce" for Jews (p. 15), and restrictions on Jewish cemeteries, such as Beheshtieh "which the Muslims had not allowed to expand, so that for centuries corpses had been placed one on top of the other" (p. 71). Ties of blood link characters in the first two novels, as some tormented characters in *Moonlight on the Avenue of Faith* are descendants of Peacock's husband, Solomon the Man, the charismatic boundary-crosser.

Notably, in Nahai's third novel *Sunday's Silence*, Blue, the snake-handling Kurdish Jew living in Appalachia, is another descendant of Solomon the Man (*Sunday's Silence*, p. 158), and grows up learning both of her grandmother's callous abandonment by and her mother's futile wait for Solomon the Man. She also learns that her mother's "Jewish blood" is to blame as it "had caused her madness, [...] that all Jews were inhabited by the devil and that he compelled them to do and say strange things" (p. 158). And as if the story of the wanderings of the Chosen People were not enough for Nahai this time around, she layers into her narrative the story of the wanderings of the Kurds, complete with a mythical origin:

They are a strange breed, these Kurds—the children of fairy-tale Jinns and their real-life lovers: five thousand years ago King Solomon ordered the Jinns in his service to search the four corners of the earth and bring him the most beautiful virgins alive. The Jinns searched far and wide, but by the time they brought the maidens back, King Solomon had died and the Jinns themselves had fallen in love with the girls. So they married the mortals and had children who belonged neither to this world nor the planet of fairies, destined to live in the neverland of exile, in perpetual movement, forever restless. (pp. 158–9)

This novel weaves Jewish identity into the widely recognized plight of the wandering Kurds, connecting only remotely to Iranian identity through association in the geographically well-versed reader's mind. The declining arc of historical national interest further diminishes in Nahai's fourth novel. Despite its Iranian setting, this novel proves to be disconnected from the first two, as the familiar bloodline of Solomon the Man disappears in this last novel, constituting a clear break from the historical connection. It also marks an end to Nahai's interest in the amalgam of Jewish and Iranian identity. The temporal setting of the novel is restricted to a short time range, from the pre- to the post-Islamic Revolution era; the suffering in the novel, however, is attributable to gender rather than religious isolation. In this setting, discernible Jewishness becomes synonymous with being lower class, being poor. Being Jewish no longer means being *mahalleh*-bound or thwarted in upward mobility, but rather denotes one's lack of ability to assimilate fully. Here, purportedly, with the new liberties, if one has enough money, one can rise out of Jewishness, like Niyaz's lover who "started out as a Jew and then quickly crossed over—because of his money and good looks—into that most coveted of all spheres, the place where a man's religion and ancestry are immaterial, where he is accepted and envied regardless of his beginnings" (*Caspian Rain*, p. 41). Unfortunately the novel's protagonist, Bahar, lacks power, money and full assimilation, and will therefore not be forgiven her transgression of boundaries. As she struggles to lose her Jewish accent and to cook "Muslim-style (meaning with more elegance)," (p. 69) "her guests can detect 'the Jewishness' in her food, in her manners and accent and choice of words, and this puts them off and makes them offer excuses the next time she invites them" (p. 71). Bahar is doomed by her roots in the lower class and her gender, not her Jewishness.

Fantasies of Flight and the Redemptive Power of Exile

Nahai's declining arc of nationalist/religious interest is paralleled by a rising arc of interest in the restrictions of gender and the potential of exile. In Nahai's first four novels, her women are all refugees of one sort or another; and as female refugees they are vulnerable and subject to mistreatment. As Jews they are part of a community seemingly doomed to wander the Earth and, as women in Jewish patriarchy, they suffer the fate of the weakest oppressed by the weak. Yet, Nahai's women dare to dream: Esther the Soothsayer of *Cry of the Peacock* escapes the isolation of her life in Bandar Abbas and leaves the caravan in Isfahan, because in her dreams she saw "a world of calm and plenty [...] women who walked the earth with pride" (p. 12). She unwittingly enters a world where "the men wore red or yellow patches on their clothes. [...] Anything a Jew touched became soiled forever. If accused of crime, a Jew could not testify in his own defense" (p. 13). Historically, this is an Iran where Jews "are forbidden to go out when it rains; for it is said the rain would wash dirt off them, which would sully the feet of the Mussulmans."[16] Esther swiftly realizes that she "had escaped the harem [...] but not her bondage" (*Peacock*, p. 13). She marries but has no power to escape the patriarchs of Juyy Bar, who have deemed her a whore at first glance and refused her acceptance. And she is condemned by a rabbi who has longed for 20 years "for the chance—the moment when he would be called to judge, to control the fate of another, set down the law" (p. 19). Having just given birth, Esther is taken from her home, her head shaved and paraded around town. The rabbi gives in to the sensuality of destructive power, the urge to destroy, knowing that "he could have done what the book really preached—asked for indulgence, demanded forgiveness, forbidden vengeance. He could have saved Esther and her child. But to do this, he would have to forgo his one chance at immortality" (p. 20); so he does not and sets in motion the cycle of female lives that will suffer in this narrative with little hope of escape. Esther's curse follows members of the community, and her supernatural abilities allow her to appear in her descendants' dreams, thus creating the link between past generations and new generations, between the ancient empire and the new monarchy.

The precedent set by Esther the Soothsayer continues in the second novel, *Moonlight on the Avenue of Faith*. Here, too, women attempt to escape and pay a horrendous price. This saga begins with the Crow, a woman who is kept so concealed and swathed by her rabbi husband in "suffocating layers of black cloth" (p. 12) that she lacks a name other than the nickname bestowed upon her by the community. One day, the suffocating hold of the patriarchal tradition and male authority that deprive her of name, freedom and voice breaks. She is heard singing as she walks through town naked and then leaves it "white as the river's foamy waters. Blond from her head down to her feet, slender and curved and scented like every young man's dream of copulation" (p. 13). She departs but the stigma of her deed remains and dooms every female descendants of hers as "it augured a series of escapes among the female members of every subsequent generation of the rabbi's offspring" (p. 14). Every escape exacts a price: the abandonment of a daughter or mother and physical or emotional retribution. The harshest of these punishments is dealt to Roxana, the last of the Crow's descendants, whose life unfolds in Iran. Roxana, the central character of *Moonlight on the Avenue of Faith*, dares to dream of flight; and one night, unable to voice her demand for love, protection, freedom, "[i]nstead of screaming [...] she opened her arms and leaned into the night" (pp. 168–9), flying away into the unknown. This woman who dares to flee suffers in the best (worst) Victorian manner. She flees the confines of a prison-like home only to be sold by the Kurdish border police into a Turkish brothel, where she is forced to sleep with hundreds of men and contracts malaria and typhoid fever. Somehow denuded of her former ability to fly, she does finally escape but only into a life of nameless and voiceless drudgery in Turkey. Decades later, as the memory and guilt of the abandonment of her daughter, Lili, wash over her, she swallows her sorrow to inflate into a 300 lb monster of a woman oozing water and bitter tears (p. 341).

The suffering of Nahai's women continues as, in *Sunday's Silence*, Blue grows up watching the progression of her mother's madness. Having eloped with Blue's father, a Sunni Muslim Kurd, Blue's mother, a "village girl," enters the mountain camp of her husband and realizes that she has made a grave mistake, that the nomadic life is not for her. Leaving is not an option as "she could not find her way out of the life she had ridden into one dark night on the back of a horse" (p. 171), thus her nightmares come to her, black snakes that rule her life and torment her. Her occasional escape between her bouts of madness is the creation of henna paintings on her palms that depict villages and landscapes. Central to all the drawings, "surrounded by walls and barriers she could not climb, was a lone woman with bewildered eyes and a crown of gold coins" (p. 170). Blue discerns that "the entire painting was a maze, that the woman at the center was searching for a path that led away from the center and off my mother's palms" (p. 170). This mother's fantasy of escape will come to fruition in her daughter, her surrogate. When the suitor from America arrives, the mother paints Blue's palms and Blue sees "the line that ran from the middle of the painting down toward my wrist—a narrow river that led out to a sea and, beyond it [...]" (p. 182). As always, Nahai exacts a terrible price for escape: first the guilt of forever abandoning a mad mother "chained to a pole outside the tents all the time" (p. 177), and then the death of Blue's daughter, "a little girl catching fire in the middle of the afternoon, running across the yard without a sound or a whimper as the flames rise around her body and over her face and head, running toward her mother with her arms open as if to embrace her, and me standing there, too stunned to utter a sound or make a move" (pp. 155–6). Blue's story, however, is one of ultimate redemption as Blue's unwillingly severed ties to mother and daughter enable her to cast off her husband and marriage.

The first three novels notwithstanding, the grimness of *Caspian Rain*, Nahai's fourth novel, is a surprise. As in the earlier works, it makes reference to the hardships of Jewish life in Iran where "Jews have been second-class citizens since Islam first arrived" (p. 12) and to "the 'Pit'—the central square of the Tehran ghetto, which is where all the Jews came from" (p. 12). The main characters' suffering and struggles are rooted in the age old battles of the sexes but they are offered no literal or figurative escape. The protagonist Bahar's immense losses stem from her ability to envision for herself an individual future in this patriarchal society. Omid, her future husband and initial harbinger of hope, notices her because of this ability, but whereas he, "has the advantage, the power to drive away or to stop, to [abandon] her to her fate or to reach forward and pull her out of her universe of failed dreamers and of women who clean rice for a living" (p. 17), she lacks power. Worse yet, he destroys that very quality that attracted him to her because he merely surmises "she won't be hard to train" (p. 23). He drops her into a world of daily slights, crushes her dreams of pursuing an education, and isolates her from her family, subjecting her to years of disinterest and humiliation while he publicly carries on an illicit affair with another woman. Bahar's life becomes one of "sadness at having sold herself for a wish, her dreams that rose like ships in the night, lit up and glorious against the reality of what she would be able to attain" (p. 36). Her world shrinks as her dreams die, as her husband proves incorrigible, and her child progressively damaged. No happy ending is reserved for Bahar, as her husband immigrates and begins a new life in America with his mistress, leaving Bahar and her daughter Yaas to post-Islamic Revolution life in Iran. Bahar, paying Nahai's high price for daring to dream, is another protagonist doomed to watch her daughter burn with only the consolation of Yaas's post-death, unsatisfying assertion that her mother Bahar's life of thwarted dreams is preferable to one containing no attempt at escape.

As *Cry of the Peacock* portrays the history of Iranian Jews and *Moonlight on the Avenue of Faith* women's fantasies of escape from their homes, men, bodies and obedience to the laws of society and nature, the attempts at flight draw increasingly larger circles and finally bridge the gap between the East and the West, Iran and the United States. Ultimately the characters are successful if they find their way West, to the land of opportunities, where they are awarded space for individualism. "Choices and chances" (*Moonlight*, p. 209) come with life in the US and the redemptive power of exile. Disillusioned Americans might define the American Dream as Fitzgerald's elusive green light on the other side; however, in its original form, the form held by immigrants, the American Dream denoted the belief in freedom, equality and the right to the pursuit of happiness. This early definition holds for Nahai's characters. In *Cry of the Peacock*, the survivors are those who immigrate to America. In *Moonlight on the Avenue of Faith*, reinvention is only successful if it occurs in the West, free of the restrictions of the East. Eastern reinventions, such as Alexandra the Cat's who reinvents herself as a displaced Russian (p. 42) or Golnaz's who reinvents herself as the German Fraulein Claude (p. 101), are all doomed to fail, as these attempts are transgressions against dominant moral, social, or sexual codes. Only those who do not subscribe to the restrictive rules and eventually turn their backs on Iran achieve a measure of happiness: Mercedez who "at sixteen [. . . stops] going to school altogether and [spends] her time mostly in Tehran, hunting for a rich Muslim man" (p. 57), and Effat who meets an Englishman, takes him to a brothel in "'New City' where [. . .] she [shows] him her bare breasts" (pp. 124–6). Ultimately, the West—"The Land of Choices and Chances" (p. 209)—is where they resurface. Mercedez, in Hollywood, "had managed to [. . .] reinvent her life [. . . ,] had become rich in her own right" (p. 226). Effat marries her Englishman and becomes "the mother of two sons and a daughter" (p. 126). As Lili, the young narrator of *Moonlight on the Avenue of Faith*, is placed in a Catholic boarding school in the United States and pines for her parents and grieves her state of quasi orphanhood, Mercedez aptly points out, "I had to cheat and lie and sleep with a dozen men just to get myself out of that ghetto and to America. Your father just handed you this freedom on a platter and let you be whoever you want. If you're smart, you'll thank him and never want to see him again" (p. 261) and Lili eventually agrees by realizing that "they had sent me across the ocean and, by doing so, given me a new destiny" (p. 263).

Regarding this Western exile, Weber of *The Jerusalem Post* aptly pointed out:

Nahai takes the enabling power of exile as her core subject, conjuring richly imagined tales of Iranian Jewish life in transition: from the Old World ghettos of Teheran, where Jewish families lived for centuries as a self-conscious minority according to strict social hierarchies and constraining codes of behavior, to the liberating air of Los Angeles, a sun-drenched golden medina where since the fall of the shah in 1979 Iranian Jews live thriving in 'a land of choices and chances' basking in perhaps the best of all possible diasporas.[17]

Blue of *Sunday's Silence* achieves a modicum of happiness by being a beneficiary of the Western belief in individual happiness. In *Caspian Rain*, unrepentant Omid and Niyaz, selfish and destructive as their affair has been, simply assume this right to happiness with America's happy ending reserved for them because "God loves some people more than others" (p. 41). Their daughter has "the luxury of being born in a place where her gender is not a curse" (p. 288).

Interestingly, Nahai's view of America is not uncritical. After all, "Americans don't get devastated and don't lose their cool at funerals because they have no idea what real loss is. It doesn't affect them as completely, as irreversibly," (*Caspian Rain*, p. 14) and one must weigh "Exile's Gains and Losses" as one has "the great good fortune of witnessing {the} community [...] easing up on the misogyny and intolerance that were byproducts of Islamic and Jewish practices [...] In exchange for" losing "the handprints of [...] ancestors on the landscape [...] the beauty of the land where history began, the glow of a sunlight that was older, more seasoned, more forgiving."[18] America is a land of chances and choices, and "you can love the old country all you want. Sometimes, exile is the best thing that can happen to a people. [...] *Maybe here, in this land of chances and choices, {the journey} does not need to end in sorrow.* [...] It is possible to know and, at last, feel at peace" (*Moonlight*, pp. 359, 371, 374).

Lovely and fascinating as Nahai's books are, they are not free of flaws. They awaken the imagination and senses with Nahai's provocative phrases evoking sensations, recasting the past, and bringing to life places neglected in today's utilitarian world. As the beauty of Nahai's writing mesmerizes the reader, however, it also serves to camouflage the negligible nature of her endings. As the enthralled reader of *Jane Eyre* strains to stir up interest in the lengthy St. John episode, so the reader of Nahai's books will vividly recall key passages but strain to even recall the book's ultimate ending. In these wan endings, the characters do not so much walk into the sunset or gloom as fade from view. In *Cry of the Peacock*, Peacock leaves the prison and goes on her conceivably unmerry way into the fledgling Islamic Republic of Iran. In *Moonlight on the Avenue of Faith*, Lili, who provides the narrative perspective at the end, is a bland being, straining to work through her emotional past. Nahai does, however, offer up a vision of reconciliation as "Roxanna's long-alienated New World daughter Lili is reconciled with her self-exiled mother and together they hover in the skies over post-shah Tehran (a startling journey of reverse migration from Los Angeles to Iran) as Roxanna unearths the repressed fragments of family history—a therapeutic act of filial bonding through memory and love."[19] The quasi-happy ending reappears in *Sunday's Silence*, as the long-suffering Blue partakes of the happy ending reserved for Nahai's liberated sexual taboo breakers. Blue makes her future happen by realizing her potential: "Make a wish... and we will imagine it to life" (p. 309). Despite this, the happy ending fails to carry the day. And, in the fourth novel, *Caspian Rain*, hopelessness reigns, the damaged Yaas's despair is contained within her name, and her life ends in self-immolation. Yet this violent act of self-destruction lacks emotional intensity as it is depicted through a subjective lens and robbed of effect, with the author hastening to yet another imaginary meeting between mother and daughter, this time Yaas and Bahar. Nahai's endings are afterthoughts, as if the author's interest lies in the path of suffering protagonists, providing an unwilling ending only because narrative convention and reader expectations require it.

In the world of Nahai, a story is an offering, one that the listener "cannot turn away from, or deny, or leave behind in the folds of my hands and on the edges of my lips" (*Sunday's Silence*, p. 1). And the intent of this storytelling? In the voice of a fictional character Nahai asserts: "When I am done, you will believe that which seems impossible to you now—that you and I are one and the same, regardless of all of our differences, that you cannot undo me without destroying yourself, that hearing my story has made you—my confessor, my judge, my enemy—it has made you my accomplice" (*Sunday's Silence*, p. 1). In her own voice, she says "the reason I started writing in the first place: to tell a good story; a story about Jews; a story that in its own small way continues the tale of this people who have had to struggle, in every generation, to ensure that their story doesn't end. And I think this is what all the other people in this room have also wanted to do—to write a word, a line, a chapter in that great story, and to make sure our story goes on."[20] In reading Nahai's novels, her reader has imbibed the Jewish Iranian story, now has knowledge of it, and can no longer deny it. That existence that has once been imagined can no longer be unmade. Thus, Nahai's novels are not scholarly examinations of Iran, but rather broadly painted accounts of Jewish life in Iran where Nahai, here in my adaptation of Amichai's words, has had to acknowledge that "all the generations before her donated her, bit by bit, binding her, demanding that she change life and death to fulfill prophesies." This she has done through an undermining of physical, regional and historical boundaries, ultimately culminating in the revelation of the redemptive power of exile and the potential of freedom.

Notes

1 Yehuda Amichai, "Jerusalem Poems: All the Generations Before Us, " tr. Harold Schimmel, *Palestine-Israel Journal*, 2:2 (1995).

2 A few Nahai characters are oddly reminiscent of Bijan Mofid's character, Elephant, in the musical animal fable *Shahr-e Ghesseh* [City of Tales]. In the 1967 musical, Elephant, a stranger, arrives in town with a broken tusk. The animal-citizens gather and opt to aid him by forcing him to conform to their norms: they break off his other tusk and plant both atop of his head like horns, and they slice off his "nose" piecemeal. Elephant lives on as a "strange animal," neither elephant nor other animal. Moshe (Muhammed the Jew) of *Cry of the Peacock* and Blue of *Sunday's Silence* are also damaged individuals who relinquish their Jewish pasts in order to conform and, thus, become isolated "strange animals." Interestingly, Blue's exile in the West affords her the liberty to seek fulfillment; whereas Moshe's life within the restrictive confines of Jewish and Muslim Iran equals being sentenced to loss and death.

240   THE JEWS OF IRAN

Eleanor J. Bader, review of *Caspian Rain*, *Library Journal Reviews* (August 15, 2007), p. 72.

Chanady, quoted in Maggie Ann Bowers, *Magic(al) Realism* (London and New York, 2004), p. 4.

Bowers, p. 4.

Bowers, p. 57.

Quoted in Bowers, p. 40.

"Authors@Google: Gina Nahai." YouTube (October 5, 2007) <http://www.youtube.com/watch?v=47KKNmrcxEY> last accessed July 2, 2014.

Edward Hower, "Spinning Jinni," review of *Moonlight on the Avenue of Faith*, in *New York Times* (March 30, 1999), sec. 7, p. 19.

David Yeroushalmi, *The Jews of Iran in the Nineteenth Century: Aspects of History, Community, and Culture* (Leiden, 2009), pp. 4–5.

Louise Titchener, "Down and Outcast in Iran: Fiction of a Jewish Family in a Harsh Land," review of *Cry of the Peacock*, *The Washington Post* (July 30, 1991), Style: C3.

Norman Shrapnel, "A Childhood Seventy Years Long," review of *Cry of the Peacock*, *The Guardian* [London] (February 6, 1991).

The correct name of the Jewish quarter or *mahalleh* in Isfahan is *Jubāreh* [editor's note].

Mahalleh is the name for the Jewish quarters that Iranian Jews were confined to by the hostility the Shi'ite clergy fueled. As Reza Shah's overt hostility to the Shi'ite clergy grew, Jews took new liberties and began to move into neighborhoods beyond the *mahalleh*.

Nahai's taking artistic liberty in referring to the *mahallehs* or the Jewish quarters in Iran as ghettos. A full discussion of the difference between the two would expand far beyond the limits of this footnote. To state two key differences, the Jewish ghettos in Europe were walled off and had gates that got locked from the outside from dusk till dawn. And unlike ghettos, *mahallehs* could technically expand horizontally [editor's note].

Benjamin, quoted in Yeroushalmi, p. 14.

Donald Weber, "Escaping Self-Exile," review of *Caspian Rain*, in *The Jerusalem Post* (October 3, 2007), p. 20.

Gina Barkhordar Nahai, "Exile's Gains and Losses," *The Jewish Journal of Greater Los Angeles* (September 3, 2008) <http://www.jewishjournal.com/opinion/article/exiles_gains_and_losses_20080903> last accessed July 2, 2014.

Weber.

Gina Barkhordar Nahai, "Want to Hear a Story?" *The Jewish Journal of Greater Los Angeles* (August 3, 2007) <http://www.jewishjournal.com/archive/results/40a32753e4e29010f138489d33c949f8/P50> last accessed July 2, 2014.

INDEX

www.ingramcontent.com/pod-product-compliance
Lightning Source LLC
Chambersburg PA
CBHW050414280326
41932CB00013BA/1861